Woodland High School
800 N. Moseley Dr.
Stockbridge, GA 30281
770-389-2784

Woodland High School
800 N. Moseley Dr.
Stockbridge, GA 30281
770-389-2784

Ceramic
Masterpieces

CERAMIC MASTERPIECES

Art,

Structure,

and Technology

W. DAVID KINGERY
PAMELA B. VANDIVER

THE FREE PRESS

A Division of Macmillan, Inc

NEW YORK

Collier Macmillan Publishers

LONDON

The Free Press
A DIVISION OF MACMILLAN, INC.
866 Third Avenue, New York, N.Y. 10022

Collier Macmillan Canada, Inc.

Printed in the United States of America

printing number

1 2 3 4 5 6 7 8 9 10

Library of Congress Cataloging-in-Publication Data

Kingery, W. David
    Ceramic masterpieces.

    Includes index.
    1. Pottery—Themes, motives.   2. Porcelain—Themes,
motives.   I. Vandiver, Pamela. B.   II. Title.
NK4235.K56   1986   738.2   85–27559
ISBN 0–02–918480–0

Designed by Raymond Solomon

The appearance of a ceramic is determined by its internal structure, which is in turn determined by the technology of its manufacture. Revolutionary new methods of study and analysis have advanced our understanding of ceramics. This book applies these new methods, connecting visual impact, internal structure, and technology for a deeper appreciation of ceramic masterpieces.

CONTENTS

LIST OF FIGURES   xi

LIST OF TABLES   xv

LIST OF COLOR PLATES   xvii

PREFACE   xix

ACKNOWLEDGMENTS   xxiii

Part I. INTRODUCTION   3

Chapter 1. AN OVERVIEW   7
   A History of Ceramics   7
   Ceramic Science   18
   Ceramic Technology   37
   Object Examination   43

Part II. CERAMIC MASTERPIECES   47

Chapter 2.   AN EGYPTIAN FAIENCE CHALICE   51

Chapter 3.   A SONG DYNASTY LONGQUAN CELADON
             JAR   69

Chapter 4.   A SONG DYNASTY JUN WARE BOWL   93

Chapter 5.   AN ISLAMIC LUSTERWARE FROM KASHAN   111

Chapter 6.   AN IZNIK TILE   123

Chapter 7.   A MEDICI PORCELAIN BOTTLE   135

Chapter 8.   A K'ANG HSI FAMILLE VERTE PORCELAIN
             PLATE   149

Chapter 9.   A BÖTTGER PORCELAIN   163

Chapter 10. A BOUCHER SOFT-PASTE UNGLAZED
             BISQUE SCULPTURE—*LA DANSEUSE*   179

Chapter 11. A WEDGWOOD JASPERWARE   195

             Part III. CERAMIC TECHNOLOGY   209

Chapter 12. SOME UNDERLYING SCIENCE   211
   Structure   211
   Capillarity   217
   Effects of Temperature   223

Chapter 13. SHAPING AND FIRING   227
   Ceramic Bodies   227
      PERMEABLE EARTHENWARE   227
      WHITE QUARTZ-PASTE BODIES   229
      VITREOUS STONEWARE   229
      WHITE PORCELAIN   230
      SLIPS AND GLAZES AS PART OF THE BODY   230
      SUMMARY   231
   Shaping and Drying   232
      MODELING (PINCH FORMING)   238
      SLAB AND COIL BUILDING   239
      SHAPING WITH PADDLE AND ANVIL   240
      MOLDING AND MOLD MAKING   241
      THROWING ON A WHEEL   242
      ASSEMBLY AND JOINING   243

SLIP CASTING 244

DRYING 244

Finishing 245

Firing 247

CHANGES IN THE BODY DURING FIRING 247

KILNS 252

Chapter 14. GLAZES AND DECORATION 261

Glazes 261

RAW GLAZES 263

FRITTED GLAZES 264

APPLICATION 264

FIRING 265

GLAZE SURFACES 266

GLAZE FIT AND ADHERENCE 267

GLAZE DEFECTS 268

Colorants, Pigments and Opacifiers 269

Slips and Underglaze Decoration 272

Overglaze Enamels, Gilding and Luster 274

Efflorescence, Ashes, Galena and Vapor Glazing 275

Part IV. STUDYING CERAMIC OBJECTS 279

Chapter 15. SEEING AND STUDYING CERAMICS 281

Visual Examination 281

Magnifying Glass, Pen Light and Needle 285

In the Study, Kitchen or Storage Area 288

At the Laboratory 292

POSING A QUESTION 293

SAMPLING REQUIREMENTS 294

CHOOSING A METHOD OF TESTING 295

DATING 297

VISUALIZING AND DESCRIBING THE
MACROSTRUCTURE (0.05-1mm) 298

VISUALIZING AND DESCRIBING THE
MICROSTRUCTURE (0.05-50μm) 300

COMPOSITIONAL ANALYSIS   302

PHYSICAL PROPERTY MEASUREMENTS   306

Replication and Ethnographic Observations   306

Identification of Fakes and Copies   308

Chapter 16. INFERENCE FROM ARTIFACTS   311

SOME SPECIAL TERMINOLOGY   315

INDEX   325

LIST OF FIGURES

1.1	Flow of History	19
1.2	Metric Units	20
1.3	K'ang Hsi Microstructure	22
1.4	Boucher Microstructure	24
1.5	Jun Glaze Microstructure	28
1.6	Mendeleeff Table	32
1.7	Phase Diagrams	34
1.8	Kaolin	38
II-1	Map	48
2.1	Chalice	52
2.2	Forming Methods	55
2.3	Xeroradiograph	57
2.4	Xeroradiograph	59
2.5	Microstructure 300X	60
2.6	Microstructure 800X	61
3.1	Jar	70
3.2	Dragon	71

3.3   Xeroradiograph   74
3.4   Cross-section   75
3.5   Kiln   78
3.6   Microstructure   82
3.7   Bubble Structure   83
3.8   Microstructure of Quartz and Anorthite   84
3.9   Composition Plot   85
3.10 Microstructure   88

4.1   Jun Bowl   95
4.2   Kiln Site   98
4.3   Cristobalite   99
4.4   Anorthite   102
4.5   Emulsion   103
4.6   Composition   104
4.7   Wollastonite   105
4.8   Copper Content   106

5.1   Kashan Plate   113
5.2   Microstructure   117
5.3   Glaze Penetration   117
5.4   Silver Particles   119
5.5   Reflection   120

6.1   Tile   124
6.2   Panel   127
6.3   Cross-section   128
6.4   Microstructure   130
6.5   Red Colorant   132

7.1   Medici Bottle   137
7.2   Medici Drawing   139
7.3   Glaze Microstructure (a, b, c)   142
7.4   Body Microstructure   144
7.5   Melting Diagram   145

8.1	K'ang Hsi Plate	150
8.2	Kiln	154
8.3	Microstructure of Body	156
8.4	Enlarged Painting	158
8.5	SEM of Hematite Crystals	159
8.6	Copper glaze Containing Quartz Crystals	160
9.1	Böttger Tea Caddy	164
9.2	Panel Designs	169
9.3	Phase Diagram	171
9.4	Böttger Microstructure (2)	172
9.5	1731 Microstructure	174
10.1	Boucher Figure	180
10.2	Molding	186
10.3	Head	187
10.4	Radiograph	188
10.5	Surface Roughness	190
10.6	Phase Diagram	191
10.7	Microstructure	193
11.1	Wedgwood Pot	196
11.2	Bas Relief	197
11.3	Microstructure—Sprig, etc.	201
11.4	Microstructure Body	203
12.1	Specular and Diffuse Reflection	215
12.2	Glass and Crystal Structure	218
12.3	Soap film	220
12.4	Surface Tension	221
12.5	Glaze Spreading	222
12.6	Firing Process	225
13.1	Deformation vs. Water Content	233
13.2	Chinastone, Corinth Illite, Hajji Feruz Montmorillonite	234

13.3   Water Content vs. Shrinkage   236

13.4   Firing—700°, 800°, 900°   248

13.5   Shematic Body   251

13.6   Kilns: a. primitive, b. Pan-Po, c. medieval   254

15.1   Magnifying Glass, Light and Needle   285

LIST OF TABLES

1.1 Some of the Compounds Used in Ceramics and Appearing in Ceramic Micro-Structures   33

2.1 Chemical Composition of Egyptian Faience   63

5.1 Chemical Composition of Lusterware Frit as Determined by Electron Microprobe Microchemical Analysis   116

8.1 Composition (weight percent) of Three Enamels Used on One Piece   157

8.2 Principal Constituents Present in K'ang Hsi Enamels (Weight Percent)   161

9.1 Chemical Composition of Böttger's Porcelain and the Later Meissen Porcelain   170

12.1 Effectiveness of Particles in Rendering a Glaze Opaque Is Determined by the Relative Index of Refraction   213

15.1 Steps Required in Choosing a Method of Testing   296

15.2 Dating Methods   298

15.3   Methods of Visualizing and Describing the Macrostructure
       (*0.05—1mm*)   300

15.4   Methods of Visualizing and Describing the Microstructure
       (*0.005–50* μ*m*)   302

15.5   Widely Available Instrumental Methods of Compositional
       Analysis   305

LIST OF COLOR PLATES

AFTER PAGE 38

I.   Blue lotus chalice of Egyptian faience, circa 1400 B.C.

II.   Xeroradiography of Egyptian blue lotus chalice.

III.   (a) Details of Egyptian faience glaze. (b) Mehrgahr shard.

IV.   Southern Song Dynasty celadon jar.

V.   Dragon on celadon jar.

VI.   Xeroradiography of Song Dynasty celadon jar.

VII.   Southern Song Dynasty jun ware bowl.

VIII.   Magnified details of jun ware glaze.

IX.   (a) Underglaze reaction layer forms a white ground for jun glaze. (b) Cooling rates are critical in developing jun glaze properties.

X.   Lusterware plate made in Kashan with an inscription dated 1208 A.D.

XI.   Closer view of Kashan Lusterware.

XII.   (a) Details of the silver luster used for the sample shown in Plate X. (b) Copper lusters often have red flash at edges.

XIII.   Sixteenth century Iznik tile with underglaze coating covered by brilliant lead-alkali silicate glaze.

XIV.   (a) Panel seen at distance appears blue. (b) Closer view of details shows the brightness of color.

XV.   (a) Magnified view of Iznik tile colors. (b) Cross section of Iznik tile painting.

XVI.   Medici porcelain square bottle made in 1581.

XVII.   Enlarged view of painting on Medici porcelain.

XVIII.   K'ang Hsi famille verte porcelain plate believed to be made in 1713.

XIX.   Closer view of K'ang Hsi design.

XX.   Two enlarged views of K'ang Hsi plate painting details.

XXI.   Tea caddy of Böttger porcelain (1713–1718).

XXII.   (a) Fluorescent analysis of Böttger porcelains illustrating use of feldspar in glaze.(b) Pigment colors.

XXIII.   Soft-paste bisquit porcelain figure, *La Danseuse*, made in 1752 at Vincennes after a design by Françoise Boucher.

XXIV.   Wedgwood jasperware chocolate pot made about 1790.

PREFACE

There are many different ways of studying ceramic objects of artistic, historic, or cultural interest. In general they involve the object's appearance—its form and decoration. Indeed, museum presentations of objects encased behind glass limit observation to one side of a piece from a distance of perhaps half a meter. Only students, curators, and private collectors can appreciate a closer view, perhaps with a hand glass, along with the tactile experience of handling the ware that is often essential to its overall effect. This alone makes even the smallest collection worthwhile.

When one first sees a ceramic, there is an immediate impression of form, color, and texture. If it is an object worthy of our attention, we want to examine it more closely, see how light, texture, color, and form interact, and place it in a context of the artist who made it, the culture from which it arose, the history of its design elements, and how it was produced. In addition to traditions of form and design, there are, for ceramics, well-defined traditions of materials and methods—traditions that specify how things are made, the palette of colors chosen, and the textures possible. Our major goal is to show students, collectors, curators, and all who love ceramics how an understanding of these traditions, and their underlying technologies, can enhance the appreciation of outstanding ceramics.

The appearance of a ceramic, for example, is based on the arrangement of atoms in the crystals and glasses of which it is made, which determines the properties of each of its constituents. On this scale it is possible to understand why fine crystal has a brilliance that distinguishes it from

ordinary window glass. The most important structural level is the arrangement and distribution of the crystalline and glassy constituents. These can
be directly observed with optical or electron microscopes; they constitute
the microstructure, which has an enormous influence on the appearance
of the final piece. Although seeing the microstructure is often beyond the
capability of the unaided eye, those who design and fashion ceramics
intuitively manipulate this level of structure to create their effects. Thus,
understanding how this leads to the results we see in the final object further
adds to our appreciation.

Beautiful objects and beautiful stories and beautiful experiences of all
kinds require the perception of an underlying sense of order and simplicity
in what otherwise seems a pretty random world. Science appreciation, like
art appreciation, lies in developing this sense of, understanding of, and
even explanations for this simplicity. And what is true of science appreciation and art appreciation is also true of the appreciation of technology—which involves an understanding of the fundamental constraints on
what can and what cannot be achieved and how a particular object has
been created by artisans and artists working within a particular technology.
That technology is an essential part of the culture and history within which
the artist worked; what is produced at a particular time and place is a
unique result of an interaction between historical, cultural, aesthetic, and
technical factors—none of which should be ignored and each of which aids
in understanding the others.

Unfortunately neither artists nor artisans have often documented exactly how or why they created their work. But recent advances in the
characterization of both the external structure and the internal microstructure and composition of tiny samples of material can permit inferences
about how, when, and where an object was made. We illustrate this with
examples and discuss the methodology. One might ask: "What good is all
this analysis, this attempt to see and understand what was often not seen
and not understood by the artist or artisan?" For us it allows an articulation
of understanding that was only intuitive for the artist; it adds an element
of appreciation.

The most useful part of this work may well be the discussion of ways
whereby one may see and study an object in greater depth. Much can be
learned from nothing more than careful observation. Much more can be
learned with the simplest of tools—penlight and magnifying glass. Setting
aside a corner of the office, study, or kitchen in which to carry out microscopic observations and simple tests should be considered by serious

students, collectors, and curators—they will certainly benefit. Finally, modern laboratory methods enable us to learn a great deal from tiny samples that can often be taken in an inconspicuous way without any apparent harm to the object. Other tests can be done without any sampling at all, and, of course, are preferred. We think, however, that when serious questions are posed that can be answered best by inconspicuous sampling, the advantages and disadvantages of such sampling should be rationally weighed. This places an obvious obligation on the curator-collector to understand what might be thus learned.

These same methods and approach are also necessary tools for the historian or archaeologist studying ceramic objects. They constitute revolutionary additions to methods of recognizing pottery types, to stylistic analyses, and to more usual laboratory studies.

We think the most important parts of the work are the ten examples of ceramic masterpieces we provide to illustrate our point of view. If these descriptions convey some sense of joy and wonder at these extraordinary accomplishments, then an interest in understanding the hows and whys of their creation will naturally follow. We ourselves are filled with pleasure and delight each time we see these wonderful creations.

W. David Kingery
Pamela B. Vandiver

ACKNOWLEDGMENTS

We are indebted to many curators for allowing us to examine, touch, and feel objects in their care, and to observe these objects with a microscope, and in some cases by radiography. Many have been generous in providing small samples of equivalent wares from which it was possible to determine microstructures and chemical analyses. Without their enthusiasm, advice, and help, this work would not have been possible.

Professor William Kelly Simpson, Curator, Dr. Edward Brovarski, Assistant Curator, and Peter Lacovara, Departmental Assistant, of the Department of Egyptian and Ancient Near Eastern Art at the Boston Museum of Fine Arts, helped us with answers to numerous questions, and allowed us to examine and photograph the Egyptian faience chalice of Chapter 2 and to sample a chipped area in a similar chalice from the same tomb at Abydos.

Our appreciation is expressed to Drs. Bo Gyllensvard and Jan Wirgin of the Museum of Far Eastern Antiquities for their help and permission to analyze shards in their care, and to Dr. James Watt and Diane Nelson of the Boston Museum of Fine Arts for their advice and permission to photograph and examine the Longquan celadon vessel of Chapter 3. We would also like to thank Betty Seed, Louise Corkhum, and Judy Tully of the Radiology Department, Cambridge Hospital, for their interest and assistance with xeroradiography.

We gratefully acknowledge the permission of the Victoria and Albert Museum to photograph and examine the jun ware bowl shown in Chapter 4. Robert Tichane and Mrs. J. Grebanier have been kind enough to give us excellent replications made by R. Tichane and J. Grebanier for our study. Rose Kerr of the Victoria and Albert Museum and Jessica Rawson of the British Museum and many others have been most helpful with discussions and suggestions.

We are grateful to the Victoria and Albert Museum for allowing us to examine and photograph the luster plate illustrated in Chapter 5. Oliver Watson of the Victoria and Albert Museum has provided much advice and encouragement as well as lusterware shards for study. Alan Caiger-Smith has discussed his work with lusterware.

We are grateful to the Musée National de Céramique de Sèvres, its curator, Mme. A. Hallé, and Mlle. E. Fontan for permission to examine and photograph the Medici porcelain bottle illustrated in Chapter 7 and the Iznik tile, Chapter 6, as well as for providing Iznik tile fragments. The Museo delle Ceramiche di Faenza and its curator, Dr. Gian Carlo Bojani, furnished a fragment of the rare Faenza Medici porcelain shard for analysis.

We wish to thank Margaret Medley, Rosemary Scott, and the Percival David Foundation of Chinese Art for permission to examine the K'ang Hsi plate shown in Chapter 8, and for providing us with a photograph and contemporary shard for analysis.

We gratefully acknowledge permission of the Musée National de Céramique at Sèvres to study and photograph the Boucher statue shown in Chapter 10 and thank A. Hallé, G. LeDuc, T. Préaud, E. Fontan, and A. d'Albis for many helpful discussions. The radiograph was done by Mlle. F. Drilhon, Laboratoire de Recherche des Musées de France, Musée du Louvre, to whom we are grateful.

The Böttger porcelain discussed in Chapter 9 and the jasperware chocolate pot illustrated in Chapter 11 are from the collection of the Metropolitan Museum of New York. We are grateful to C. LeCorbieller and J. McNab for permission to examine and photograph these objects and to Arnold Mountford, Curator, and David Barker of the Archaeology Department of the Stoke-on-Trent Museum and Art Gallery for providing us with a seventeenth century jasperware shard.

We also wish to thank David Lange, Electron Microprobe Laboratory, Geology Department, Harvard University, for assistance with microprobe analyses; Leonard Sudenfeld, Massachusetts Institute of Technology, for help with scanning electron microscopy; Yet-Ming Chiang, Massachusetts Institute of Technology, for scanning transmission electron microscopy; and Yusuke Moriyoshi of the National Institute for Inorganic Materials, Japan, for transmission electron microscopy.

We are particularly grateful to Rose Kerr and Oliver Watson of the Victoria and Albert Museum, Rosemary Scott of the Percival David Foundation of Chinese Art, Derek Gilman of the British Museum, Bill Sargent of the Peabody Museum, and Christine Ann Webb and Lauriston Ward for reviewing sections of an early draft and contributing many perceptive and helpful comments.

Many students have worked with us in developing our understanding; particular help has come from I-Wen Huang, Shari Yokota, and David Smith. Tony Centorino has done an excellent job of typing and retyping. John Mara drafted most of the line drawings with great skill. Most important, editorial assistant Susan Rosevear has been invaluable in many ways, persevering through several plans and drafts.

Finally, we are indebted to Edward Rothstein and Erwin Glikes of the Free Press and Sidney Solomon and Raymond Solomon, of Publishers Creative Services Inc., for their enthusiasm and support in actually turning all this into a book.

Ceramic
Masterpieces

PART *I*

INTRODUCTION

*C*eramics are formed from clay or claylike materials, which, after being mixed with water, are plastically shaped, dried, and heated to form a rocklike product. Usually the ware is coated with a thin layer of adherent glass, or glaze. Sometimes it is left unglazed; this is called bisque or bisquit. Painted decoration may be applied under or over the glaze, and the glaze may be transparent or opaque; clear, white, or colored; with a surface that is glossy, matte, or rough. The unlimited possibilities of form, texture, design, color, and optical effects make ceramics a wonderful medium for artistic expression. Utilitarian, luxury, and art wares mirror the needs and tastes of the society and culture within which they were created.

Sparked by the emergence and enormous growth of high-technology ceramics over the past two decades, there has been a revolution in our understanding of the science and technology underlying the production and properties of all ceramics. This has been accompanied by the development of new methods of microscopic observation and analysis. The time seems ripe to apply this new understanding and these new techniques to the interpretation of outstanding ceramic wares—masterpieces—made throughout the ages. This approach is accessible to the typical nonscientist student, curator, devotee, or collector since the essential idea is simple: each ware has a particular structure that determines the properties of the ceramic. By "structure" we mean the composition and arrangement of the physically and chemically different constituents that make up a ware. A fired glaze, for example, may consist of bubbles and various crystalline

3

particles suspended in a glass medium. The amount, size, and distribution
of the bubbles and particles in the glaze, together with its overall thickness
and the nature of the underlying body, determine its appearance. An
example: glazes with many fine particles dispersed through the glass are
white and opaque, thus serving as an excellent ground for painting. The
structure results from the raw materials selected and the technology used
to apply and fire the glaze. This linkage of technology, structure, and
visual impact is both simple and important. By concentrating on the origin
of structure and its influence on visual impact, we can bring together and
begin to understand what otherwise seem widely divergent observations
and interpretations.

Modern ceramics have been developed mostly in response to needs for
new products or devices that could not be made from existing materials.
Ordinary spark plug insulators were among the first "high tech" ceramics.
They came about as a result of the revolution in transportation through
the emergence of the automobile and aircraft during the early part of this
century. As more powerful engines were developed, temperatures increased, and greater requirements were placed on the spark plug ceramic
insulator. This led, first, to the reinvention of a composition very similar
to the Böttger porcelain described in Chapter 9; and then to revolutionary
new compositions manufactured to close specifications and based on an
artificial raw material (chemically purified aluminum oxide) rather than
the traditional clays and minerals previously used. Although spark plugs
have become such standard products that they are not seen as part of the
latest, electronics-based high-tech revolution, their pattern of development
is similar to that of most new ceramics.

During the past 30 years, new ceramic materials have been created as
part of the development of nuclear power (which uses uranium oxide ceramics as the principal fuel), and for modern steel production (which requires sophisticated high-temperature ceramics), for insulating coatings of
missiles and space shuttles, for automatic manufacturing procedures that
employ ceramic cutting tools, and particularly for computers and communication devices. Some of these new ceramics, such as sensors developed
for automatic control systems, are at the beginning of their history; others,
such as uranium oxide fuel for nuclear reactors, are now mature products.
Ceramics are being developed at such a rapid pace that no other class of
materials includes as large a proportion and variety of new products and
properties.

If the development pattern for these new high-tech ceramics seems
familiar to those interested in traditional wares, it is because modern ways

follow an ancient precedent. The first contrived ceramic, Egyptian faience (described in Chapter 2), was developed in the Near East and Mediterranean region in response to the desire for ceramics with clear, bright colors. The discoveries of Medici porcelain (Chapter 7), soft-paste porcelain (Chapter 10), and Böttger porcelain (Chapter 9) were the result of determined research efforts aimed at finding new compositions with the visual impact of white Chinese porcelain. In these developments, technological, cultural, geographical, aesthetic, and utilitarian requirements and objectives are so intertwined that no one of these histories can be fully appreciated independently of the others.

CHAPTER 1

AN OVERVIEW

*I*n this chapter we first review a history of how ceramics are made and then discuss ways in which modern ceramic science and technology can contribute to our interpretation and appreciation of the visual effects obtained. For the most part, the artisans and artists who created this history have not told us how they proceeded—indeed, new and valuable techniques have most often been treated as closely held secrets. We must learn by examining the objects themselves.

A HISTORY OF CERAMICS

The earliest fired ceramic products thus far discovered are the molded figures from Dolne Vestonice in Czechoslovakia, which were made about 24,000 years ago. Fired clay vessels began to be produced in the Near East about 10,000 years ago; these vessels were utilitarian, undecorated, fired at a relatively low temperature, and seem to have been derived from brickmaking practices. By 6400 B.C. pottery making was a well-developed craft. Carefully made ware was often coated with a specially prepared clay suspension, or "slip," to form a surface or slip layer of a finer consistency. Both utilitarian and aesthetic aims were achieved by burnishing (that is, polishing) the damp surface of the pot with a smooth stone to form a sheen. The resulting surface was more attractive as well as less porous. Decorations were both incised and impressed. Red decorations were achieved by an ochrous iron-oxide pigment applied before firing; for black decorations, paints based on manganese oxide pigments were employed. Both types of paints had been used for thousands of years—for body decoration, burial objects, and cave paintings—so their use on fired ceramics is hardly surprising. When ochre pigments are fired in a smoky atmosphere deficient in oxygen, they give up some of their oxygen to the atmosphere and form reduced-oxygen-content compounds, which are black. This phenomenon was already being utilized in the sixth millennium B.C. to form black decorations from widely available, iron-containing ochres and clays.

In Mesopotamia during the Halaf period, 5,500–,000 B.C., these techniques had become more sophisticated and were used to produce beautiful polychrome wares. The clay suspensions employed as paints before firing were carefully prepared by allowing the coarser particles to settle out, and using only very fine particles. Probably a bit of ash was added to help keep the particles from settling out, and also to enhance sintering (the hardening and densification of a body that occurs on heating without substantial melting). The ware was fired to form a glossy clay surface. Glossy sintered black decoration resulted when the ware was fired in a smoky (that is, reducing) atmosphere; glossy red coatings were made by firing in an air-rich (oxidizing) atmosphere. Thus by manipulating the kiln atmosphere, the color of the ware could be controlled.

During the late fourth and third millennia, the sophisticated use of this technology, which required knowledgeable control of kiln atmospheres during the firing process, was widespread. It was perfected in Attic black-on-red ware, circa 700–300 B.C. Electron microscopy and microchemical analysis have allowed us to determine the special composition and structure of the glossy sintered paint layer. Thus we are very sure of this relationship between the technology and its visual results.

Quantity production of ceramics began during the fourth millennium B.C. in the Near East, and later in other parts of the world as urban centers developed; with these came specialized ceramic production and extensive use of the potter's wheel and fired earthenware molds. The potter's wheel provides the momentum for continuous rotation while a lump of clay is formed (thrown) into the shape of a vessel. By pressing a slab of clay onto or into a mold, it can be quickly shaped, and removed when it becomes stiff; the process is repeated again and again. These technical developments revolutionized the form and shape of ware that hitherto had been hand-molded by assembling pinches or coils or slabs of the prepared clay. Wheel throwing, followed by carving, trimming, and turning, along with the use of molds, became the standard production methods in Europe and Asia.

In the New World, molds were used, but not the potter's wheel.

From early production through Roman times, earthenware of many sizes, shapes, and styles was made everywhere utilizing this repertoire of tools and techniques. There were periods when geometric designs predominated, others when shape was most important, others when sophisticated painting was the greatest concern, and yet others in which black-on-gray or black-on-red ware was especially well executed, but the basic underlying techniques continued in a way almost disconnected from gyrations of style and design. In many societies earthenware is being made today using production methods practiced since the fourth millennium B.C.—careful preparation and purification of the clay; the addition of non-plastic additives, slips, and painted, impressed, and carved decoration; the joining together of separately formed parts; paddle and anvil consolidation; modeling; throwing on the potter's wheel; forming in molds; and using kilns with controlled atmospheres and temperatures.

Earthenware, however, is not the only ceramic tradition. The first truly new ceramic body composition evolved in Egypt and Mesopotamia about 4500 B.C. and is generally called Egyptian faience. A paste was made by crushing and grinding quartz pebbles and mixing the powder with sodium and calcium salts obtained from desert deposits called natron and malachite ore containing copper. Shapes were formed by hand or in molds. During drying the salt solution migrated to the surface of the damp objects, where the water evaporated and an "efflorescent" salt layer was deposited. On firing at about 900°C, the white quartz body became coated with a surface glaze colored blue by copper oxide (a sample is described in Chapter 2). Improvements in technique were made over the millennia: a bit of clay was added for workability; a less pure sand was used and only the slip layer made from pure quartz; a vapor glazing process was employed; the glaze was premelted before being applied to the surface; polychrome patterns, inlaid and painted, enhanced the ware's appearance.

The goal achieved by the development of Egyptian faience was the provision of a white body to serve as a ground for the beautiful clear blue color. This objective—to form a white ground for colored decoration—underlies many of the important technological developments in ceramics. The simplest solution was to apply a white clay slip over a buff body, as was done in the Near East in the ninth and tenth centuries A.D., perhaps in response to the white porcelains that began to be imported from China during the T'ang Dynasty (618–906 A.D.). By the ninth and tenth centuries A.D., glass melting and glass blowing were a developed technology, and a modification of Egyptian faience was invented. This consisted of crushing and grinding quartz, which was mixed with a pre-melted glass formed as a fine "frit" powder by grinding or pouring the molten glass into water and a small fraction, 10–15 percent of highly plastic white clay. The quartz-frit-clay ware became the Near Eastern equivalent of porcelain; an early thirteenth century sample of such ware made at Kashan, Persia, and decorated with a gold luster painting is illustrated in Chapter 5. A similar, but crude body, in which only the slip layer involved pure white quartz, was used for the sixteenth century Iznik tile described in Chapter 6. The best Seljuk ware of the thirteenth century, and later seventeenth century "Gombroon" ware, exported from that port (modern Bandar Abbas) on the Persian Gulf, used more frit, less clay, and longer firing times to achieve a particularly hard, white translucent product. To enhance the translucency, this ware was sometimes pierced with small holes that filled with glaze to make "rice grain" porcelain, a technique later used in China and Japan.

A quite different ceramic tradition that ultimately led to fine porcelain began in China where the widespread availability of mineral deposits of "china stone" and china clays (kaolins) and the early development of high-temperature kilns led to the production of stoneware as early as the Shang Dynasty (1027–771 B.C.) that was equivalent to the German stoneware first made during late Medieval times. The necessary temperatures were achieved in three different types of Chinese kilns: the "horseshoe" kiln of the north, the hill-climbing "dragon" kiln of the south, and the egg-shaped kiln of Ching-te-Chen. All were built partly underground in a porous, sandy soil, and all were heavily insulated above ground; all had effective chimneys to give a good draft and a long, hot flame. As a result temperatures of about 1200°C were achieved during the Shang and Zhou "proto-porcelain" period when stonewares were first made. Kiln temperatures gradually increased to about 1300°C by the T'ang Dynasty (618–906 A.D.), during which dense white porcelain was being produced for export. In contrast, kilns of the Near East were built with large fireboxes for bulky fuel, had relatively poor insulation, and were particularly suited for rapid firing at temperatures of 1000°C or so, but could not achieve temperatures of 1200°C. The importance of different raw materials and the development of high kiln temperatures in contributing to the history of Chinese ceramics as compared with their Near Eastern counterparts can hardly be exaggerated.

The first Chinese glazes, that is, fully melted glassy coatings, appeared during the later Shang Dynasty (1027–771 B.C.). They had a high lime content, and appreciable quantities of alkali, iron, and phosphorous oxides, which lowered the melting temperature and allowed a glaze to form during firing at 1200°C. The principal constituent of these first glazes was probably the ash of the soft pine used for kiln firing. Pine ash has a high lime content, but a variable composition, and as production developed, calcined limestone was mixed with the ash in increasing quantities until it became the principal constituent, as in the beautiful Song Dynasty celadon described in Chapter 3 and the jun ware of Chapter 4. Throughout the Song Dynasty, wares were probably made from a single natural mineral mixture of quartz, clay, feldspar, and mica, called china stone or petuntse. As production expanded, a white-burning clay (kaolin) began to be added (early in the Yuan Dynasty) to make forming easier; alkalies that lowered the melting point gradually replaced a portion of the lime content in the glaze.

Successful glazes became widely used in the Near East rather later than in China, mostly because of the lower firing temperatures (up to about 1000°C) on which the technology was based. Alkaline glazes molten in this temperature range have rather poor penetration and adhesion and a higher contraction on cooling than does a clay body; they tend to flake off the surface. Bodies with a higher quartz content, such as Egyptian faience, have a high contraction on cooling and are the best choice for low-melting alkaline glazes. But these wares are difficult to shape and have rather poor physical properties for utilitarian ware. Alkaline glazes similar in composition to glasses were used on limey clay bodies (which have a high contraction on cooling) beginning about 2300 B.C., but only came into wide use when lead oxide began to be used. Glaze compositions with a substantial lead content flow out over the surface, penetrate to form a good glaze–body bond, and have less contraction, which makes them usable on earthenware bodies. Lead-alkali glazes were used on Near Eastern pottery and brick beginning about 500 B.C., but lead glazes for vessels did not become widespread until the Roman era, when they were employed in both the Near East and China. The use of tin oxide as a white opacifier pigment became common in the ninth century A.D. by Islamic potters trying to replicate the whiteness of imported Chinese porcelains.

Famous T'ang Dynasty earthenware tomb figures and "splash decorated" vessels with a lead glaze colored yellow with additions of iron, blue with additions of cobalt, and green with additions of copper, were widely seen. However, the rapid decrease in viscosity with temperature of the lead glazes, and the tendency for these glazes to spread over the surface to give a good smooth coating, also causes the colors to run together. As a result precise designs were not easy to accomplish, although a number of techniques similar to those for cloisonne enamels on metal were utilized to separate the colors.

The ninth century A.D. Islamic invention of overglaze painting with metallic lusters on a tin-opacified white glaze ground introduced a major change in the nature of pottery decoration (a Kashan plate is described in Chapter 5). This revolutionary technique brought the technology of pigment preparation and the role of painters to center stage in luxury ceramic production. Later in the thirteenth and fourteenth centuries, the painting of scenes on Islamic wares in underglaze blue had a major influence on Chinese and worldwide conceptions of what ceramics should look like; the famous Ming underglaze blue and white porcelains were influenced by the Islamic wares. Underglaze decoration in the Near East was perfected in the bright polychrome Isnik tile described in Chapter 6. Overglaze enamels had been used on occasion in China, but Islamic pottery painters were the first to develop a class of ware (minai) with scenes painted in overglaze enamels, a form of ware perfected by the Chinese using their wonderful white, porcelain ground. It is represented here by an early eighteenth century K'ang Hsi plate painted in the *famille verte* palette (shown in Chapter 8).

Techniques for manufacturing the opaque white tin glaze as a ground for overpainting, first with luster and then with other enamels, spread throughout Spain, to Italy, and then to all of Europe, where "maiolica" became the dominant mode of European luxury pottery manufacture. And, following the earlier Islamic lead, the nature of the whole process changed; the shapes of the ware, and even the firing of the clay, became secondary to the preparation of the white ground and the rich palette of ceramic colors already developed by the end of the fifteenth century. Designs were painted directly on the unfired tin glaze layer and then coated (usually) with a lead overglaze, a virtuoso method in which no mistakes could be tolerated. The most time-consuming, and skillful, work was that of the painter, whose role became increasingly important. The Italian city-states bordering the sea, particularly Venice, carried on extensive trade with the Near East, and thus had indirect contacts with China as well. Italian maiolica was influenced by Oriental blue-and-white porcelain and by the colorful Iznik wares from Turkey. However, by the middle of the sixteenth century, carefully executed paintings of stories and historical scenes in a wholly European style became dominant.

During the sixteenth and seventeenth centuries, maiolica manufacture—known as "faience" in France, "delftware" in Holland—was the principal luxury ceramic throughout Europe. It was at this time that large quantities of Chinese wares began to come into Europe by sea routes. Maiolica did not have the translucency, strength, or hardness of porcelain, and there were extensive European efforts to make "real" porcelain.

There are reports of Venetian efforts to reproduce Chinese porcelain during the fifteenth century, and certainly milk glass with enamel decoration was produced in the sixteenth century. There were many reports of efforts to replicate Chinese wares, and some documentary descriptions, during the sixteenth century, but no regular production was established, and no examples exist that illustrate the degree of success actually achieved. The first successful European manufacture of porcelain was accomplished in Florence in 1575–1587 under the patronage of the Grand Duke Francesco I de Medici, and is usually referred to as Medici porcelain. A sample of this historically important material is shown in Chapter 7. According to a 1575 letter of the Venetian ambassador to Florence, a "Levantine" pointed out the road to a success after ten years of effort supported by the grand duke, who was an amateur alchemist and had a laboratory where he melted minerals and carried out chemical experiments. The Medici porcelain was an adaptation of Persian compositions to Italian methods. Instead of melting a frit, as in Persia, the alkali constituent was a glazemaker's sintered "marzacotta." This was made by heating, at the rear of the firebox, during the unglazed ware's bisque firing, a mixture of three parts of crushed sand and one part of calcined wine lees used as a source of alkali. The reacted alkali silicate marzacotta was milled and mixed with sand and clay to form a body that, when fired to a temperature of about 1100°C, was translucent. However, as almost every example deformed during firing and losses in firing must have been substantial, it is no surprise that production ended with the death of Francesco I in 1587.

After the Medici near-success, another hundred years passed that saw the increasing importation of Chinese ware, and increasing pressure for European production of its equivalent. Although earlier ware may well have been made at Paris or Rouen, the first successful European porcelain production seems to have been established near Paris at St. Cloud on the road to Versailles. An Englishman, Dr. Martin Lister, visited the factory in 1698 and was told that the first success was achieved in 1695 after 25 years of experimentation. There is no documentary evidence as to exactly how this ware was made, but Dr. Lister was told that at St. Cloud they "made a thing not unlike frit for glass to be wrought up with the clay," and later descriptions indicate how a mixture of soda ash, sea salt, potassium nitrate, sand, and lime were finely milled together and heated for a long period of time, as had been done with Medici porcelain. The resulting sinter was mixed with additional lime and a calcerous clay from Argenteuil, thrown or pressed to shape, trimmed or turned, and bisque-fired before applying a lead silicate glaze. The success of this material, as compared with the Medici body, lay in the high lime content, which made effective firing possible. Its overall similarity to the Medici formulation is striking, and it clearly is the culmination of a technical tradition that can be traced back to the Egyptian faience of 4500 B.C. A sculpture made of this soft-paste porcelain at Vincennes in 1752 is illustrated in Chapter 10.

During this same period, Augustus the Strong, elector of Saxony and king of Poland, was a compulsive collector of Chinese porcelain. At his court was Count von Tschirnhaus, a physicist famous for his experiments with high temperatures and mineral fusions achieved with burning mirrors. He was a foreign member of the French Royal Academy, carried out studies of mineral resources of Saxony, and established glasshouses and faience factories. In 1694 he wrote to his friend, Liebnitz, that he had "no more than a little piece of artificial porcelain." His research program was aimed specifically at the manufacture of porcelain, and he was assisted by Johann Friedrich Böttger, who had completed an apothecary's apprenticeship in Berlin. Much has been written but little is really known about the experiments studying the response of different soils and mixtures to von Tschirnhaus' mirrors and lenses. In any event, shortly before von Tschirnhaus' death in 1708, Böttger succeeded in making a dense red stoneware that was clearly an imitation of the Chinese Yi-Hsing ware (some was shaped in molds taken from the Yi-Hsing samples). Böttger's colors indicate a firing temperature of 1200–1300°C, equivalent to the temperatures then being used by German stoneware manufacturers in horizontal gas-flow furnaces to manufacture their salt-glazed product. By combining a white clay with gypsum and pushing his furnaces to the highest possible temperatures, Böttger achieved a European equivalent to white Chinese porcelain, as described in Chapter 9. Most descriptions of Böttger's invention focus on the composition used, but a principal secret of his success lay in achieving the kiln temperature necessary for satisfactory firing. During the next ten years, the advantages of feldspar as a flux to replace lime were recognized, and after Böttger's death in 1719, the Meissen formula was modified to that still used for modern European hard porcelain.

By the early eighteenth century, therefore, the Near Eastern quartz-frit-clay porcelain, the Chinese clay-quartz-feldspar porcelain, and the Islamic tin-glaze faience all were being manufactured in Europe, resulting in a worldwide trade in ceramics. Ceramic developments became part of the chemical and industrial revolutions of eighteenth century Europe; with trade came the widespread and rapid dissemination of technology. Meissen workers moved to Vienna and began porcelain production in 1720; soon thereafter migrating workers brought their knowledge of materials and methods to Hochst, Furstenburg, Nymphenburg, Strasburg, Frankenthal, Berlin, St. Petersburg, and Venice, among others. In France the story was much the same; from the original production of soft paste at St. Cloud, virtually identical production methods were employed at Chantilly, Mennecy, Vincennes, and elsewhere. In England the first porcelain (soft paste) was manufactured at Chelsea in 1742 by Nicholas Sprimont, who was born in France and familiar with expatriate Huguenot artisans.

The planned research program to develop porcelain at Meissen was only one of the more spectacular successes in a general atmosphere of experimentation with various techniques throughout Europe. The careful preparation and salt-glaze methods of the immigrant Dutch Eler brothers in Staffordshire during the 1690s became the standards for Staffordshire production. A Jesuit priest, Père d'Entrecolles, sent letters from China to France in 1712, and again in 1722, describing raw materials and manufacturing methods. He included samples, which were given to the famous chemist René Reaumur for analysis. Reaumur found that one of the ingredients, kaolin, was infusable, whereas the other, petuntse, fused readily in his furnace. He theorized that Chinese porcelain consisted of a mixture of an infusible earth with a fusibly constituent, a conclusion reached only after many factories had applied the same considerations in actually making ware. Reaumur also invented a method of heating glass packed in a mixture of gypsum and sand to make a fibrous crystalline product called "Reaumur porcelain," which was widely discussed, but seems never to have been produced.

In England the first porcelain made at Chelsea was almost immediately modified by adding bone ash to the calcined frit, probably to increase the whiteness of the material. At Worcester soapstone was employed as a kaolin replacement. By the end of the century, beginning about 1796, the entire frit was replaced by a calcined, but not fused, bone ash used in combination with feldspar as the low-melting ingredient. The typical English formula for "bone china," for which Spode is given the credit, was six parts bone ash, four parts china stone, and three and a half parts china clay. Fired at 1200–1250°C, a strong, white translucent porcelain resulted, which remains the premier porcelain (bone china) manufactured in England.

The addition of calcined flints to produce a whiter body when used with the available ball clay was begun in 1720 by Astbury in England, who was impressed by the clear white color of flint milled after calcination. It became the staple of the fine white earthenware production of the Staffordshire potteries.

Perhaps no one exemplifies the century more than Josiah Wedgwood, who was born in 1730, apprenticed as a potter to his brother, and entered the business for himself in 1759 making wheel-thrown, lead-glazed earthenware. An experimentalist, his improvements in body and glaze led to a very successful dinnerware manufacturing plant. He applied an improved engine-turning lathe in which the ware is moved horizontally in synchronism with its rotation to make fluted designs; this machinery is still being used. He recognized that the turning process gave rise to a surface sheen roughly equivalent to burnishing. He also did compositional experiments to improve a body known as Egyptian black, or basalte, which had a high iron content. These developments took a special turn when Wedgwood borrowed a copy of the book *Compendium of Egyptian, Etruscan, Greek, Roman and Gallic Antiquities*, by Count Caylus. Wedgwood and his partner, Thomas Bentley, began manufacturing and marketing ornamental ware modeled on their ideas of antiquarian and classic art. The combination of careful raw-material selection, grinding and purification, precise body preparation, controlled engine turning, and sprigged decorations made Wedgwood's colored, unglazed stonewares a great success.

An increasing part of Wedgwood's production became ornamental wares, particularly medallions and cameos. He wished to make a body he could color in imitation of various gemstones and which would take a polish. By 1773 he had developed a fine, white terra-cotta body that contained a small amount of barium carbonate. A year later he developed a composition using barium sulfate, of which a variety called *cawk* was abundant in Derbyshire. Early in 1776 Wedgwood wrote to his partner Bentley that the jasper composition he preferred was one part flint, six parts barium sulfate, three parts potter's clay, and one-quarter part gypsum. At that time his mixing was done in secret and the nature of this composition was very closely held.

The eighteenth century was also the time of the chemical and industrial revolutions in Europe; each was influenced strongly by and, in turn, influenced ceramic developments. While the preparation of colors and glazes had been an important part of maiolica manufacture for more than two centuries, and the first soft-paste porcelain made at St. Cloud used a tin-opacified lead glaze well known in maiolica manufacture, clear glazes became the norm for both soft-paste and hard-paste porcelain and were used in conjunction with separately fired overglaze enamels. Once body compositions and firing procedures were settled on, the major technical effort was devoted to modeling, to expanding the color palette, and to developing new decorative techniques. The beginning of this period coincided with the introduction of *famille rose* decoration in Chinese porcelain. These colors were known as "foreign colors" in China, and the extensive trade contacts between Europe and the Orient led to the exchange of designs and enamel formulations. New colors were developed and new flux compositions for enamels that contained bismuth oxide and borax additions to the basic lead or lead alkali silicates evolved. The decorating process became increasingly complex. Toward the end of the century, as many as nine successive firings might be required for different colors using different fluxes and at different temperatures.

The development of porcelain manufacture at Meissen was supported by the state, but it was intended to be, and eventually did become, a self-sustained enterprise that paid its way by producing wares for sale and export. The 1712 and 1722 letters of Pere d'Entrecolles describing Chinese porcelain manufacture during the reign of K'ang Hsi were rather garbled, and probably less helpful in formulating compositions than is generally believed. However, they were widely disseminated, and the description of porcelain-making methods also appeared in an English translation of DuHalde's history of China. These descriptions of a system in which separate specialists mined, milled, and purified the material, supplied it to specialist factories for the manufacture of shapes, with other specialists operating the kilns, and still others doing the painting and enameling, are known to have had a major influence on Wedgwood, who is credited with being the first European manufacturer to organize his factory using such a division of labor. The standard ceramic factory became a production facility with special materials preparation and independent formulators, modelers, mold makers, repairers, glazers, furnacemen, painters, and so forth. Indeed much of the ware manufactured in Staffordshire was sent to Chelsea for painting or to Liverpool for the application of printed decoration.

By the end of the eighteenth century, this extraordinary period of European ceramic development had pretty much run its course. The basics of body formulations, manufacturing methods, and decorative techniques were in place. At the French National Manufacture at Sevres, Brongniart abandoned the production of soft-paste wares in 1804, and the continent settled on hard porcelain. In England, bone china and fine earthenware became the norm. The quality and cost of European ware made it a major export product. Many of the developments we have not discussed (for example, the history of vapor glazing, the use of platinum for silver luster, parian porcelain, and Belleek ware) and local traditions (we have not even mentioned Korea or Japan) are essentially variations on these major themes. As a beginning toward understanding the relationship of technology, aesthetics, and tradition, we have focused on the principal streams of technological development illustrated in Figure 1.1, because this is the best way to see the connections between what are often pictured as isolated wares rather than as parts of an integrated story.

CERAMIC SCIENCE

By ceramic science we mean an ability to apply principles of chemistry and physics to ceramic systems in a way that is useful and makes their behavior comprehensible. Ceramic science developed gradually over the past hundred years or so, but took a giant step forward in the last decade with the general availability of electron microscopes with a magnification sufficiently great to reveal the details of internal microstructures. Methods of microchemical analysis have also developed that allow us to determine the composition of constituents in the size range where they have a strong influence on ceramic processes and the resulting visual characteristics [about 0.0001 to 0.001 mm (millimeter)]. As a consequence of these advances, we have entered a new era where even a little understanding of ceramic science can contribute much to one's interpretation and appreciation of ceramic objects of archaeological, historic, and artistic interest.

A basic tenet of ceramic science is that materials selection and processing beget structure, and that structure begets visual impact and other properties. By structure, we mean the nature of various parts of a body or glaze and how they are arranged or put together to construct the whole. Structure in the millimeter and centimeter range of the metric system of units (Figure 1.2) is called the *macrostructure*—for example, how a handle is luted on the body. On a finer scale, at a magnification of 100–100,000X, we can actually see the size, shape, and arrangement of the individual "phases" in the body or glaze; with modern analytical instruments we can determine the chemical composition and atomic arrangement of each of these different constituent phases. (*Phase*, a word derived from the different physical states—i.e., vapor, liquid, crystal, glass—is commonly used to describe each of the separate constituents coexisting in a particular microstructure.) This analysis of the *microstructure* turns out to be a powerful tool because this is the level of structure near the wavelength of light that most strongly affects optical properties and visual effects.

Finally, by spectroscopic and diffraction methods, the internal structure of the individual atoms that make up the ceramic and their arrangement in the crystalline or glassy phases can be determined. These arrangements are of interest to us in their role of determining melting behavior and glass

about 22000 BC-Earliest known fired clay figures

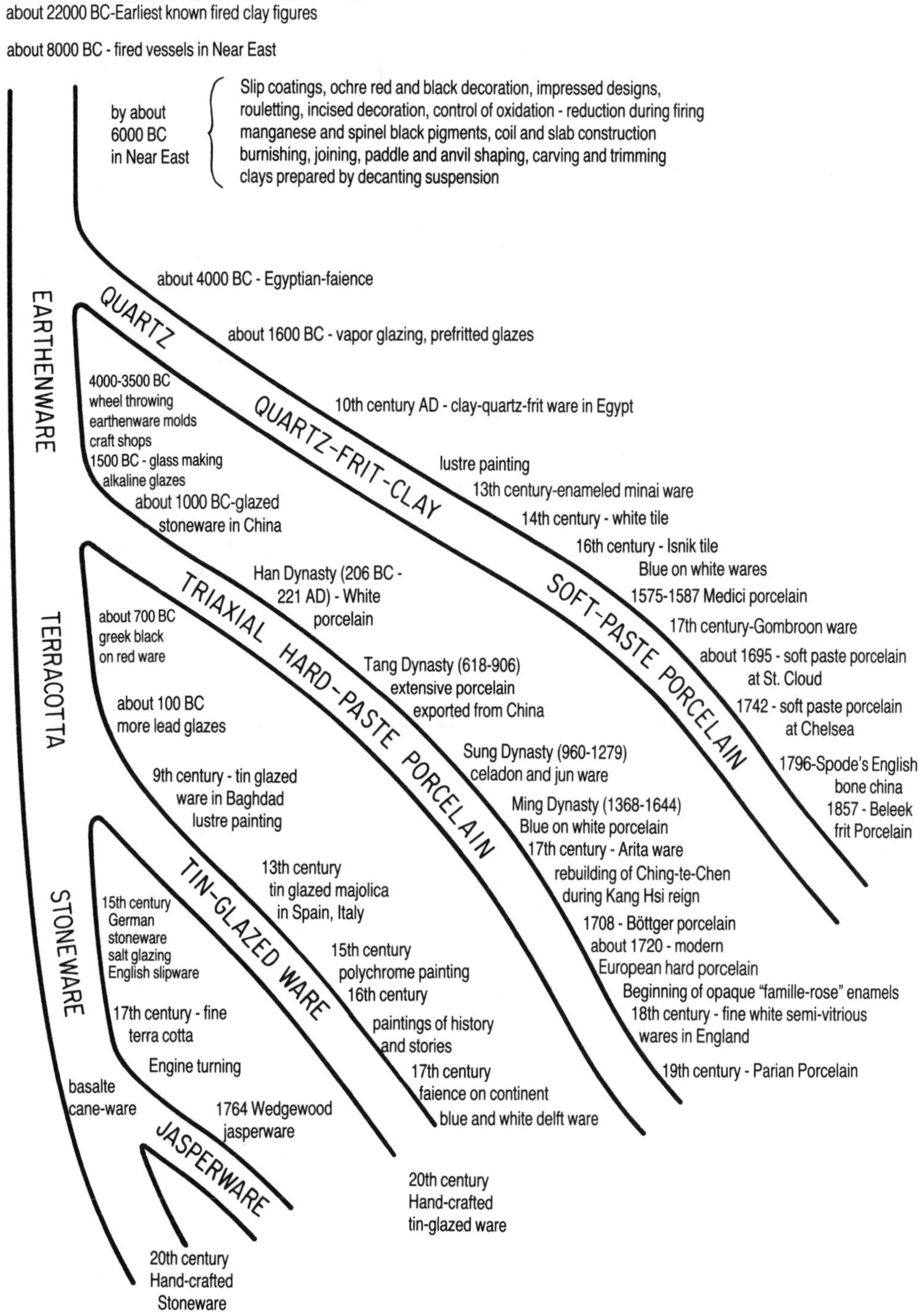

about 8000 BC - fired vessels in Near East

EARTHENWARE

by about
6000 BC
in Near East
{ Slip coatings, ochre red and black decoration, impressed designs,
rouletting, incised decoration, control of oxidation - reduction during firing
manganese and spinel black pigments, coil and slab construction
burnishing, joining, paddle and anvil shaping, carving and trimming
clays prepared by decanting suspension }

QUARTZ

about 4000 BC - Egyptian-faience

about 1600 BC - vapor glazing, prefritted glazes

4000-3500 BC
wheel throwing
earthenware molds
craft shops
1500 BC - glass making
alkaline glazes
about 1000 BC-glazed
stoneware in China

QUARTZ-FRIT-CLAY

10th century AD - clay-quartz-frit ware in Egypt

lustre painting
13th century-enameled minai ware
14th century - white tile
16th century - Isnik tile
Blue on white wares

SOFT-PASTE PORCELAIN

1575-1587 Medici porcelain
17th century-Gombroon ware
about 1695 - soft paste porcelain
at St. Cloud
1742 - soft paste porcelain
at Chelsea
1796-Spode's English
bone china
1857 - Beleek
frit Porcelain

TERRACOTTA

Han Dynasty (206 BC -
221 AD) - White
porcelain

about 700 BC
greek black
on red ware

Tang Dynasty (618-906)
extensive porcelain
exported from China

about 100 BC
more lead glazes

TRIAXIAL HARD-PASTE PORCELAIN

Sung Dynasty (960-1279)
celadon and jun ware

9th century - tin glazed
ware in Baghdad
lustre painting

Ming Dynasty (1368-1644)
Blue on white porcelain
17th century - Arita ware
rebuilding of Ching-te-Chen
during Kang Hsi reign
1708 - Böttger porcelain
about 1720 - modern
European hard porcelain
Beginning of opaque "famille-rose" enamels
18th century - fine white semi-vitrious
wares in England
19th century - Parian Porcelain

STONEWARE

TIN-GLAZED WARE

13th century
tin glazed majolica
in Spain, Italy

15th century
German
stoneware
salt glazing
English slipware

15th century
polychrome painting
16th century

paintings of history
and stories

17th century - fine
terra cotta

17th century
faience on continent
blue and white delft ware

Engine turning

basalte
cane-ware

JASPERWARE

1764 Wedgewood
jasperware

20th century
Hand-crafted
tin-glazed ware

20th century
Hand-crafted
Stoneware

Figure 1.1. The flow of ceramic history illustrates the mainstreams of earthenware, terra-cotta, and stoneware; of "triaxial" hard-paste porcelain; of quartz-based bodies; and of tin-glazed ware. Some important shaping and decorative techniques are illustrated, but the diagram is far from complete.

formation. They also are our colorants—particularly the group called the
transition elements, which includes copper, cobalt, manganese, chromium,
and iron.

For each of the objects discussed in Part II we shall explicitly determine
the macrostructure, which tells us much about the forming procedures;
the microstructure, which connects the raw materials selection and processing methods to the visual effects achieved; and the individual constituent
compositions, which affect behavior during firing and contribute to the
color and other properties of the ware. None of these different levels of
structure can be ignored, but the microstructure is most revealing, and
therefore most important. It is studied by polishing a small sample, some-

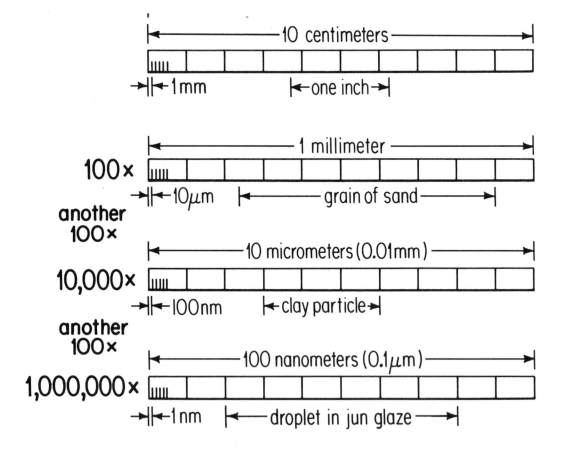

Figure 1.2. Metric units are the standard international units of
measure. There are 2.54 centimeters (cm) in 1 inch. A thousandth
of a meter is a millimeter (mm); a millionth of a meter is a micrometer (μm), about twice the wavelength of light; a billionth
of a meter is called a nanometer (nm).

times etching the surface to give better contrast between the different constituent phases, and then observing it with optical or electron microscopes.

As an example, consider the microstructures of the eighteenth century K'ang Hsi Chinese porcelain described in Chapter 8 and its contemporary, the French soft-paste porcelain of Chapter 10. Shown at the same magnification in Figures 1.3 and 1.4, they are similar in many respects but quite different in others. Quartz was an important ingredient in each of these wares, but it turns up in the fired body in rather different ways. In the K'ang Hsi body, which was fired for several hours at the high temperature of 1250–1300°C, the quartz has partially dissolved in the surrounding viscous potassium-aluminum-silicate liquid, leaving residual rounded quartz particles, and even some pools of liquid from which the quartz particle has completely dissolved and disappeared. On cooling, the viscous liquid solidifies as a glass. In contrast, the quartz particles originally present in the soft-paste porcelain have mostly been changed to multiple grains of another crystalline form of silica, cristobalite, as a result of as long as 90 hours in contact with a more fluid alkali-silicate liquid at a temperature of about 1000°C. The quite different microstructures indicate the nature of the firing procedures used.

The microstructures also determine the strength of these different wares. Around the quartz particles in the K'ang Hsi porcelain cracks have developed to accommodate the contraction of quartz on cooling as it changes crystalline form at 573°C. These cracks act as stress concentrators, lowering the fracture strength as compared with the properties of a nearly quartz-free body such as the Böttger porcelain of Chapter 9. In the soft-paste ware, the cristobalite transforms to another crystalline form on cooling, with a volume change similar to that of quartz, but at a temperature near 200°C. This transformation also leads to high strains, but cracks occur at the interface between the cristobalite grains and the rest of the body, rather than in the glass. As a result of the cristobalite content, the ware is less strong and more subject to cracking when its temperature is changed rapidly. The fracture surface has a sugary texture rather than the smooth fracture seen in hard-paste porcelain. The microstructure of the Böttger porcelain, of which a replica is shown in Chapter 9, has less quartz than the Chinese ware and, as a result, is the strongest and most thermal shock-resistant porcelain ever made.

The particles of the clay constituent of the K'ang Hsi porcelain are much smaller than the quartz. The clay is not seen in the microstructure because it has completely decomposed to form the tiny mullite crystals

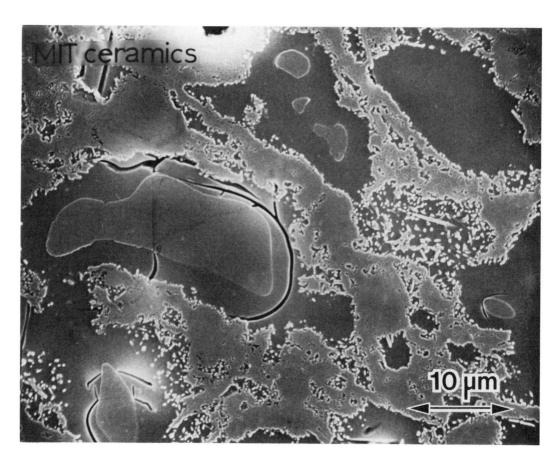

Figure 1.3. The microstructure of eighteenth century K'ang Hsi Chinese porcelain. Large quartz particles are mostly dissolved in the alkali-silicate glass.
Tiny crystals of mullite derived from the clay material, and also from the
feldspar, are immersed in the continuous glass phase. The fissures adjacent
to the quartz grains (exaggerated by the etchant used) result from differential
contraction on cooling (1000X). The sketch is provided to help identify the
constituent phases present.

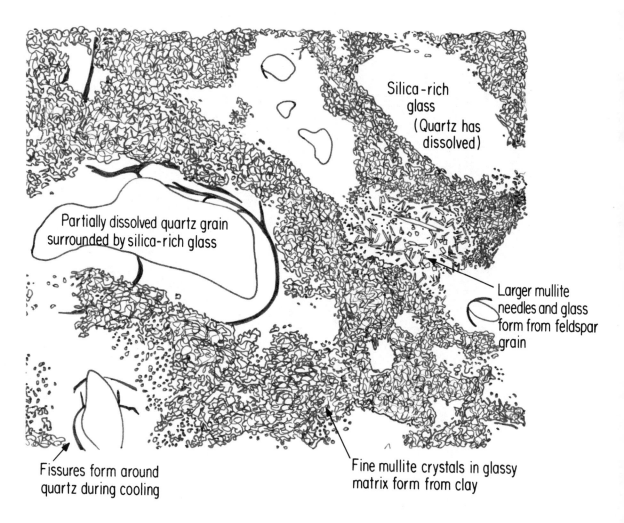

Silica-rich glass (Quartz has dissolved)

Partially dissolved quartz grain surrounded by silica-rich glass

Larger mullite needles and glass form from feldspar grain

Fine mullite crystals in glassy matrix form from clay

Fissures form around quartz during cooling

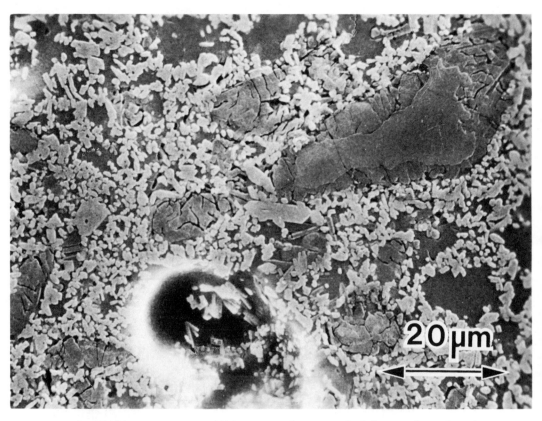

Figure 1.4. The microstructure of European soft-paste porcelain contains cristobalite grains derived from quartz in the body formulation. Large quartz
grains are not completely transformed. There are also many smaller crystals
of calcium silicate (wollastonite). The crystalline constituents are immersed
in a continuous glass phase (1000X). The labeled sketch is provided to help
identify the phases present.

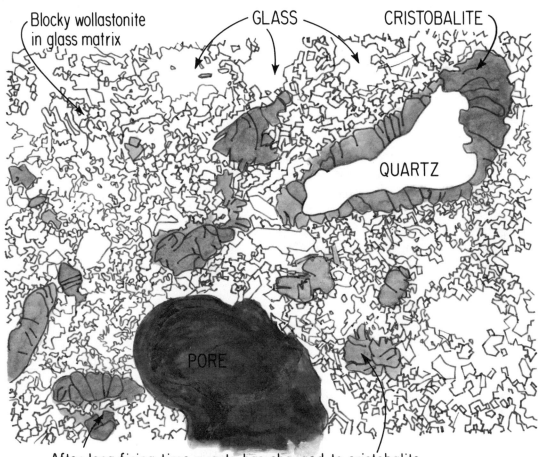

Blocky wollastonite in glass matrix

GLASS

CRISTOBALITE

QUARTZ

PORE

After long firing time quartz has changed to cristobalite form of silica embedded in the glass phase. Feldspar, the third principal raw material, melts and then reacts to form mullite, and the location of one residual feldspar grain can be seen where larger rodlike crystals of mullite occur in the glass matrix. In contrast the fine crystals distributed in the glassy matrix of the soft-paste porcelain are chunky crystallites of wollastonite, $CaSiO_3$. These form during firing as a result of the high lime, high silica, and low aluminum oxide content of this composition. In both hard-paste and soft-paste porcelain, the microstructures of fine crystals, together with larger silica crystals distributed in a glass matrix, afford comparable translucency.

The hard porcelain achieves this white translucent structure using relatively high alumina content derived from the clay and feldspar, which permits good plasticity and formability, but requires a high firing temperature. In contrast the soft-paste porcelain requires a low clay content to give a low alumina content. This formulation allows a lower firing temperature, but provides a less plastic body. From the amount and composition of the different phases, both the body formulation and resulting properties can be inferred.

Another microstructure determined at a higher magnification is illustrated in Figure 1.5, which shows the internal structure of the jun glaze discussed in Chapter 4. In a thin cross section viewed with a transmission electron microscope, it is easy to see that an emulsion much like an oil–vinegar salad dressing is formed in the glaze and solidifies on cooling. The size of the particles and their composition give the jun glaze its typical lustrous translucent blue color. At a lower magnification, Figure 1.5b, it can be seen that there are also "white cloud" areas within which wollastonite, $CaSiO_3$, forms as tiny particles precipitating from lime-rich regions of the glaze. The best glazes have these cloudy formations on a scale just at the limit of naked-eye resolution, about 0.1 mm. For optimal visual impact, these glazes both must have compositional variations with local regions rich in lime and be cooled slowly. Cooling too quickly or a uniform composition without lime-rich regions leads to flat, uninteresting results. Thus from the microstructure we can infer the process involved, understand the scarcity of really outstanding jun ware, and appreciate the source of the ware's powerful visual impact.

Each constituent phase in a ceramic microstructure has its own composition, which determines its individual properties. Since silicon and oxygen together make up about 75 percent of the earth's crust, it is not suprising that silica (SiO_2) and silicates are the principal phases present in ceramic microstructures. In silicates the ratio of oxygen to silicon is the main factor determining their properties. When melted, pure quartz (silicon dioxide, SiO_2) forms a viscous liquid that cools to room temperature as a solid noncrystalline glass, with a very high melting point (1710°C). When added to silica, alkalies such as soda (Na_2O) and potash (K_2O), alkaline earths such as lime (CaO) and magnesia (MgO), and baria (BaO) and other low-oxygen-content compounds such as lead oxide (PbO) markedly lower the melting temperature; they act as "fluxes," but still allow glass to form on cooling. The relative oxygen content and other properties depend on the atomic structure of the elements in a regular way. Materials with similar characteristics are grouped in various areas of Mendeleeff's periodic table of the elements such as shown in Figure 1.6. The "transition elements" that are used for most of our colorants are also shown. A few common names and shorthand chemical designations of materials used and phases commonly occurring in ceramics are listed in Table 1.1.

The relative amount of each phase present in the microstructure during firing and on cooling is fixed by the overall composition, temperature, and oxygen pressure in a way that can be derived from the nineteenth century thermodynamics of J. Willard Gibbs, a professor at Yale University, and perhaps the most influential scientist America has produced. By following his rules, we can prepare what is called a "phase diagram" that maps the regions of composition and temperature at which particular constituent phases exist. Experimentally it is very tedious to work out the phases at every possible temperature and composition for a complete range of mixtures. (When the mixture has more than three components, the task is overwhelming, and we usually take advantage of the similarities of constituents in the same column of Mendeleeff's table to group them together.) From the experimental data, we make a map of the mixture composition such as shown in Figure 1.7, where each point corresponds to a particular mixture of three ingredients. Then we draw contours of the melting temperatures that are analogous to the elevation contours on a geographical terrain map. Lines are shown indicating the temperature at which the entire mixture is completely melted.

For the hard porcelain composition shown as *p* in Figure 1.7, complete melting does not take place until the temperature is raised to over 1600°C, but the first liquid forms at 990°C. This temperature difference (990° − 1650°) is called the melting range, and is very large for porcelain compositions such as this one. If this composition were fired for a long time at a temperature of 1300°C, there would be a viscous silicate liquid together with mullite and silica. A cut through the contours at one constant temperature such as 1300°C is called an isothermal diagram (Figure 1.7b).

Figure 1.5. (a) At high magnification the microstructure of a jun glaze is seen to consist of an emulsion of one glass composition in another. The spherical particles have a higher iron and calcium content and contribute to the blue color (100,000X). The sketch is provided to help identify the phases present.

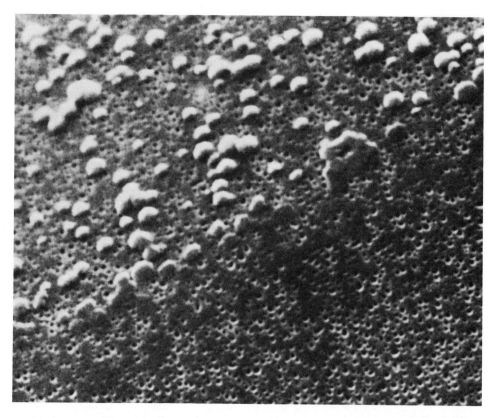

Figure 1.5. (b) An etched surface at somewhat lower magnification shows that the emulsion structure is accompanied in certain regions by tiny particles of a crystalline calcium silicate, or wollastonite. This gives rise to the "white cloud" areas found in the best samples (10,000X). The sketch is provided to help identify the phases present.

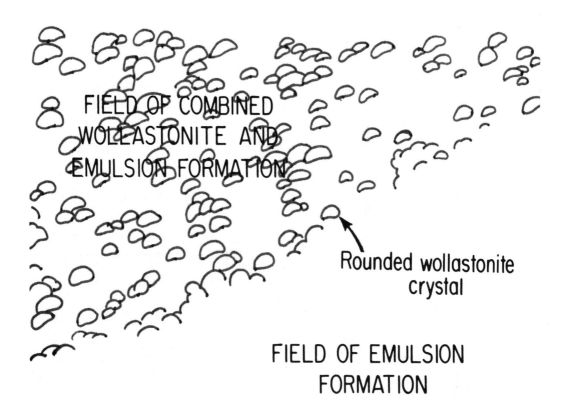

FIELD OF COMBINED
WOLLASTONITE AND
EMULSION FORMATION

Rounded wollastonite
crystal

FIELD OF EMULSION
FORMATION

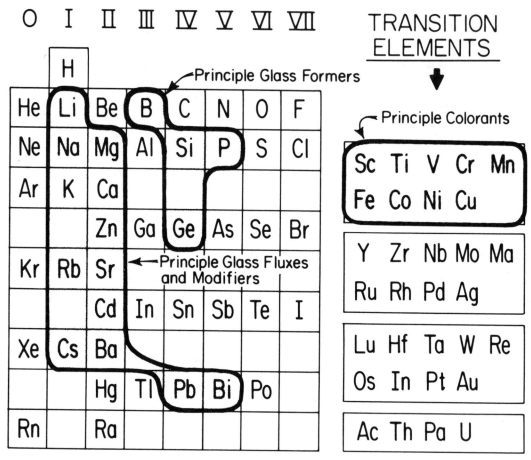

— ELEMENTAL GROUPS —

The Rare earth elements are not shown.

Figure 1.6. Mendeleeff's periodic table of the elements illustrates regions of alkali and alkaline earths, which are rather large ions on the left-hand side of the table. These sharply lower the melting point of glass formers, which are rather small ions in the central region. The colored transition elements form a separate group.

TABLE 1.1

Some of the Compounds Used in Ceramics and Appearing in Ceramic Micro-Structures.

Compound	Chemical Symbol	Compound	Chemical Symbol
Alumina	Al_2O_3	Iron oxide	
Anorthite (calcium feldspar)	$CaO \cdot Al_2O_3 \cdot 2SiO_2$	Hematite	Fe_2O_3
Antimony oxide	Sb_2O_5	Magnetite	Fe_3O_4
Arsenic oxide	As_2O_3	Lead oxide	
Boric Oxide	B_2O_3	Litharge	PbO
Borax	$Na_2B_4O_7 \cdot 10H_2O$	Red lead	Pb_3O_4
Calcium carbonate (limestone)	$CaCO_3$	White lead	$2PbCO_3 \cdot Pb(OH)_2$
Calcium silicate (wollastonite)	$CaSiO_3$	Magnesia	MgO
Clay		Mullite	$3Al_2O_3 \cdot 2SiO_2$
Kaolinite	$Al_2Si_2O_5(OH)_4$	Potassia	K_2O
Montmorillonite	$(Al,Mg)_2(Al,Si)_4O_{10}(OH)_2$	Potassium carbonate (pearl ash)	K_2CO_3
Feldspar		Silica	
Potash	$K_2O \cdot Al_2O_3 \cdot 6SiO_2$	Quartz	SiO_2
Soda	$Na_2O \cdot Al_2O_3 6SiO_2$	Cristobalite	SiO_2
Glasses		Tridymite	SiO_2
Soda-lime-silicate	varies	Soda	Na_2O
Lead-silicate	varies	Sodium carbonate (soda ash)	Na_2CO_3
Lead-alkali-silicate	varies	Talc	$Mg_3Si_4O_{10}(OH)_2$
		Tin oxide	SnO_2

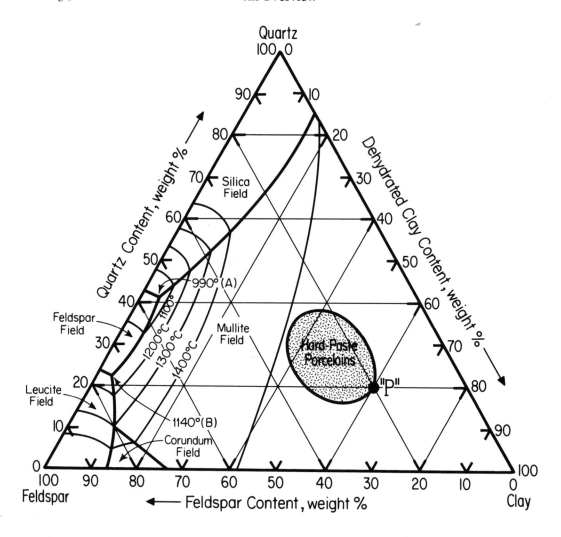

Figure 1.7. Phase diagrams showing the behavior
of mixtures of feldspar, clay, and quartz. Any
point on the diagram shows the relative amounts
of the constituents (check that "p" on the edge
of the hard-paste porcelain region is 60 dehydrated clay–20 feldspar–20 quartz). Diagram (a)
shows the temperature contours at which a particular composition is completely molten. The
different regions indicate the last crystalline
phase to melt on heating.

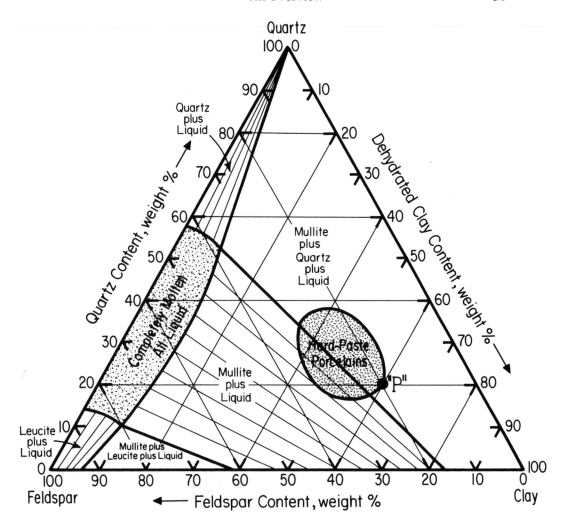

Diagram (b) shows a constant temperature "isothermal" cut through (a) at 1300° C. After a long enough time has passed for all the quartz to dissolve that is going to dissolve, the region of hard-paste porcelain may or may not contain residual quartz, depending on the original composition.

Some composition regions are completely molten; others have a crystalline solid plus a liquid (such as mullite plus liquid); and still others consist of two crystalline solids and a liquid (one of these is labeled mullite plus silica plus liquid A). Hard porcelain compositions exhibit initial melting at 990°C and may or may not have residual quartz along with mullite and a viscous silicate liquid at 1300°C. K'ang Hsi ware does (Chapter 8); Böttger porcelain does not. Phase diagrams serve as maps explaining how changes in mixtures or firing temperatures will affect the resulting microstructure.

Another extremely important concept in ceramics relates to surface properties and the resulting capillary behavior of liquids. We know that it takes a great deal of energy to grind something up and form small particles that have a lot of surface area. Thus it seems only natural that nature would try to regain some of this energy by having the particles first agglomerate into clumps and then, on heating, to "sinter" or join together into a continuous agglomerate with decreased surface area; and this is exactly what takes place. The rate at which agglomerates form and coalesce on heating depends primarily on the amount of liquid formed, so that a practical understanding of firing behavior is based on both determination of the liquid present and the capillary forces. These capillary forces are the same as those that make a soap bubble spherical and a molded ceramic shape shrink during drying and firing. Very small particles agglomerate and sinter faster than larger particles; particles with a little liquid present agglomerate more rapidly and densify further than those that have none. These results ensue because the capillary force increases as the radius of the surface becomes smaller.

An example of this was Attic vase painting during the period 700–300 B.C. A slip made from clay and water had a bit of potash added to separate the individual particles. After the larger particles settled out, the finest portion of the clay still in suspension was extracted or decanted to use as paint. The smaller particle size and potash content combined to make the paint agglomerate and sinter to form a smooth glossy surface without completely melting, as a glaze would. This is capillarity at work.

These three concepts of ceramic science—the nature and importance of the different levels of structure, the role of capillarity and particle size, and the representation of melting and solidification behavior—are enough for most of our purposes. They are discussed more extensively in Chapter 4.

CERAMIC TECHNOLOGY

As with ceramic science, we do not expect the student, curator, collector, or the person who simply enjoys ceramics to become a technologist. Nevertheless, an understanding of how things can be shaped, decorated, and fired is necessary to create a true picture of the nature of ceramics. The methods used for preparing materials, forming and joining shapes, finishing, decorating, and firing determine the outcome, and also set limits on what it is possible to accomplish. Inventions of new methods, such as the potter's wheel or engine turning; of new materials, such as the *famille rose* palette of colors; and of new ideas, such as painting ceramic plates and vessels with scenes from stories, myths, or history; are technologically as well as culturally and aesthetically based. Understanding ceramic methods and their limitations is also essential if one is to draw proper inferences from archaeological and historical objects—neither stylistic analyses, nor chemistry, physics, and statistics are in themselves sufficient.

Impure clays for buff or red or gray earthenwares are widely available; purification by mixing the clay with water and settling out the sticks and stones has been done from very early times. Natural clays (Figure 1.8) have a fine particle size and a platey particle shape. When well dispersed so that each particle is separated from its neighbor by a water film that prevents sticking, they are very plastic. They also have a high drying shrinkage as a result of the contraction that occurs when the many lubricating water films that separate the particles evaporate during drying. Excessive drying shrinkage causes warping and cracking. Natural clays are often mixed with a nonplastic material such as sand or grog (fired ware that is crushed and ground) to decrease this shrinkage.

The properties of a clay are also affected by the soluble salts present—alkalies such as soda and potash tend to stabilize suspensions and allow the finer-particle-size material to be separated by decanting off the surface layer, but they also increase drying shrinkage and lower the stiffness of plastic masses. Alkaline earths such as lime and magnesia tend to stiffen clay–water suspensions, and also firm up plastic masses, cut down on drying shrinkage, and make them more workable. The chemistry of these effects is complex and depends on the type of clay; even today desired results must be obtained by trial and error. Developing a workable body involves a judicious mixture of clay and nonplastic, together with control of the salts present.

Workable clay pastes have been shaped somewhere at some time by every conceivable method. Pinch forming and hand modeling, slab and

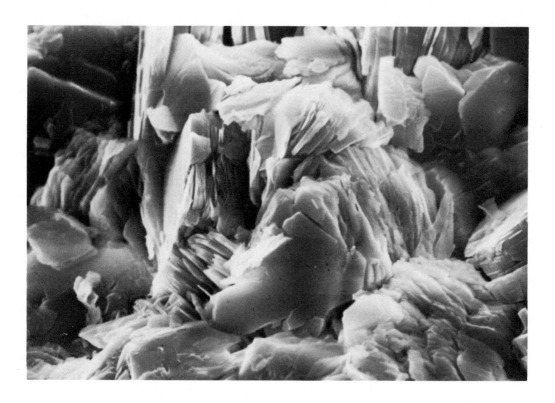

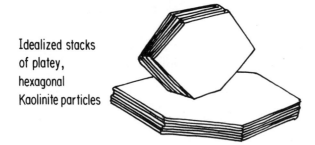

Idealized stacks
of platey,
hexagonal
Kaolinite particles

Figure 1.8. The individual particles of kaolin are
fine platelets with a thickness of less than 0.5
μm. They frequently occur as stacks of platelets
that require intensive mixing to break up into
individual particles. When separated by water
films, the platelets slide over one another to give
good plasticity to a clay–water paste (3700X).

Plate I. This 18-cm-high blue lotus chalice made of Egyptian faience was excavated at Abydos, Egypt and dated to the middle part of the Eighteenth Dynasty (1504–1349 B.C.). It is on display at the Boston Museum of Fine Arts (no. 1901.7396, gift of the Egyptian Exploration Fund). Egyptian faience, which provides a white ground for the blue color in the glaze, was widely produced in the Near East and Mediterranean regions, and a similar product is still made by bead makers in Iran. By the Eighteenth Dynasty, ceramic manufacturing techniques had been fully developed in Egypt, and were extensively employed. (Courtesy of the Boston Museum of Fine Arts.)

Plate II. X-rays transmitted through the chalice and developed on a Xerox plate (xeroradiography) show its internal structure as seen from the side. The chalice was made in two pieces. Material added inside the base to strengthen the joint can be seen, along with the carved decoration. The white spots are porosity, always present in ceramics molded at low pressures. These features are identified in Figure 2.3.

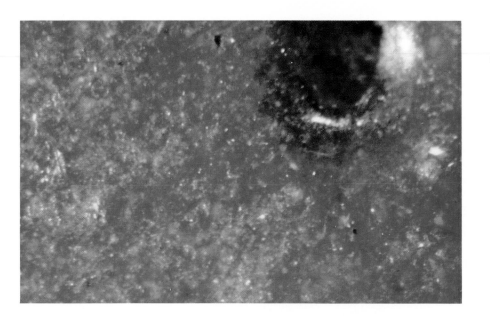

Plate III. (a) When viewed with a 10X magnifying glass, separate quartz particles can be distinguished at the interface of the glaze and underlying white layer. They give the glaze a translucent appearance. During the relatively low-temperature firing, the viscous alkaline glaze saturated with silica does not spread out to wet the underlying body. As a result "crawling" of the glaze to leave uncoated areas is a fairly common defect. (b) This shard from Mehrgahr in Pakistan was made about 2800 B.C. It was first fired in a reducing atmosphere to form a black glassy glaze and gray body at the highest temperature, and then cooled in air to reoxidize the permeable body to a pink color. That this was the processing method used is definitely indicated by the fact that the thin areas of the "black" are reddish. There are similar samples in many museums.

Plate IV. The Song Dynasty (960–1279 A.D.) was the classical period of Chinese ceramics. This celadon jar, created in the twelfth century A.D. near the market town of Longquan, is on display at the Boston Museum of Fine Arts (no. 35-734). Celadons vary from opaque to clear, and range in color from olive green to gray-green. The best ware, such as the jar illustrated, has a deep, lustrous, translucent blue-green glaze that is jadelike in appearance. (Courtesy of the Boston Museum of Fine Arts).

Plate V. The dragon encircling the neck of the jar was modeled and joined in place when the jar was partially dried. The fine parallel circumferential grooves in the clay body resulting from trimming are seen at the rim of the jar. The reddish color of the clay body at the unglazed rim results from the oxidation of iron during cooling.

Plate VI. When developed on a Xerox plate (xeroradiography), transmitted x-rays of the celadon jar illustrate horizontal throwing marks on the interior and an incised pattern on the exterior. A joint can be seen between the body and the separately thrown neck and there is typical porosity in the hand-modeled dragon. Cracks occur at some of the luted joints where the dragon was attached to the vessel while still plastic. Features of this radiograph are illustrated in Figure 3.3.

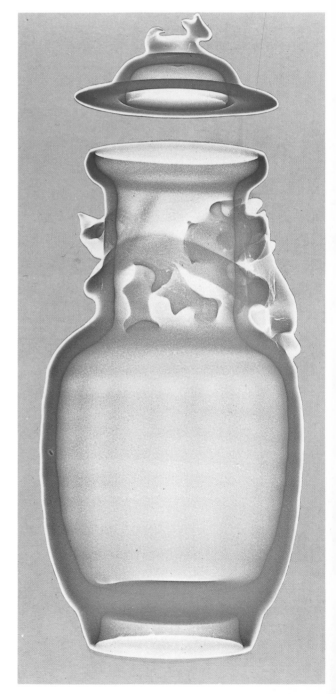

Plate XXIII. *La Danseuse*, modeled at Vincennes in 1752 after a design by François Boucher, was one of the first series of bisquit figures made in soft-paste porcelain. Earlier glazed figures were not as precisely molded. *La Danseuse* represents the attainment of full technical competence in the production of French soft-paste porcelain, together with the introduction of recognized artists as participants in French ceramic manufacture. The bonnet has been restored. (Courtesy National Musée de Céramique, Sèvres, France, no. 20-069.)

Plate XXIV. One of the most remarkable innovators of the eighteenth century was Josiah Wedgwood, inventor of "jasperware," which began production in 1774. This chocolate pitcher from about 1790 was made of cobalt-blue jasper dip with appliqué decoration based on a design by Lady Elizabeth Templeton, and modeled by William Hackwood. The tip of the spout has been repaired. (Collection of the Metropolitan Museum of Art, New York. Gift of Ferdinand Herman, 1912.)

coil building, consolidation and shaping with a paddle and anvil, forming in a mold, throwing on a wheel, slip casting—and mechanized versions of each of these processes and combinations of them—have all been used. Most complicated shapes require the assembly of separate parts, which is done after partial drying. The surfaces to be joined are roughened and some clay slip is added to stick the pieces together. The biggest problem with assembling separate parts is that clay bodies shrink as they dry; if the two parts have a different degree of wetness, they will shrink differently, and either warpage or cracks will result. Thus the water content of two parts to be joined should be low (so that further shrinkage is slight) and identical.

For producing outstanding wares, the skill and extent of finishing operations after initial shaping and partial drying are particularly important. While the clay is still soft, designs may be impressed or rouletted on the surface. When the clay has dried to a stiff "leather-hard" state where the drying shrinkage has nearly ended, ware can be trimmed to shape, designs carved and incised, and the foot formed. Wedgwood introduced the engine lathe, which moves the piece back and forth as it is being turned; when these motions are synchronized, a variety of special shapes can be obtained. While plastic clay has good dry strength, quartz-frit and soft-paste bodies with little clay require the addition of an organic binder to provide sufficient strength for finishing—a mixture of black soap and parchment glue was used at Sevres, and natural gums have been used in the Near East.

Surface finishing of fine wares by slip coating with a different color or texture of clay, and the special preparation of such coating materials, was an early and continuing development. There is better consolidation and alignment of the surface layer if slightly damp ware is burnished with a pebble, wooden tool, or leather polisher. Both Böttger at Meissen and Wedgwood in England polished their unglazed ware. In quartz bodies, such as Egyptian faience (Chapter 2) and Iznik tile (Chapter 6), cheaper interior compositions were coated with a more expensive surface layer made of pure and finely milled quartz pebbles. The entire development of tin-glazed ware as a ground for painting (maiolica) was based on coating an earthenware body with a white surface layer suitable for the painter's work.

The great differences that arose between the ceramic traditions of the Near East and of China can be attributed to the availability of raw materials and to kiln design. China has many natural deposits of feldspar, quartz, and mica mixed with kaolin that are suitable for use in stoneware without other additions. They are high melting, and only those with a high iron content could be used at firing temperatures below 1000°C or so. Near Eastern clays fire well at 900–1000°C, but have sufficient alkaline impurities present that they melt when the temperature exceeds about 1100–1200°C. In China the alkali constituent of ceramics was derived from insoluble mineral feldspar and mica; in the Near East the alkali component was derived from desert deposits of natron, or potash derived from desert plants, both of which dissolve in water and so had to be sintered or fused with sand or quartz to form an alkali silicate.

To form a glassy glaze on a clay body, it is necessary that the glaze have a relatively small contraction on cooling and good penetration of and interaction with the underlying body. The most successful glazes have been the lime-alkali-aluminum-silicate glazes first developed in China, and the lead-alkali-silicate glazes first developed in the Near East. A quite different method of forming a glassy surface coating is by reaction of an alkaline vapor with the surface of a silicate body to form a molten alkali silicate. This was first used during the Middle Kingdom in Egypt for Egyptian faience and is still employed in Iran for manufacturing glazed beads. If the quartz paste bead is immersed in a "glazing powder" consisting of quartz, lime, alkali, copper, and carbon, the alkaline vapors react with the silicate surface to form a liquid coating while the ware simultaneously shrinks away from the surrounding powder. In medieval Germany a related process of salt glazing stoneware by adding mineral salt to the kiln at a temperature of 1200°C or so was widely used. This became the standard method for fine English stoneware during the seventeenth and early eighteenth centuries. "Smear" glazing was also employed in which the alkaline glaze composition was smeared over the inside of a closed clay saggar containing the unglazed ware so that when it vaporized during firing, it deposited on the enclosed ware, forming a thin, adherent, porefree, alkali-silicate glass coating.

Color has always been an essential ingredient in ceramic masterpieces, being extensively used for Egyptian faience and for glass objects in the Near Eastern and Mediterranean region during the second millenium B.C. Efforts to use these colorants in lead-alkali-silicate glazes on earthenware were not so successful because the brown color of the fired clay gives a muddy appearance to the glaze.

In every culture once control of the technology was achieved and white ceramics appeared, attention focused on colorants, methods of decoration, and pictorial representation, and the painter's role became primary. Actually this was first seen in Greek black-on-red ware. The underglaze palette of Chinese porcelain and European hard porcelain was limited to the most stable colors and focused on blue and white decoration. A wider range of underglaze colors could be developed to be compatible with the lower firing temperature of lead-alkali-silicate glazes, as we illustrate with an Iznik tile in Chapter 6. Overglaze painting of detailed scenes from life and story began with the use of overglaze metallic lusters in ninth century Islam and was almost certainly derived from techniques of glass decoration. A Persian example of this technique is illustrated in Chapter 5. For luster a fine mixture of an inert powder (often ocher) with a copper or silver compound in a suspension containing vinegar was painted on the surface of the glazed ware. When the ware was reheated to a dull red heat in a mildly reducing atmosphere, the copper or silver first diffused into the glaze, and a surface layer of dispersed metallic particles formed. When the residual powder was cleaned off after firing, a glossy metallic decoration remained.

Painting over a fired glaze with colored enamels became extensive, both in Europe and in China, during the early seventeenth century. During the middle part of that century, the end of the Ming Dynasty saw political disturbances in China, and Japan began to export Arita ware, porcelain with overglaze decoration, extensively. Subsequently made mostly for the home market, it became the famous Imari ware. Toward the end of the seventeenth century, when tranquility returned to China and Ching-te-Chen was rebuilt under the leadership of K'ang Hsi, enamelled painted wares of great perfection were made, as illustrated in Chapter 8.

The painting on unfired, porous, lead-tin underglazes did not allow for much variation in the depth of color, nor did the *famille verte* palette in which most of the colors were in solution in the low-melting lead-silicate and lead-alkali-silicate glasses, resulting in paints much like watercolors. Early in the eighteenth century, in both Europe and China (beginning with the *famille rose* palette, 1720–1730), enamels consisting of a low-melting glass medium to which pigments were added became common, and painting techniques became more sophisticated. With pigmented enamels variations in tint could be achieved by laying on the color more or less thickly (impasto technique), and the style of overglaze enamels came to resemble oil painting. Boron oxide, fluorspar, and bismuth oxide were added to the spectrum of low-melting glass constituents and methods of gilding with gold were developed. Decoration processes became more and more complex—for some wares made at Sèvres, as many as seven separate firings were required—and new materials prepared by chemists continued to come into use.

By the end of the eighteenth century, chemical science and analytical techniques had developed to the point where color preparation was a specialized part of chemical technology. Constituents were reacted with one another under controlled conditions to form a large variety of hues and tints not found in nature. Blue cobalt oxide, for example, was reacted with pegmatite to form "Sèvres blue"; with pegmatite plus rouge and manganese oxide to form "Sèvres blue-black"; with pegmatite, clay, and nickel oxide to form "Delft blue"; and so on. One of the popular eighteenth century pigments was purple of Cassius, formed by precipitation of gold with tin chloride. Reproducible results for these colors could be obtained only by careful control of the reaction process and careful attention to the raw materials employed. More and more, color preparation came to be the realm of the chemist.

All ceramic designs were hand painted until the invention of the transfer printing process by Sadler and Green of Liverpool, England, in 1756. Using an engraved copper plate and special ink containing the mixed ceramic flux and pigment, a design was printed on paper, which could then be placed on the curved surface of ware and rubbed down to transfer the ink onto the glaze surface. This process of printing on a flat plate and transferring the design to the curved pottery surface was a major development in the mass production of decorated ceramics. During the latter part of the eighteenth century, much English ware was sent to Liverpool for decoration. In the related lithographic decalcomania process, several colors are printed on paper with a waterproof organic medium such as varnish. The decals are applied to a tacky varnish coating on the glazed ware, and then the ware is immersed in water to float off the paper, leaving the transfer design ready to be fired. In the printing of decals, sometimes only a varnish layer is printed and the dry color dusted on the tacky layer. A similar process is used for laying uniform color grounds. First the uncolored areas are reserved by painting with a sugar and dye solution. After drying, a linseed oil layer is brushed on and smoothed to a uniform surface without brush marks; then the powdered flux–color mix is dusted on the oil, where it adheres as a uniform layer. After drying, water is used to remove the sugar-coated reserved areas and the piece is ready for firing or further decoration.

Other major technological developments of the latter part of the eighteenth century were related mostly to the general adoption of a system specialized labor, in which one person prepared the raw materials, another threw the rough shape, another trimmed the foot, and still another applied the glaze; there also were separate modelers, repairers, decorators, and firemen for the kiln. This factory system, associated first with water power and then the steam engine (James Watt, inventor of the steam engine, was owner of a small pottery, and also a member of the Lunar Society of Birmingham, where he knew Josiah Wedgwood), led to the more efficient production of uniform good-quality ware for a wider market.

OBJECT EXAMINATION

To infer how and from what an object was made, and to understand how its appearance and special properties arose, we must focus our examination on its internal structure, which is the key to the relationship between a processing method and its result. To observe internal structure, it is necessary to extract a minute sample for examination. That was not possible for the museum objects described in the next chapter, so we combined close external visual and microscopic examination of the object with microscopic and analytical studies of a sample taken from a broken piece of similar ware recovered from the same site, of the same time period, and with the same characteristics and decoration. As we elsewhere acknowledge, we are indebted to many museum curators, both for allowing us to study whole objects in their care, and for providing us with equivalent shards or damaged pieces from which a sample could be taken with no harm done.

The whole objects were examined visually, and by feeling the surface smoothness or roughness, contours, and form. The surface was viewed in light reflected at a low angle from the surface, which enhances variations in surface smoothness, shows up pinholes and glaze defects, and makes obvious areas of overglaze decoration. Particularly on the inside of vessels, a ridge can often be seen or felt where separately formed parts were joined together. Finger marks from throwing can be seen, and the thickness of the base and walls discerned. For the jun ware described in Chapter 4, finger marks where the bowl was held for dipping in glaze are clearly visible. This examination was extended by using a 10X magnifying glass for a more detailed view. The magnifying glass, in concert with a light reflected at a low angle, brings out turning, trimming, and smoothing marks on the surface and on the foot; allows the bubble structure of glazes to be discerned; and shows up glaze inhomogeneities. The enlarged view often makes apparent the order in which forming and decorative steps occurred by showing one process overlying another.

Finally, particularly interesting features of the object itself were examined under a "zoom" binocular microscope with a magnification range from 10X to 80X—the type of microscope available in all museum conservation laboratories and most high school science laboratories. The steadier view and wide range of magnification allow one to make a more relaxed study of such features as turning marks, joints, glaze defects, pigment buildup, and brush strokes, as well as which features overlay other features, variations in pigment types and color, flow lines in the glaze, and pores in the body. Also, our microscope has a camera attachment that allows us to photograph and record particularly interesting features.

For each new type of ware one examines, it takes quite a long time to see features that in retrospect seem quite obvious. For this we have found no substitute for just spending more time looking at and thinking about each object. Curators and collectors have, of course, the luxury of daily contact with different examples of the same type of ware seen in various lighting conditions. This allows them to recognize particular features of each type, often without explicitly articulating the reasons for their judgments.

For some samples—the Egyptian faience chalice of Chapter 2, the Song Dynasty celadon of Chapter 3, and the Boucher soft-paste figure of Chapter 10—we used x-ray radiography to detail the internal structure further. Film radiography (Chapter 10) shows a greater gradation and detail of structure, but the use of Xerox plates in xeroradiography (Chapters 2 and 3) emphasizes edge effects and tends to show up cracks and porosity with great clarity. Internal cavities, pore and temper orientation, cracks and fissures, and areas of low and variable density can be seen.

These macroscopic observations and surface microscopy are particularly useful in identifying the forming, shaping, and joining methods used in the manufacture of an object. Thoughtful interpretation of the macrostructure has served that purpose for each of the objects we describe in the next section.

With core samples drilled out with a diamond drill, or samples chipped from one edge of a slab sheared or cut from a corner of a broken object or shard, we investigated the internal microstructure and chemistry. We usually started with a polished section observed with both an optical microscope and a scanning electron microscope. (These techniques and the instruments used are described in Chapter 15.) We have also used scanning electron microscopy with etched samples, in which the topographic relief often better indicates microstructural relationships. For most samples we also carried out quantitative chemical analyses of each phase using an electron microprobe. In a few cases where the microstructure has a very fine scale structure, such as the jun glaze of Chapter 4, we thinned a sample for transmission electron microscopy and scanning transmission electron microscopy chemical analysis. Both electron diffraction and x-ray diffraction structural analyses were done. The particular experimental methods we used most depended partly on the equipment available, but mostly on their utility in determining the macrostructure and the microstructure, which are the essential indicators of the ceramic processes used and of the visual impact achieved. If we were facing other questions, we would be using other techniques.

Through our tests we determined the constituents present along with their size, shape, amount, crystal (or glass) structure, and chemical composition, as well as the overall sample chemical composition. From this information we inferred the materials from which the objects were probably made and how they were processed. The microstructure determination also allows us to explain resulting visual effects such as translucency, color, light scattering in transmission, iridescence, gloss, and reflectivity.

Finally, we have replicated in our laboratory many of the materials and techniques inferred, to assure ourselves that these processes actually work. A number of these studies have been carried out as student projects. In other cases we have relied on the fact that modern artisans are still using the method described.

The interpretation of structure requires application of both the principles of ceramic science and a knowledge of ceramic technology. Examples of what we can learn about specific objects and the technology used to make them are given in Part II.

RECOMMENDED READING

Brongniart, Alexandre, *Traite des Arts Céramiques*, Dessain and Joira, Paris (1977). (Facsimile of 1877 edition.) Brogniart's treatise covers the technology and its history in great detail as it was known in the nineteenth century (in French).

Charleston, Robert J. (ed.), *World Ceramics*, Chartwell Books, Secaucus, N.J. (1976). A comprehensive and profusely illustrated history by a collection of illustrious authors.

Cooper, Emmanuel, *A History of Pottery*, St. Martin's Press, New York (1972). A concise history of the different types of pottery and some of the technology involved from neolithic times to the present.

Norton, F. H., *Elements of Ceramics*, Addison-Wesley Publishing Co., Cambridge, Mass. (1952). Probably too technical for many readers, but a clear, straightforward exposition of ceramic fundamentals and practice.

PART II

CERAMIC
MASTERPIECES

*I*n selecting a small number of superb, historically important ceramic objects for examination and study, we have been guided by historical significance, by technological interest, by the aesthetic appeal of form, design, and texture, and by the quality of craftsmanship.

In this volume we pass over the early and continuing tradition of earthenware and focus our attention on wares in which the selection or preparation of special materials as a replacement for everyday clays is a key feature of the technology. This technique was first seen in Egypt and Mesopotamia at about 4000 B.C., during which period a ware called Egyptian faience was formed based on crushed quartz. The name is an unfortunate choice since it suggests a similarity to French faience where none exists. Egyptian faience was the premier luxury ware of the eastern Mediterranean region for several millennia and a fine example is examined in Chapter 2. As shown in Figure II.1, the production of the finest ceramic wares was first centered in the Near East, in China, Korea, and Japan, and, more recently, in Europe. We have two examples of fine monochrome wares from the Song Dynasty of China, which some connoisseurs consider the finest hour of ceramic history. Celadon wares such as illustrated in Chapter 3 were made in great quantity in southern China and exported throughout the world. In contrast, the jun wares produced at about the

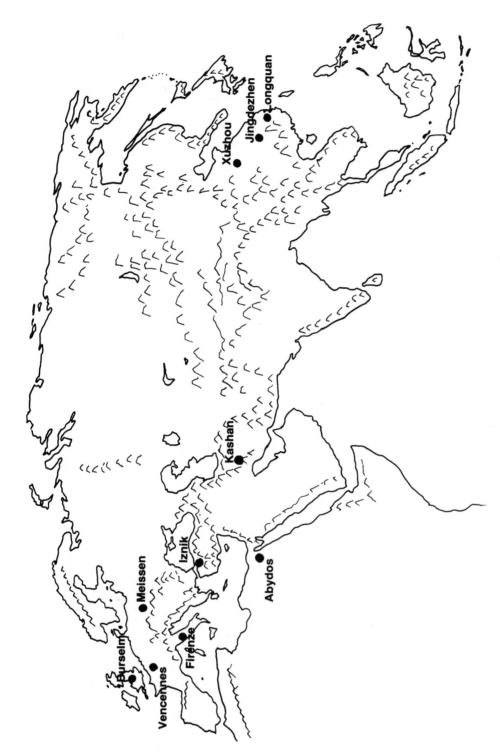

Figure II-1. Sites in Europe, the near East and China, where the ceramic masterpieces described in this book were created or discovered.

same time in northern China were fairly crude and only became collectibles in the Ming Dynasty. Both wares reflect the superb achievement of deep lustrous glazes with the feeling of the best jade, and may be thought of as a consciously contrived construction of articles that are fully the equivalent of precious stones.

In the Middle East the Islamic culture fostered a special creative capacity for generating and combining technical accomplishments and new art forms. The quartz-frit-clay body used for the Kashan lusterware plate of Chapter 5 and for the Iznik tile of Chapter 6 was clearly a lineal descendant of Egyptian faience, but the decorative styles were new. The lusterware plate emphasized the role of the painter, and its brilliant gold finish was impressively rich. By using thick underglaze decoration in bright colors under a brilliant lead-alkali-silicate glaze, the Iznik potters created a sparkling jewel-like product in which a variety of symmetries created an interesting design.

During the sixteenth century, Chinese and Islamic blue and white porcelains were being imported to Europe. These hard, white transparent wares with bright blue decorations inspired many attempts to make equivalent wares. Although there are reports of other successes, the earliest European porcelain of which we have examples was made at Florence under the patronage of Grand Duke Francesco I in the period 1575–1587. It combined a Persian formula with Italian maiolica methods, but had a short firing range. Production was discontinued when Don Francesco died. An outstanding example is illustrated in Chapter 7. Basically similar methods became successful when adapted to a high-lime composition at St. Cloud circa 1695 to produce what we call soft-paste porcelain. The ware subsequently was manufactured at many factories near Paris and elsewhere; the example we have selected to illustrate in Chapter 10 is a sculpture made at Vincennes in 1752 after a design by François Boucher.

Meanwhile in China, K'ang Hsi, second emperor of the Ching Dynasty, had reorganized porcelain production and had rebuilt and given imperial support to the ceramic complex at Ching-te-Chen. Here ware of unequaled technical virtuosity was made during his and following reigns. The example shown in Chapter 8 illustrates the level of quality achieved and helps us understand why Europeans became so addicted to these wares.

After a thoroughly modern type of research program initiated by Count von Tschirnhaus, Johann Friedrich Böttger succeeded in making a European product equivalent to the Chinese wares, and we study a sample of Böttger porcelain in Chapter 9. We end our illustration of particular pieces with a factory-produced example of Josiah Wedgwood's jasperware. The jasperware body is a rare example of a completely new compositional invention, and came at a time when the factory production methods pioneered in Europe by Wedgwood made fine-quality luxury ceramics available to a much wider audience than hitherto had been the case.

CHAPTER 2

AN EGYPTIAN FAIENCE CHALICE

*D*uring the 4000 years before late Roman times, Egyptian faience was widely produced in the Near East and eastern Mediterranean region, and it is still being made in Iran for beads and stone paste vessels.

Egyptian faience is important in the history of ceramics as the first "contrived" nonclay body developed as a white ground for the use of blue-green colors in imitation of lapis lazuli and turquoise. The blue lotus chalice shown in Plate I and Figure 2.1 was excavated from Cemetery D at Abydos and is dated by tomb pottery to the middle part of the Eighteenth Dynasty, between the reigns of Thutmosis III and Amenophis III (ca. 1479–1353 B.C.). Although Egyptian faience is difficult to shape, the chalice displays a masterful control of raw materials in achieving a pleasing flowerlike form and in the exquisite symmetry of carving and incising. The technology has been optimized to combine brilliant color with a soft, diffuse reflectance—qualities admired in polished stone vessels. Egyptian faience was esteemed as an inexpensive substitute for more expensive semiprecious stones and as a means of producing larger and more complicated objects than was possible with stone. The success of such imitation is found in the confusion over the Egyptian terms for true lapis and imitation lapis, or Egyptian faience.

The blue lotus chalice, which is on display at the Boston Museum of Fine Arts (no. 1901.7396), was presented together with a similar chalice

Figure 2.1. This 13-cm-tall blue lotus chalice made of Egyptian faience was excavated at Abydos, Egypt, and dated to the mid-Eighteenth Dynasty (1504–1349 B.C.). It is on display at the Boston Museum of Fine Arts (no. 1901.7396, gift of the Egyptian Exploration Fund). Egyptian faience, which provides a white ground for the blue color in the glaze, was widely produced in the Near East and Mediterranean regions, and a similar product is still made by bead makers in Iran. By the Eighteenth Dynasty, manufacturing techniques had been fully developed in Egypt, and were extensively employed. (See Plate I.) (Courtesy of the Boston Museum of Fine Arts.)

as a gift of the Egyptian Exploration Fund in 1901 in recompense for the museum's support of excavations at Abydos. From predynastic times Abydos was a favorite place of burial, and later became a shrine and religious center. The site was originally identified with the god Osiris, ruler of the netherworld. Egyptians from all parts of the country had tombs constructed at Abydos and, according to the excavators, each tried to secure a place as near the Osiris enclosure as possible. The two chalices were excavated from Tomb 115, a rich grave deposit in which the entombed treasures testify to the Egyptian belief in the afterlife. Tomb 115 had been plundered in antiquity and was the site for a later burial, and so other, early grave goods probably had been removed. This tomb is not described in the excavation report, but MacIver and Mace[1] provide a general description of these tombs as mastabas—that is, as having an outer court surrounding a single chamber made of bricks standing about four to five feet in height with the remains of a sprung arch roof and an offering chamber over the doorway. The mummy was set below ground, but MacIver and Mace report that no single burial in Cemetery D was found intact.

This Egyptian faience goblet was made at a very expansive time in Egyptian history, when power and wealth were at a high point. Both Thutmosis III and Amenophis III (1504–1349 B.C.) did extensive rebuilding at the temple of Osiris at Abydos. During the Eighteenth Dynasty (1570–1307 B.C.), Egyptian control extended over Nubia to the south and over Palestine and Syria to the east, bordering on the Hittite empire in the north and Mesopotamia in the east. There was extensive foreign trade in Nubian gold, wood, skins, and other luxury materials, as well as tribute exacted from the Hittites, Hurrians, and Babylonians. It was a period of prosperity and growth. Just prior to this time, manufacturing methods for Egyptian faience had been fully developed and these basic methods were implemented in diverse and elaborate ways to produce master works, often considered unusual in Egyptian art for their naturalistic style.

The blue lotus chalice represents the culmination of a process of development for Egyptian faience that began about 4000 B.C. The earliest examples are beads and amulets, which are found along with more numerous carved and glazed steatite or soapstone objects. Modeling of this early faience was followed by surface grinding in a manner similar to stoneworking methods. The manufacturing technique, as well as the similarity of form and color, support the idea that these materials were first developed as substitutes for turquoise, lapis lazuli, and malachite, stones rare in Egypt. The process was widely used throughout the Near East, but most of the best preserved samples have been found in Egypt.

In the arid environment of the Near East, blue and green are colors of special significance that long have been considered omens of good luck. In Egyptian literature and ritual, the bright blue color and lotus flower are related to good fortune and fertility. The ability to produce objects in various shapes and sizes, in these colors, and even to cover large expanses of wall with faience tile (as in the South Tomb of the Step Pyramid of Djoser at Saqqara), was certainly prized. Egyptian faience was used as tile and as inlays in jewelry, furniture, and games, and was modeled into ceremonial objects and cult figurines. The middle part of the second millennium saw a new spirit of artistic and technological achievement as new methods of production emerged and as tour-de-force crafted objects were produced, sometimes in polychrome, or in complex forms with parts individually modeled and molded.

Egyptian faience was made by modeling or molding a mixture of finely ground quartz or sand and small amounts of lime and alkali, plus copper salts that furnished the blue-green color. A mixture of such raw materials with water is stiff at first, but becomes soft and flowing when it begins to be deformed; if deformed too rapidly, it cracks. During drying the soluble salts migrate to the surface and a layer of effloresced salts is deposited as the water evaporates (Figure 2.2a). Upon firing, these salts react with the quartz body to form the glaze layer. Where drying is more rapid, more salts are deposited and so the glaze is thicker. Under the base and in the interior of cups where drying is slower, the glaze is thinner. Self-glazing by the firing of effloresced salts was the prime method of manufacture during the third millennium.

By the beginning of the New Kingdom, two other, quite different ways of making a glaze had been developed; these have been replicated in the laboratory. One involved a slow roasting process, in which the quartz-paste body was modeled, then embedded in a special glazing powder (Figure 2.1c). The powder contained a high content of lime (CaO) so that it remained solid at the firing temperature. Alkali and copper compounds in the powder migrated to and reacted with the surface to form the glaze. After cooling the object was easily removed from the friable, porous glazing powder. The thickness of the glaze is fairly uniform over the entire body, which would shrink away from the surrounding powder during firing, but internal surfaces, concave areas, and holes had little glaze. This method was used to manufacture some of the Abydos beads, and, according to Kieffer and Allibert,[2] the Hippopotamus from Meir, dated at about 1971–1892 B.C. No examples of this process from the Old Kingdom have been found. The process is still used in Qom, Iran, in the manufacture of the popular bright-blue donkey beads.

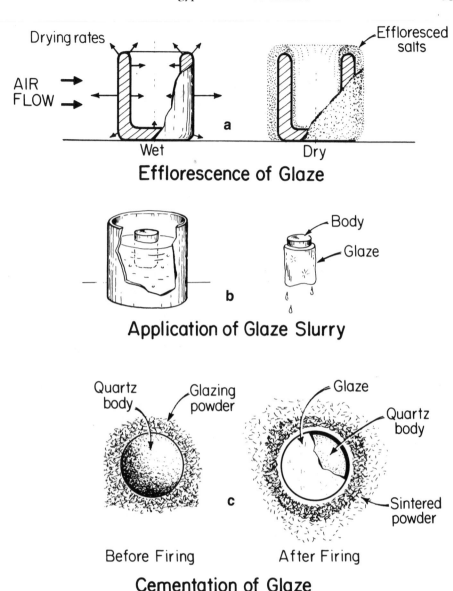

Figure 2.2. Three different methods were used to form a glaze on Egyptian faience. (a) The first method was to incorporate soluble salts in the mixing water or body composition. As the water moved to the surface and evaporated, these salts deposited as an effloresced layer. (b) Some ware used a prefritted glass that was ground for use as a glaze. This finely ground glass was added to water to form a slurry and applied by painting or dipping. (c) A third method was to embed and fire the quartz body in a special glazing powder. Glaze constituents migrated to and reacted with the quartz surface.

The third method of forming a glaze surface was to heat the mixed glaze constituents to form a glass, and then to grind this glass to a fine powder to be dispersed in water and applied to the surface by dipping or painting (Figure 2.2b). With this method, one sometimes sees drips or runs or a thick rim at the base of the glaze. Examples of this glazing technique have been found in many Kerma tiles dating to the Second Intermediate Period (1668–1570 B.C.). However, there is no archaeological evidence of a glass industry in Egypt at this time, and this is a subject for further research.

Egyptian faience chalices emerged at the beginning of the Eighteenth Dynasty with little apparent evidence of prior development. A sequence of stylistic changes from thick-walled, short-stemmed, wide-mouthed vessels to slender, trumpet-shaped forms with elaborate relief decoration has been suggested. The relief appeared first in the form of a lotus with possible associations with the goddess Hathor and the symbolism of rebirth. Later the relief decoration consisted of bands with narrative scenes at the rim of vessels that were probably used for drinking rather than as offeratory vessels. The Museum of Fine Arts chalice is midway in this development. The lotus petals and leaves are cut back in low relief and subtly modeled. The cup is more elaborately conceived and finely worked than earlier examples.

The blue lotus chalice was shaped in two sections. The upper cup was molded into a concave mold, probably made of porous, fired earthenware. The mold, possibly of Nile mud (the widespread brown firing clay of Egypt, which has good plasticity), might have been thrown in a wheel, turned to its final shape, and then fired at a moderate temperature, resulting in low firing shrinkage and the porosity necessary for it to function as a mold. The base may have been made in a similar mold, or possibly formed around a rod as a cylinder and then flared open at one end. After molding, the two parts of the chalice were removed from the molds before shrinkage occurred and joined together with a small amount of quartz-alkali paste. To strengthen the join, a plug of body material was inserted inside the foot, as can be seen in the xeroradiograph shown as Plate II and Figure 2.3. A coil was placed outside the base where the cylinder joins the cup; the join lines can be seen with a low-power microscope. The cup and base had to be joined when they were still damp or cracks would have developed as a result of unequal shrinkage of the two parts and the joining coil. However, when damp, the ware does not have much strength; the cup was joined to the base slightly off center so that when the chalice was set aside to dry, it tilted toward the side with the least support, and so is not

Figure 2.3. X-rays transmitted through the chalice and developed on a Xerox plate (xeroradiography) show its internal structure as seen from the side. The chalice was made in two pieces. Material added inside the base to strengthen the joint can be seen, along with the carved decoration. The white spots are porosity, always present in ceramics molded at low pressures. (See Plate II.)

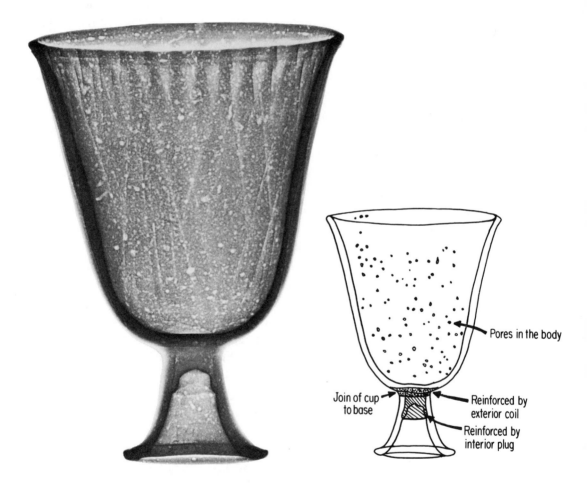

perfectly symmetrical (Figure 2.4). Once the cup was dry enough to be handled without changing its shape, the relief decoration was incised on the surface and the space between the petals and upper border cut back or scraped away to form the beautifully symmetrical lotus design.

There are five sepals, or leaves, and 35 petals incised and carved in low relief on the chalice, and arranged in fivefold symmetry. A blue lotus actually has four green sepals and 12 to 16 petals, so a certain amount of artistic license was exercised. The cup is 13 cm (centimeters), or 5 ¼ inches, tall, slightly larger than an average modern glass tumbler, and yet fits comfortably in the hand. The chalice has a strong bilateral or twofold symmetry, and the base form mirrors the cup form. The cup of the chalice is as wide as it is tall, but the eye is deceived by the vertical design. To create this visual effect, the sepals were made the same length as the petals, and a double vertical line was used to delineate the spine of the sepals, and reinforce this verticality. Three petals were placed between each petal and sepal near the rim. The increased number of petals fills space at the rim and supplies a visual reason for the flaring of the cup at the lip. The complexity of the design is increased at the rim, as is the depth of relief, thus serving to focus the attention of the viewer on the lip of the chalice. The lip is further emphasized by a double horizontal band; in contrast, the foot is deemphasized by its lack of decoration and the simple shape of the basal rim.

Carving and incising the lotus relief removed the effloresced layer from the surface, thus eliminating the formation of a glaze during firing. A clever technique was employed to add an effloresced salt layer sufficient to form a glaze. When almost dry, the chalice was dipped into a slurry suspension prepared from a finely ground mixture of milled white quartz and alkali to build up a layer about 0.5 mm thick on the surface. The slurry contained soluble alkali, lime, and copper salts, which migrated to the surface and formed an efflorescent layer during drying. Figures 2.5 and 2.6 illustrate the microstructure of the underlying body. The interior of the body has a grayish-brown tint resulting from iron impurities and is coated with a fine, white quartz layer and glaze. The internal surface of the cup and the inside of the base dried at a much slower rate than the external surfaces. As a result the glaze layer is thinner on these surfaces, particularly inside the base.

Inside the cup, however, the added slip and glaze end in a slightly thickened rim about a third the way up from the bottom. The white alkali-rich efflorescing layer was applied by dipping the chalice into a slurry; first one end and then the other. There are horizontal facets near the interior

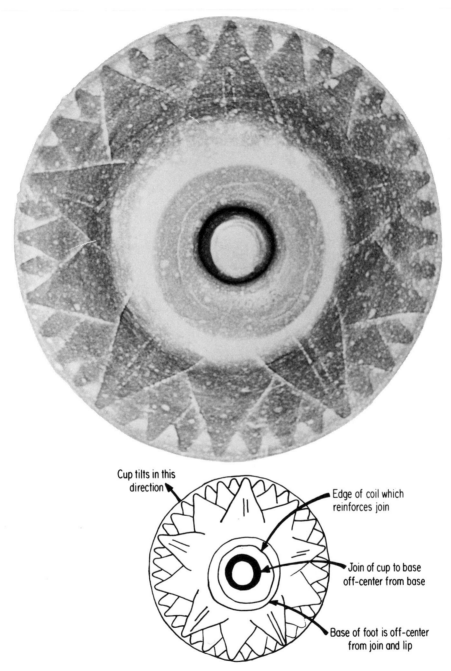

Figure 2.4. Xeroradiograph of the chalice from above gives a special view of the beautifully symmetrical lotus pattern formed by incising and scraping the dry ware. The inner dark circle is the join, surrounded by the base, and the outer circle is the cup. The cup is tilted to the upper left.

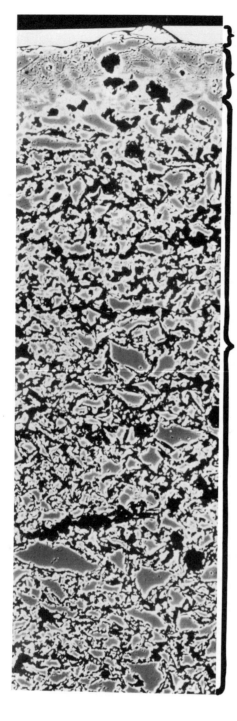

Blue Glaze

White Quartz
Layer

Impure, Quartz
Interior of Body

1 mm

Figure 2.5. The micro-structure of the body, fine white powdered quartz, and glaze illustrates how a small fraction of liquid silicate formed at the firing temperature bonds the quartz particles together. Salts deposited on the surface form the glaze (300X).

of the lip and the foot where excess slurry was removed and the surface layer smoothed. The slurry did not reach all the way to the bottom of the bowl or foot during dipping. Where no white layer was added, the grayish body color comes to the surface and the effloresced glaze from the body is quite thin. Once the slurry stiffened on the surface and began to dry, the leaves, petals, and sepal spines were outlined with shallow grooves, and the bands at the top and bottom of the cup reworked.

A relatively thick slurry was necessary to form the white quartz-alkali-copper layer. When the chalice was dipped into the slurry, bubbles formed between the slurry and body along some of the incised decoration. During

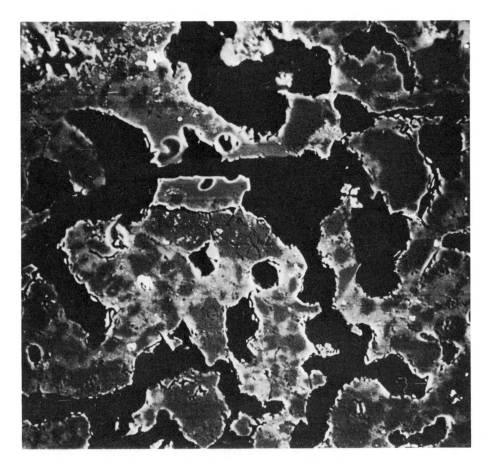

Figure 2.6. Microstructure of white-quartz layer showing the glass envelope that affords cohesion of the angular quartz particles and acts as a high-viscosity bonding material during firing (800X).

reworking and drying, a thin surface layer of salts effloresced, but during firing the alkali-lime-silicate glass that formed did not spread out to wet the underlying body, as a lead glaze would. As a result the glaze has "crawled" at the sepal spines, edges of the petals, and in many areas of flat surface, leaving residual holes such as shown in Plate III. This glaze defect is fairly common in Egyptian faience objects.

The blue lotus chalice was the result of a lengthy and complex manufacturing process requiring a greater number of steps and a greater degree of precision than found in the manufacture of objects from earlier periods. The body was molded, joined, and carved; the glaze was formed by a combination of efflorescence and application methods. This sequence required relatively tight control of the moisture content of the vessel. For instance, if the two molded parts had been too dry, the join would have cracked. If the join or vessel had been too wet when the slurry layer was applied, warping and flow cracks would have resulted. If the vessel had been too dry, the slurry would have delaminated on drying. If the body had been too dry during incising, the fine detail would have been lost because the body tends to powder and break down. Thus there not only was a complex manufacturing procedure involved, but the necessity to carry out certain operations at various stages of drying. All this demanded mastery of the process as well as conceptual sophistication on the part of the artisan regarding the complexity of design and degree of risk in execution.

The internal structure of the chalice, Figure 2.5, consists of angular quartz particles of about 0.01 to 0.2 mm with little added natron; lime and iron impurities are present, which impart a grayish-white color. To make it sufficiently strong for carving, it must have included an organic gum addition such as used by modern Iranian bead makers. A white quartz surface layer of finer particle size and a larger amount of copper, alkali and salt additives lies between the inner body and glaze; the glaze penetrates about halfway into this intermediate layer. Figure 2.6 shows how the quartz particles are dispersed in and held together by viscous glass bonds. The microstructure in Figure 2.5 also shows a network of cracks, which are the result of pressing the gritty paste into the mold.

Chemical analyses done with an electron microprobe as described in Chapter 15 are reported in Table 2.1. We see that the interior of the body has very little residual alkali but retains the insoluble lime and iron impurities. The intermediate white quartz layer contains more alkali and copper, showing that the slurry used was made up with more of these constituents to form the efflorescent glaze. The soda content of the glaze

TABLE 2.1

Average Chemical Compositions of the Interior Body, the White Quartz Layer, the Glass Bond in the Quartz Layer (see Figure 1.7), and the Glaze. The Values Reported are Averages of Five to Seven Individual Determinations to Account for Variations in the Local Areas Analyzed. Errors that Can Easily Creep Into This Sort of Analysis Are Discussed in Chapter 15.

	Overall Composition of the Interior Body	Overall Composition of the White Layer	Composition of the Glass Bond in the White Layer	Composition of the Glaze
Silica, SiO_2	98.9	94.0	77.6	80.
Alumina, Al_2O_3	0.04	0.4	0.5	0.6
Titania, TiO_2	—	0.04	0.03	0.04
Calcia, CaO	0.4	0.5	1.4	1.7
Magnesia, MgO	—	0.07	0.1	0.3
Soda, Na_2O	<.1	0.25	9.7	10.8
Potassia, K_2O	—	0.1	0.3	0.5
Copper Oxide, CuO	<.5	2.19	7.7	4.8
Iron Oxide, FeO	0.5	0.4	0.4	1.0
Phosphorus pentoxide, P_2O_5	—	0.07	0.29	0.1
Chlorine, Cl	—	0.2	1.4	1.1
Sulfate, SO_3	—	0.15	0.4	0.2
Lead Oxide, PbO	—	—	0.08	0.05
Tin Oxide, SnO_2	—	0.1	0.16	—
Baria, BaO	—	—	0.05	—
Total	99.84	98.47	100.11	101.19

increases to become 40 times greater than the interior concentration as a result of the efflorescence; copper is less soluble, and its concentration only increases by a factor of two. The electron microprobe is able to focus on the glass regions between particles shown in Figure 2.5, and the compositions of this material and the glaze are also given in Table 2.1. These compositions are quite similar, corresponding to the reaction between the quartz grains and a mixture of malachite copper ore and desert alkali natron. The high chlorine and sulfur content and low phosphorous are indicative of natron as the source of alkali.

The firing temperature for this glaze must have been in the range of 900–1000°C, probably closer to 900°C. A lower temperature would have resulted in a lower silica content; a higher temperature would have given a smoother, glossier surface. As shown in Plate III, the glaze has not spread out to wet the underlying body, where a bubble or crack or finger mark in the slip has caused a local defect. Malachite copper ore is insoluble in pure water, and the presence of substantial chlorine and sulfate derived from the desert natron are thought to be helpful in its efflorescence, but this is an area in which more research is needed. Dissolved in the glaze, the iron oxide impurity contributes a greenish hue, but it is inconsequential in comparison with the copper oxide. The leadfree, low-calcia glaze has a strong blue color.

In cross section (Figure 2.5), the glaze is seen to be transparent. However, when one looks directly at the surface of the chalice, the glaze appears soft and translucent in texture and mottled with small white inclusions. A 10X magnifying glass reveals that quartz particles are dispersed in a transition region at the interface with the underlying white ground as shown in Plate III. These underlying quartz particles scatter the reflected light, giving a soft diffuse appearance to the glaze. This special visual impact is almost never replicated in modern "reproductions" of Egyptian faience, which have a substantial amount of clay in the body and a low-melting lead-alkali-borosilicate glaze.

The brown, iron-containing sedimentary clays of Egypt, often referred to as Nile mud, are easy to shape, form, and fire into a satisfactory ware. On such a body, a transparent alkaline copper glaze has a muddy color; in addition, there is little glaze penetration into the body at the firing temperatures used and the contraction on cooling can cause it to delaminate or spall from the underlying body. The quartz-paste Egyptian faience body, which is white in color and has a high contraction on cooling, was a quite remarkable technical solution to the problem of achieving a brilliant blue-green equivalent of turquoise, lapis lazuli, and malachite. Egyptian faience, the earliest artificial gemstone, was the forerunner of a long tra- dition of "contrived," nonclay ceramics, including Islamic quartz-frit-clay porcelain, Medici porcelain, and French soft-paste porcelain. The ability to model and mold a variety of sizes, shapes, and colors was obviously attractive since the technology was practiced throughout the Near Eastern and Mediterranean world. However, the limited workability meant that modeling and molding rather than throwing were the prime methods of manufacture.

Research has shown that after an initial period of technological exper- imentation during predynastic times (ca. 4800–3050 B.C.) in which stone- working methods were used to form beads and amulets, the efflorescence method of glazing was adopted and became a conservative tradition during the third millennium. During the Middle Kingdom, at least as early as the reign of Senwosret I (1971–1928 B.C.), a method of glazing by roasting in a special glazing powder was also used. In the New Kingdom (1550–1070 B.C.), there was a greater diversity of shapes, glazes were also applied as slurries, and the body material was sometimes mixed with powdered col- ored glasses. Many of these second millennium objects represent tour-de- force craftsmanship and rank as artistic and technical masterworks. The faience goblet we have studied was made at a time of great power and wealth in Egyptian history and Egyptian faience was held in high esteem as an art material. A variety of visual effects were investigated and exploited in an atmosphere of technological innovation. The chalice illustrated is an outstanding example of this creative period in Egypt's history.

RECOMMENDED READING

Baines, J., and J. Malek, *Atlas of Ancient Egypt*, Facts on File Publications, New York, 1980. A general reference on Egyptian culture and society with a geographical framework and copious color illustrations.

Lucas, A., and J. R. Harris, *Ancient Egyptian Materials and Industries*, Ar- nold, London, 1962, revised edition. One chapter gives a traditional description of Egyptian faience. A great deal of information on other crafts and raw materials is thoughtfully presented in other chapters.

Stone, J. F. S., and L. C. Thomas, "Use and Distribution of Faience in the Ancient East and Prehistoric Europe," *Proceedings of the Prehistoric Society*, 22 (5), p. 40ff. (1956). The classical historical review of faience development in the Near East and Egypt, accompanied by analyses using semiquantitative emission spectroscopy.

REFERENCES*

1. MacIver, D., and A. Mace, *El Amrah and Abydos, 1899–1901*, London (1902), pp. 47, 72, 89. Archaeological report of the finds from Abydos, including a description of the two faience chalices.

2. Brovarski, E., Angela Millward Jones, and P. Vandiver, "Faience Vessels," in *Egypt's Golden Age: The Art of Living in the New Kingdom, 1558–1085 B.C.*, edited by E. Brovarski, Museum of Fine Arts, Boston (1982), pp. 140–151. A description of the chalice is given, and the chalice is fitted into the historical artistic context of other chalices in Egypt. This and other objects are used as touchstones to develop an appreciation of daily life in the New Kingdom.

3. Petrie, W. M. F., *The Arts and Crafts of Ancient Egypt*, Foulis, London, 1909, pp. 107–119. A review of glass and glaze technology as reconstructed at the turn of the century, with particular emphasis on objects that represent the first known instance of a type or process.

4. Beck, H., "Notes on Glazed Stones," in *Ancient Egypt and the East*, pp. 19–37 (June 1934). A survey of glazed steatite and glazed quartz as precursors of faience. The usefulness of a low-power microscope is emphasized to observe characteristics both on the surface and in cross section.

5. Binns, C. F., et al., "An Experiment in Egyptian Blue Glaze," *Journal of the American Ceramic Society*, 15, pp. 71–72 (1932). The first brief description of the firing of effloresced salts as a glazing technique.

6. Noble, J. V., "The Technique of Egyptian Faience," *American Journal of Archaeology*, 73, pp. 435–439 (1969). A description of efflorescence glazing combined with documentation of replication experiments.

7. Wulff, H. E., et al., "Egyptian Faience: A Possible Survival in Iran," *Archaeology*, 21, pp. 98–107 (1968). The manufacture of modern donkey beads in Qom, Iran, is documented, together with analyses of raw materials and investigation of the process using microstructural evaluation.

8. Kiefer, C., and A. Allibert, "Pharoanic Blue Ceramics: The Process of Self-Glazing," *Archaeology*, 24, pp. 107–117 (1971). A description of several techniques of cementation glazing and documentation of the replication of an Egyptian faience Hippopotamus.

9. Vandiver, P., "Technological Change in Egyptian Faience," in *Archaeological Ceramics*, J. S. Olin and A. D. Franklin, editors, Smithsonian Institution Press, 1982, pp. 167–179. A review of the three methods of glazing faience and a proposed sequence of their usage and the forming of faience in Egypt.

10. Tite, M. S., I. C. Freestone, and M. Bimson, "Egyptian Faience: An Investigation of the Methods of Production," *Archaeometry*, 25 (1) (1983), pp. 17–27. Microstructure is used to determine the method of glazing faience.

11. Kaczmarczyk, A., and R. E. M. Hedges, *Ancient Egyptian Faience*, Aris and Phillips, Warminster (1983). Analysis of colorants in Egyptian faience and their change with time. An appendix by P. Vandiver describes manufacturing methods of particular objects.

12. *Scientific Studies of Early Vitreous Materials*, British Museum Occasional Papers, in press (1986). A collection of papers reviewing the current state of research on Egyptian faience.

13. Harris, J. R., *Lexicographical Studies in Ancient Egyptian Minerals*, Akademie-Verlag, Berlin (1961), pp. 124 ff.

*Reference lists throughout include sources referred to in text as well as those suitable for further study.

CHAPTER 3

A SONG DYNASTY LONGQUAN CELADON JAR

Song (Sung) Dynasty (960–1279 A.D.) celadon is commonly considered the highest achievement of classical Chinese ceramics. The celadon jar shown in Figure 3.1 and Plate IV has the appearance of green jade with a slight hint of blue. There are subtle variations in color, in the modeled and carved surface, and in the soft, diffuse reflectance—all of which are similar to jade in form and texture. Thus celadon, like Egyptian faience, is a ceramic recreation of a semiprecious material. The celadon jar is equivalent in beauty to carved jade, but celadon vessels, unlike jade, could be made in sufficient quantity for export. The best celadons were made in the inland valleys near the market town of Longquan (Lung Ch'uan), southwest of Shanghai in Zhejiang (Chekiang) province during the middle and late Southern Song period (1127–1279 A.D.). The Longquan potters were able to produce a popular and aesthetically pleasing ware that was different from previous green glazed ware and of higher quality. Northern celadons were olive green and had a thinner glaze than the Longquan celadons; celadons made in the south and southwest, including those made to imitate Longquan celadons, were of poor quality with regard to body and glaze. Later Yuan Dynasty (1271–1368 B.C.) celadons made at Longquan have a greener color and a clearer, more transparent glaze, and lack the subtle depth of Southern Song Longquan celadons.

The technology underlying celadon production was quite sophisticated

Figure 3.1. Southern Song Dynasty celadon jar created in the twelfth century A.D. in Zhejiang province near the market town of Longquan, southwest of Shanghai (Boston Museum of Fine Arts, no. 35-734). Similar vessels have recently been found in tomb deposits. (See Plate IV.) (Courtesy of the Boston Museum of Fine Arts.)

Figure 3.2. The dragon encircling the neck of the jar was modeled and joined in place when the jar was partially dried. The fine parallel circumferential grooves resulting in the clay body from trimming are seen at the rim of the jar. The reddish color of the clay body at the unglazed rim results from the oxidation of iron during cooling. (See Plate V.)

and based on generations of trial and error; it was an empirically developed, craft-based technology. The superb craftsmanship required to produce celadon is revealed in its complex shape, which required the joining of thrown, modeled, and molded parts, and care in drying to prevent cracking. A high degree of control of both chemical composition and heat treatment was necessary to produce the green, jadelike texture of the glaze. The celadon glaze has subtle variations in green tint caused by variations in glaze thickness resulting from carving and incising of the body prior to application of the glaze. This is very different from the effloresced glaze on the Egyptian faience chalice, which has an even thickness that follows the contours of incised lines.

Song celadons are based on a long history of technological development and aesthetic appreciation. Chinese art historians have recognized the continuity of this development, making a distinction only between porous, low-fired red, cream, or gray wares, which they call pottery, and the dense, high-fired, white wares, which have sonorous ring, but which are divided into porcelain and stoneware by Westerners. Celadon is a Western term, perhaps a corruption of the name of Sultan Saladin who made a gift of 40 pieces of such ware to the Sultan of Damascus in 1171, or from the gray-green dress of the shepherd Celadon in a seventeenth century dramatization of Honore d'Urfe's pastoral *Astree*. The Islamic myth that a poisoned substance placed in a celadon vessel would be revealed to the owner further distinguished this ware.

High-fired green-glazed wares were first produced during the Shang Dynasty (1500–1066 B.C.). During the third century A.D., green-glazed Yue (Yueh) wares were first seen in eastern Zhejiang province. Yue wares look very different from the classical Longquan celadons. The glazes are thinner, almost transparent, and tend to flow. The underlying grayish-white body shows through the glaze. The glaze composition is different, being more highly fluxed with lime, but the shaping and firing techniques are the same. The classic Longquan celadon with a deep, lustrous, translucent blue-green glaze, such as the jar in Plate IV, was first produced during the mid-Southern Song Dynasty (twelfth century). The middle and late Southern Song was a period of great expansion and prosperity. A monetarist economy, mechanisms of credit and industrial organization supported economic growth. Many new kilns were founded; archaeologists have located the sites of more than a hundred on the banks of the Ou River in southern Zhejiang. Maritime and inland water-borne communication and transportation improved, and a major ceramic production area was centered around Longquan. However, there was little contact with northern China because of the Jin invasion, and pottery production in the north had fallen into decline. In the twelfth and thirteenth centuries, the central government tried to restrict the export of gold, silver, and copper but nevertheless was required to pay tribute to northern tribes to prevent their invasion of the south. Overseas trade was promoted to obtain revenue. Silks and ceramics were exported in vast numbers to Japan, Southeast Asia, Indonesia, and the Philippines, as well as to East Africa and the Middle East. Recent excavations have confirmed that Longquan celadons were not only a major object of foreign trade but also were popular within China, being shipped to many different regions, and even copied in the south in Fujian (Fukien) province.

Figure 3.1 and Plate IV show a superb example of Longquan celadon, a wheel-thrown, blue-green vessel with a modeled dragon encircling the neck and lotus petals carved and incised over the horizontal throwing rings of the body. An enlarged view of the dragon is shown in Figure 3.2 and Plate V. The basic shape of this vessel was formed by throwing on a potter's wheel a body that was quite plastic but had a limited working range. That is, the clay changes from too stiff to too fluid with only a small change in water content, requiring the potter to shape the vessel rapidly and limiting the size of vessel that can be thrown. The body is ideally suited for the small bowls that are most characteristic of Longquan production. Making a vessel as large and complex as the one shown here required great skill and joining together of prethrown sections. Circumferential grooves 5 to 10 mm apart on the interior of the body indicate the throwing process and can be seen in the xeroradiograph shown in Figure 3.3 and Plate VI. The wall was thinned at the top of the body, but it is thicker where the body joins the neck. A xeroradiograph taken at a different angle revealed a join line where the neck was attached to the shoulder. The neck was thrown separately and joined to the body after neck and body were sufficiently stiff to support the weight but not yet dry. The base was trimmed with a pointed wooden or metal tool, leaving a foot rim with an indented center. Marks from trimming are present as fine parallel, circumferential grooves about 0.8 mm apart on the bottom. The base is uneven in thickness, as can be seen in the xeroradiograph.

The dragon was modeled from two lumps of clay and then the legs were shaped in an open-face mold and added to the body; joins within the body and between the body and legs can be seen in the radiograph. Two small animals, perhaps tigers or dogs, were modeled and attached to the neck and lid. Porosity in the body and legs of the dragon is randomly oriented, indicating that very little extension of the clay took place during

74

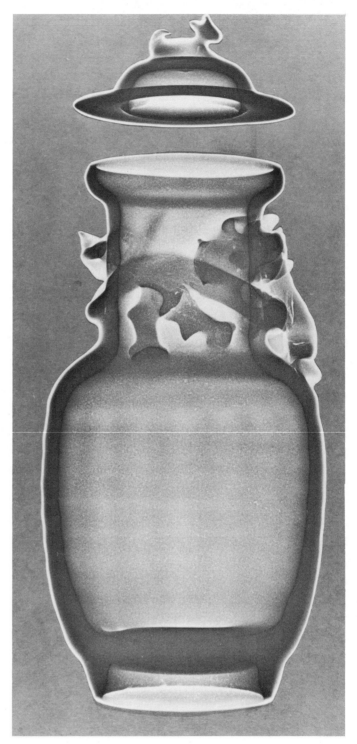

Figure 3.3. A xeroradiograph of the jar shows indications of horizontal throwing marks on the interior, an incised lotus pattern on the exterior of the body, and the join between the separately thrown neck and body. Typical porosity, seen as fine white dots in the xeroradiograph, appears in the hand-modeled dragon as rounded and un-aligned, whereas pores in the thrown body are aligned in a diagonal spiral. Cracks are present at some of the luted joints where the dragon was attached to the vessel when still plastic. (Xeroradiograph by Betty Seed and Louise Corkham.) (See Plate VI.)

modeling; in contrast, groups of pores in the body are aligned in an upward spiral direction as a result of the considerable force required to raise the initial body form. Because there was virtually no extension of the body in the base, there is no pore alignment there. The dragon was wetter than the body when it was formed around and joined to the neck. As a result there was greater shrinkage during drying and cracks developed at many of the joins. One can be seen in the xeroradiograph where the dragon's paw is attached to the shoulder of the vessel.

After the jar was dried to the leather-hard state, the surface pattern was incised by cutting away clay to leave 16 vertical panels. A horizontal cross section cut through the body and glaze at right angles to the direction of the petals is shown in Figure 3.4. This process was very delicate because the vertical grooves vary in depth in direct relationship to the throwing ridges on the interior and exterior surfaces of the vessel. Then the outline of the lotus petals near the top of the body and the leaves near the base of the body were incised with a pointed tool held at an acute angle. The

Figure 3.4. A horizontal cross section cut through the incised lotus decoration illustrates the nearly white body of this piece with a layer of glaze on each side. The glaze layers reveal the structure of bubbles throughout the glaze. The interior of the vessel is shown in the lower glaze layer. The incised pattern of the lotus petals is shown in the upper glaze layer, with the greater glaze thickness over the incised decoration providing a darker blue-green color and the thinner glaze thickness along the ridge giving a lighter color (10X).

glaze is thicker and appears darker along the incised lines whereas it is thinner and thus lighter along the ridges.

Some of the ware made during the Song Dynasty was bisque fired (or biscuit fired) at a low temperature before glazing. This jar was made with a single firing. Before the ware was completely dry, the interior glaze was applied by pouring a liquid glaze slip in and then quickly out again so that the body would not become too wet. Most likely the outer surface was dampened and the external glaze blown on through a bamboo tube with a piece of silk gauze over the end. The liquid glaze slurry would disperse as fine droplets through the gauze, then adhere and build up as a layer on the surface of the pot, much as in the modern process of spray painting. To build up the desired thickness, two or more applications were probably made, and each allowed to dry partially before the next one so that excessive water buildup was avoided. Excess glaze was wiped off the foot and lip.

After drying, the ware was placed on a plaque of unfired clay inside a saggar, a protective ceramic container, for firing in a hill-climbing dragon kiln, an example of which is shown in Figure 3.5. Saggers found at Southern Song kiln sites were made of clay bodies capable of withstanding repeated high-temperature firings. The saggers were designed efficiently to contain the shapes being fired, and were stacked on top of each other in columns. Simple or lightweight shapes were set in the sagger on a plague of unfired refractory clay similar to that used for the sagger. Complex or weighty shapes were placed on an unfired support of the same clay as the vessel. Thus allowance was made for the shrinkage of the vessel during firing by having a support that would shrink at the same rate and in the same temperature range; otherwise cracking at the base would often result. If the glaze ran or impurities in the sagger clay melted to form pockets of glass, the support would prevent the ware from sticking to the sagger. The purpose of this detailed description is to suggest the sophistication of an empirically based craft technology.

The hill-climbing dragon kiln consisted of a long chamber in the form of a tunnel that was built on the side of a hill at a slope of about 15 to 20 degrees. The fire was begun in a firebox at the base of the kiln and the upper part of the kiln acted like a chimney, serving to preheat the ware placed higher up the hill. When the pottery in the lower part of the kiln had reached firing temperature, a fire hole in the side of the kiln further up the hill was stoked with wood, brush, and twigs to bring the next section up to temperature. As the fire location was gradually moved upward to other fire holes, the heat from ware in the lower part of the kiln served to preheat the incoming combustion air and at the same time to cool the ware in the lower part of the kiln quite rapidly. This type of kiln is very efficient for firing large amounts of ware because both the incoming air and the ware above the fire are preheated. Equally efficient kilns were not designed in the West until late in the nineteenth century.

Many refinements in design show the technical sophistication of these kilns. The path of the flame was controlled in each section by the careful arrangement of saggers. Saggers were packed into a dense fire wall between sections so that each section would reach the proper peak temperature. Placement of ware not only varied over individual sections, but also over the length of the kiln. Smaller ware that required less time to preheat was placed at the bottom of the kiln to minimize firing losses. Less important ware was placed at the top of the kiln where the oxidation of the gas is difficult to control and which is fired at the end of the two- to three-day firing when workers are fatigued. During the Yuan Dynasty, the dragon kiln design evolved into a multiple-chamber or step kiln in which divisions between sections were constructed as walls with holes of optimal size and location for the control of draft. This effective design has continued in use and is often seen in China today.

Kilns of various sizes were in use during the Song Dynasty; in the larger ones, as many as 100,000 pieces were progressively brought up to a temperature of 1200°C (2200°F) in a single firing. The time, temperature, and atmosphere of firing are critical to ware quality. Much of the ware was fired at too low a temperature and appears opaque, or at too high a temperature and appears transparent. If fired in too much reduction, with insufficient air mixed with the combustion gases, the ware appears gray; if fired in too much oxidation, with too much air present, the ware becomes too bright a green in color. In addition, either condition (too much gas or too much air) in the mixture lowers the flame temperature and is detrimental to an efficient firing. Much of the celadon ware had to be rejected because of warping or cracking, as the tremendous piles of ceramic debris near kilns attest.

As we look more closely at the jar, we see that the dragon is the visual focus; the oval curves of the lid and body entice the eye back toward the dragon. The carved lotus petal design brings the eye upward across the expanse of the body, with each petal acting as an arrow to fix the focus on the dragon. The basal ring stabilizes and supports the oval body, and the convex profile curve of the base reinforces the return of the eye upward. The base and lid both bring the eye to the center of focus, but each in a different way. The horizontal rim of the lid stops the eye, whereas the dome of the lid can be viewed as an extension of the neck, which pierces

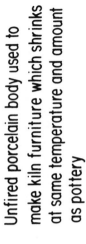

Unfired porcelain body used to make kiln furniture which shrinks at same temperature and amount as pottery

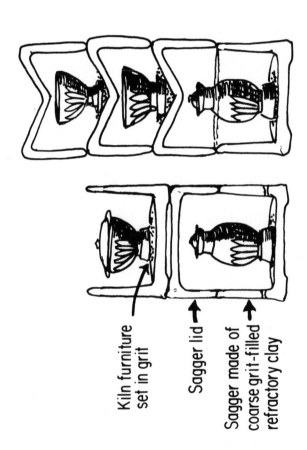

Kiln furniture set in grit

Sagger lid

Sagger made of coarse grit-filled refractory clay

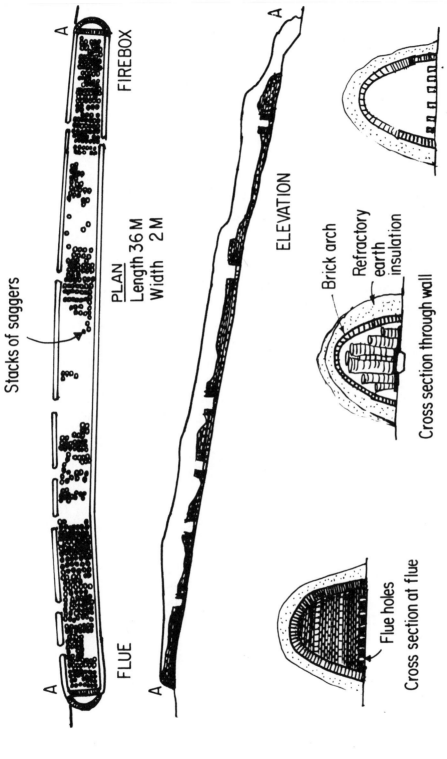

Figure 3.5. Plan and elevation of a twelfth century hill-climbing "dragon" kiln excavated near Longquan. The kiln, which held large quantities of war, was two meters across and 30 meters long. Some saggers were left in the kiln, showing that smaller wares were stacked in the lower part of the kiln. Two types of saggers were found; the schematic drawing illustrates their stacking. Cross sections of the kiln are shown at the lower firebox, the middle, and the uppermost flue.

the rim of the lid. This rim is supported in turn by the outward curved lip of the vessel, an element that provides a gradual transition to the lid rim. While the dome circles the eye downward, the small tiger or dog accents the change of direction.

The dragon is an intricate visual element that holds our attention because of its complex shape and the surface textures that have been modeled, molded, and incised, as well as because of its cultural associations. The dragon in Chinese mythology is a heavenly beast, representing the eastern direction; it is a symbol of strength, longevity, and the status quo, and is identified throughout most of Chinese history as a totem and symbol of the emperor. The body of the dragon encircles the neck of the vessel, giving a sense of visual tension to the jar and acting as if to constrict the vessel's diameter. As the dragon's body curves up and down around the neck, this impression of constriction is reinforced. The curves in the shape of the dragon are much sharper than in the vessel and hold the attention of the viewer, requiring rotation of the vessel to capture the entire shape and stance of the dragon. The lotus flower acts as a ground above which the dragon floats, while simultaneously acting as a repetitive design element that focuses the eye on the dragon as the vessel is turned in the hands. The constricted neck of the jar emphasizes the activity and strength of the dragon, and yet visually appears to pierce the lid. One possible interpretation of the horizontal elements is as the roof of heaven, with the vessel symbolizing the function of the dragon, and thus the emperor, in the binding of heaven and earth.

If we investigate the microstructure, analyze the overall bulk composition, and comprehend the local variations in composition that produce the visual impact of Longquan celadons, we can add another level of understanding and appreciation. The body is made of a mixture of finely ground china stone and a lesser amount of clay material. During firing the clay component breaks down and transforms into tiny mullite crystallites and a small amount of silicate glass, as shown in Figure 3.6. The mica and feldspar constituents melt to form a silicate glass; additional mullite forms in this glass as needlelike prisms. The quartz particles slowly dissolve in the silicate glass. Because more quartz particles dissolve at higher temperatures, stoneware and porcelain have the amazing property that the glass portion of the body becomes stiffer as the temperature rises. This resistance to slumping in the kiln is further strengthened by the growth of the needlelike mullite crystals, which form an intergrown matlike network, akin to that of modern fiber-reinforced composites. As a result the Longquan celadons could be fired over a fairly large range of temperature in the massive dragon kilns without warping or slumping.

Fired celadon clay bodies range in color from a light yellowish cream to red on exposed surfaces that have reoxidized by reaction with the air on cooling. The color of the interior ranges from almost white to gray, caused by a reducing atmosphere in the kiln and its chemical interaction with the iron impurity. As the fuel burns in the fire holes of the kiln, it forms a long, hot reducing flame necessary to obtain a high, uniform temperature. As a result the iron in the body is present partly in the glass phase and partly as magnetite particles that impart an overall gray color. In the best ware, most of the iron is dissolved in the glassy matrix to form an off-white bluish cast. As seen in Figure 3.4, the body has an almost white color corresponding to high-quality raw materials of low iron content and the achievement of a well-fired structure.

The most important feature of the celadons is the translucent jadelike depth of the glaze. This has often been ascribed to the scattering of light by bubbles and by undissolved quartz particles in the glaze. The bubbles and quartz grains are about a tenth of a millimeter in size, and can just be seen with the unaided eye. The bubbles, as viewed with a hand magnifying lens, are shown in Figures 3.4 and 3.7; they scatter light and add internal reflections that increase the brilliance of the glaze. Quartz particles, such as shown in Figure 3.8a, add to the translucency but do not produce the lustrous celadon texture. Although bubbles affect the visual impact, they do not explain the outstanding appearance of Longquan celadon as compared with the earlier Yue or later Yuan Dynasty wares.

The soft, silky luster of celadon glazes results from the interaction of light with fine anorthite and wollastonite crystals smaller than a micrometer in size that have formed in the glaze, as shown in Figures 3.8, 3.9, and 3.10. Anorthite is a calcium-aluminum silicate and has a needlelike morphology; wollastonite is a calcium silicate with a rounded appearance. Each of these crystalline phases can form in a viscous glass where there is not a lot of mixing if the temperature is maintained for a suitable length of time, and, most important of all, if the composition of the glass is similar to that of the crystal. This last requirement is the key to understanding the technology of truly outstanding celadon glazes.

Microchemical analysis reveals that local compositional variations occur in the glazes on a scale of less than one tenth of a millimeter. As shown

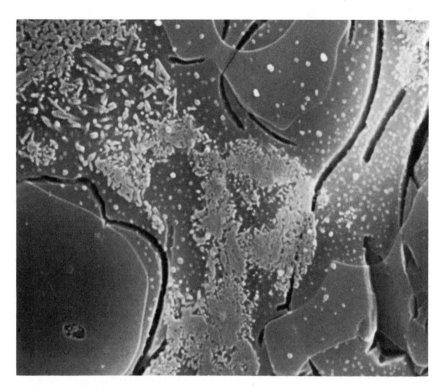

Figure 3.6. The microstructure of the body consists of partially dissolved quartz particles, each surrounded by cracks caused by the contraction of the quartz during cooling. This shrinkage occurs suddenly at about 573°C. Surrounding the quartz particles is a glass of high silica composition. Fine needlelike mullite crystals have formed along with glass in those regions originally composed of clay. Larger mullite crystals have formed in an area that was originally composed of a micaceous feldspar. This micrograph was prepared by grinding and polishing a small piece of the body until it was very smooth, and then dissolving a small amount of the glass in an acid bath in order to see the size and shape of the crystals. During this etching process, cracks around the quartz particles were enlarged slightly (1000X).

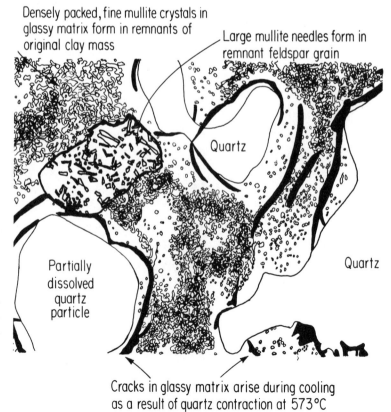

Densely packed, fine mullite crystals in glassy matrix form in remnants of original clay mass

Large mullite needles form in remnant feldspar grain

Quartz

Partially dissolved quartz particle

Quartz

Cracks in glassy matrix arise during cooling as a result of quartz contraction at 573°C

Figure 3.7. The bubble structure of the glaze is visible from the top surface at 2X and from the cross section at 10X. Anorthite and wollastonite crystallites in the glaze are too small to be seen here. A thin surface layer in the lower cross section has a yellowish-brown tint.

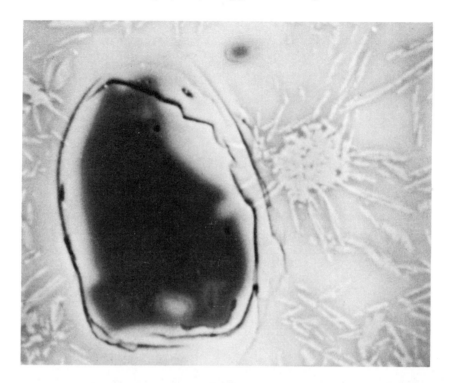

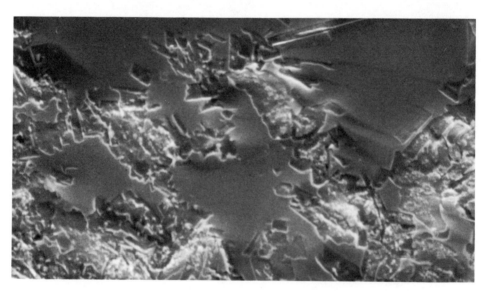

Figure 3.8. At higher magnification we see a residual quartz particle in the glaze that is surrounded by much finer anorthite crystallites in the top micrograph (5000X). The lower micrograph shows a cluster of anorthite crystals that have been etched away (5000X).

in Figure 3.9, the calcia (CaO) content varies from 5 percent near the body to 11 percent near the surface. The variation in lime content vacillates between the extreme values, while the alumina (Al_2O_3) content also varies from 14.1 to 16.2 percent. In regions of the glaze where there is high lime, there are low values for alumina, and in the microstructure a lot of wollastonite is found. Needles of anorthite are abundant in areas where the alumina content is high and lime content low. A local region high in calcia content and with a great deal of wollastonite is shown in Figure 3.10. This micrograph is particularly interesting because it also shows that the high-calcia regions are more fluid than the high-alumina regions. The high-calcia region has been carried to the surface of the glaze with a bubble that has popped at the surface. We conclude that local variations in composition lead to local changes in the type and amount of crystals that form in the glaze.

If we relate the compositions shown in Figure 3.9 to the raw materials used to formulate the glaze, more of the celadon technology comes to light. The calcia content comes from calcined limestone, whereas the alumina comes mainly from the china stone and clay. The glaze batch was made up of finely ground china stone similar to that used in the body but with a smaller clay content, together with an addition of burnt lime and ash. To account for the compositional and microstructure variations shown in Figure 3.9, the lime must have been added without the fine grinding or levigation used for the china stone and clay. Limestone (calcium carbonate, $CaCO_3$), when heated above about 800°C, decomposes to form burnt lime (calcium oxide, CaO) with the evolution of carbon dioxide. The resultant product is a soft powder, which was used as a glaze material without further grinding. Not grinding the lime was clearly aimed at producing the desired glaze texture.

Furthermore, observation of the microstructure of the glaze cross section reveals a layer of concentrated crystals at the boundaries between multiple glaze applications. The thickness of this celadon glaze sample was built up by applying two layers of glaze with some drying in between. During drying evaporation of water from the surface led to a slightly alkali-rich surface layer; this, with the presence of fine clay particles, tended to nucleate an enhanced layer of anorthite crystals.

The green color results from the presence of about 1 percent iron oxide in solution in the glaze, which is green when fired in reducing conditions. During the high-temperature reduction firing, the glaze is in contact with the combustion gases entering the kiln and the upper tenth of a millimeter or so has a yellowish-brown-amber tinge resulting from sulfur and carbon

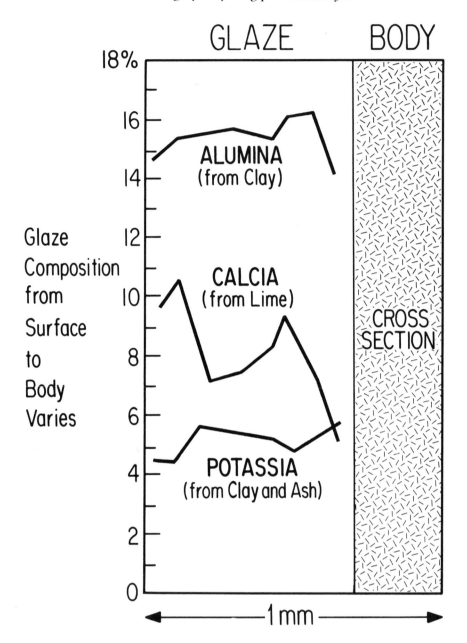

Figure 3.9. A plot of the chemical contents of calcia (CaO) from lime, alumina (Al_2O) from china clay, and potassia (K_2O) from ash and china stone, which are shown on the left side in weight percent. Along the bottom the cross section of the glaze is represented; zero is at the surface of the glaze and 0.7 mm at the interface of the glaze and body. The amount and location of compositional variability can be visualized in this plot. This analysis shows variations of about a tenth of a millimeter in the particle size of the lime added to make the glaze.

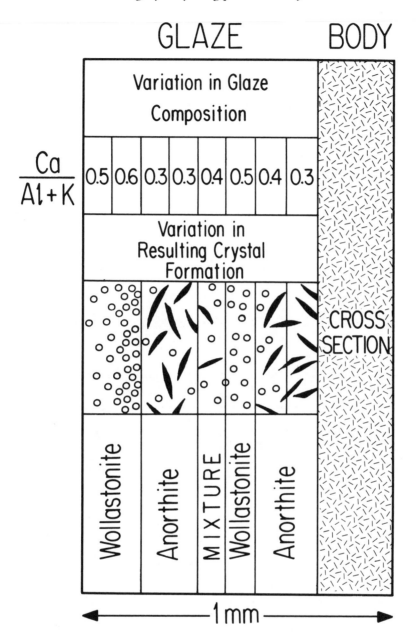

Figure 3.9. (cont) Different crystals were found in these different glass compositions, as shown along the top scale, although these were not included in the analysis. Such compositional variations produced the jadelike texture of Longquan celadon glazes.

contamination. The effect of light passing through differently colored layers contributes to the feeling of depth.

To obtain the combination of depth, translucency, color, and brightness desired, it is necessary to have the proper iron content, along with a mixture of anorthite, quartz, and wollastonite that accounts for about a quarter of the total glaze volume. To dissolve a portion of the quartz, to maintain the proper bubble size and concentration, and to develop optimal anorthite and wollastonite crystallization, the firing temperature and time of firing must be well controlled at a temperature near 1200°C. If the firing temperature is too low, the bubbles are smaller and constitute a smaller volume fraction, and there is a substantial amount of undissolved quartz and clay and larger amounts of anorthite crystals than in the properly fired ware. Low firing temperatures result in a whitish, almost opaque product. In

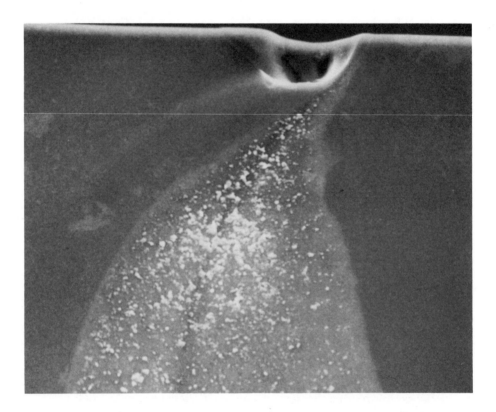

Figure 3.10. The local changes in composition shown in Figure 3.9 lead to local variations in the crystals that form in the glaze. These fine crystals are beyond resolution with the naked eye, but lend a texture and interest to fine celadon glazes that lead to its favorable comparison with jade.

the best ware, the bubbles have grown and increased in number, the quartz has mostly dissolved, and the anorthite crystals precipitate as dense clusters of crystallite needles amid high-lime regions of spherical wollastonite crystallites. In samples fired too long at too high a temperature, all the quartz has dissolved, only large bubbles that contribute little to translucence, remain, and there are no anorthite or wollastonite precipitates; overfired samples are clear and transparent. Severe limits on obtaining the best product are set by the rates of solution and precipitation of the wollastonite and anorthite crystals, and thus the firing temperature could not be too high or too low, or the time too short or too long. That Longquan potters could not always anticipate outstanding results is clear from the hills of wasters at ancient kiln sites.

Accomplishing the appearance of high-quality celadon required the proper selection and preparation of raw materials, the development of reproducible production methods, and high-temperature firing in a controlled atmosphere. From the microstructure and composition, we can deduce the nature of the processes and controls required to produce celadon; and we can reconstruct the ceramic technology in a way that is not otherwise possible. By using large-particle-size lime as a glaze constituent, by incomplete mixing of the glaze, and by good control of firing, Longquan potters were able to produce the desired color and texture of their celadons. According to the practices and goals of modern ceramic production in which homogeneity, fineness of particle size, high-temperature transparent glazes, and fast, efficient firing are sought, the manufacture of Longquan celadon would be unlikely, if not impossible, today. European porcelain glazes of the same overall composition are clear, transparent, and bright, just like the overfired Longquan rejects. A completely different way of thinking about making ceramics has prevailed since the development of porcelain in Europe that embodies a mental set antithetical to that responsible for the Longquan celadons.

The Longquan celadon glazes represent a ceramic analog to the microstructure of jade developed empirically by a sophisticated craft technology. The desired visual impact was deemed worthy of the effort to develop, perfect, and perpetuate a unique set of production steps, composition, and controls that was able to manufacture reproducibly a product that modern science-based technology finds quite difficult to replicate. Jade (in China, nephrite) has a structure of fibrous felted aggregates that lie just beyond resolution by the unaided eye. The solution to the problem of reproducing jade in a ceramic medium involved the develoment of a complex multi-component microstructure with a range of granular and fibrous constituents on a similar fine scale. This result was not achieved in the earlier high-fired green-glazed Yue wares in which the high-lime glaze composition formed a fluid, glossy coating, or in the Yuan procelains in which the raw materials were more finely ground and the firing temperature higher.

RECOMMENDED READING

Articles on Chinese ceramics, in *Ceramics and Civilization*, Volume I, W. D. Kingery, (ed.), American Ceramic Society, Columbus, Ohio (1985). Three articles, two by Chinese scholars, with recent interpretations of the development of porcelain, colorants, and glazes in China.

Palmgren, Nils, Walter Steger, and Nils Sundius, *Sung Sherds*, Almquist and Wiksell, Stockholm, Sweden (1963). Description and analysis of shards from known kiln sites collected in the 1930s. A standard of photographic excellence.

Tichane, R., *Those Celadon Blues*, New York State Institute for Glaze Research, Painted Post, N.Y. (1978).

Wood, N. *Oriental Glazes*, Pitman, London (1978). A modern description of glaze compositions and raw materials.

REFERENCES

1. Chou Jen, Chang Fu-k'ang and Cheng Yung-fu, "Technical Studies on Lung Ch'uan Celadons of Successive Dynasties," *K'ao-ku hsueh-pao*, no. 1, pp. 131–156 (1973). A thorough study of the composition and manufacture of Longquan celadons. A translation has been made by Dr. P. Proctor, East Asian Department of the Royal Ontario Museum.

2. Tregear, M., *Song Ceramics*, Rizzoli Int'l. Public., New York, 1982.

3. Wirgin, J., "Song Ceramic Design," *Bull. Museum Far Eastern Antiquities*, vol. 42, 1970, Stockholm, Sweden.

4. Gompertz, G. St. G. M., *Chinese Celadon Wares*, Faber, London (1958). Art historical description of celadon wares.

5. Tregear, M., P. Hughes-Stanton, and R. Kerr, (eds.), *Kiln Sites of Ancient China: Recent Finds of Pottery and Porcelain*, London, Oriental Ceramic Society, 1980 (no. 97). An important display of Chinese shard material and the significance of shards from known sites in reevaluating whole vessels in Western collections are discussed.

6. Lau, M., (ed.), *Exhibition of Ceramic Finds from Ancient Kilns in China*, Hong Kong, Fung Ping Shan Museum, 1981, pp. 43–45. Same catalog as reference 3, but with color photographs and an excellent introductory essay by a leading Chinese archaeologist.

7. Chou Jen, and Lee Chia Chih, "An Investigation on the Technological Aspects of Chinese Ancient Ceramics," *Archaeology Reports*, vol. I, Science Press, Beijing (1960). An overview of the development of Chinese ceramic technology.

8. Li Jiazhi (same as Lee Chia Chih), "Formation and Development of the Green Glazes in Zhejiang Province," *Proceedings of International Conference on Ancient Chinese Pottery and Porcelain*, November 1982, Shanghai, Institute of Ceramics, 1986. An overview of the development of green glazed wares in China.

9. Chen Xianqiu, Chen Shiping, Zhou Xuelin, Li Jiazhi, Zhu Boqian, Mou Yongkand, and Wang Jiying, "A Fundamental Research on Ceramics of Southern Song Altar Guan Ware and Longquan Ware," *Proceedings of International Conference on Ancient Chinese Pottery and Porcelain*, November 1982, Shanghai, Institute of Ceramics, in press. A brief description of research on guan and celadon.

10. Addis, J. M., *Chinese Ceramics from Datable Tombs, and Some Other Dated Materials*, P. Wilson Pub., London (1978), p. 86 (no. 36). The importance of tomb deposits in fixing dates for different types of ware is stressed.

11. Ishii, T., "Experiments on the Kinuta Blue Celadon Glaze," *Trans. Brit. Ceram. Soc.*, vol. 29 (1930), pp. 360–387. An early attempt at replicating celadon is described.

12. Heatherington, A. L., *Chinese Ceramic Glazes*, Cambridge (1937) or South Pasadena, Calif. (1947). A discussion of the chemistry of many glaze effects.

13. Stull, R. T., and W. L. Howat, "Influences of Variable Silica and Alumina on Porcelain Glazes of Constant RO," *Trans. Am. Cer. Soc.*, 14 (1912), pp. 62–70, and "Deformation Temperatures of Some Porcelain Glazes," *Trans. Am. Cer. Soc.*, 16 (1914), pp. 454–460. Descriptions of European glaze practice, composition, and the relation to visual appearance.

14. Vandiver, P. B., and W. D. Kingery, "The Composition and Structure of Chinese Song Dynasty Celadon Glazes from Longquan," *Bull. Am. Cer. Soc.*, 63(4), (1984), pp. 612–616. An analysis of the variations in microstructure and compositions of five Longquan celadon shards.

CHAPTER 4

A SONG DYNASTY
JUN WARE BOWL

*J*un (Ch'un) ware, such as shown in Figure 4.1 and Plate VII, is one of the most beautiful of the Song Dynasty ceramics. The glaze is thick and flowing, and ranges in color from greenish-blue to grayish-blue to lavender. In the best-quality jun ware, of which this bowl is an example, there is a blue or lavender opalescence, with a lustrous yet cloudy appearance. Like the Longquan celadon, the technical and aesthetic achievement for which jun ware is most appreciated is the glaze.

Unlike Eqyptian faience and Longquan celadon, in which the shaping, joining, and finishing required a difficult and complex sequence of steps, the forming of the jun ware was simple, even crude. The straightforward, unpretentious forms for the most part were thrown on a wheel. Technical mastery of the formulation, application, and heat treatment of the glaze contributed the visual impact of this ware. Of all the glazes we have studied, the jun glaze is by far the most difficult for modern potters to replicate. The jun glaze is unusual for its jewel-like appearance, for its depth and translucency. The blue opalescence is interspersed with white cloudy regions and bubbles, enhanced with freely applied splashes and brush strokes of copper decoration that produce a variegated blue, red, and purple texture; details of this are shown in the enlargements of Plate VIII. Producing excellent examples of jun ware was difficult, requiring control of both chemical composition and firing. The degree of technical control required of the jun-ware potters can be seen in the varied appearance and quality of museum objects.

Jun wares were made over a wide geographical region of northern China for a long period of time, beginning in the Northern Song (960–1127 A.D.) and continuing into the Jin and Yuan, and well into the Ming period (1368–1644 A.D.). They were produced primarily in Henan (Honan) province at a number of kilns, of which the two best known were Linru xian and Yu xian. The ceramic production center around Linru xian is also known for the production of the olive-green northern celadons. During the fourteenth century, wares of large size and considerable weight, characterized by dark, compact bodies and colored purple, were produced at kilns in Zhenging Fu in neighboring Hebei (Hopei) province. However, the finest jun wares appear to have been produced in Henan during the Northern Song and Jin Dynasties, such as the jun bowl in Figure 4.1 and Plate VII.

Jun ware was never exported as the Southern Song celadons were, and its place in Chinese connoisseurship is not fully understood. Some authorities report that this ware was not collected until the Ming Dynasty, while others speculate that the prized ch'ai ware was the predecessor of jun. Before the beginning of the Song Dynasty, the ceramic known as ch'ai ware, of which we have no examples, was described as made in Henan and being the "blue of the sky after rain as seen in the rifts of the clouds." Western scholarship has evolved a developmental sequence for the jun wares. Early jun pieces had no carved or incised decoration on the simple, thrown shapes, primarily bowls, dishes, and saucers. The best known early jun shape is the rounded hemispherical bowl with slightly incurving rim. In the early twelfth century, copper oxide was used to paint or splash red and purple decoration in abstract designs. During the thirteenth century, the painted decoration became more precise and the shapes more complex, often having flower-shaped bosses and scrolled feet. Quantities of incense burners were produced. In the late thirteenth and the fourteenth centuries, large flower pots and basins with molded, lobed patterns and numbered one through ten in ascending sizes were common. The glazes were more opaque than those produced in the twelfth century. Recent Chinese archaeological excavations have called into question this sequence of stylistic development. The future of jun scholarship is at an exciting crossroads, which will develop as excavations connect wares to particular kiln sites and fix the dates of ceramic production with tomb deposits.

The jun ware bowl of Plate VII has a simple, round shape formed by throwing on a potter's wheel to develop the symmetrical profile with a wall

Figure 4.1. Southern Song Dynasty jun ware bowl created in the twelfth century A.D. in Honan province in northern China. (Courtesy of the Board of Trustees of the Victoria and Albert Museum, Eumorofopoulos Collection, C.845-1936.) (See Plate VII.)

thickness of 5–6 mm. After throwing, the bowl was dried to a leather-hard state, turned over, set on the wheel, and the foot ring trimmed to the present shape. The throwing, as with most jun ware shapes, required no special skill, nor was there much risk of loss during production. The forms have a certain attractive crude robustness. The foot is often uneven or has bits of clay adhering to the base ring; there are often throwing marks or trimming marks left unsmoothed at the lip and foot. The glaze is often uneven, and has run at the lip and dripped at the base. The painting is often haphazard and uncontrolled. Vessels are often thick-walled and feel heavier than expected when handled. However, there is within this seemingly crude tradition an energetic yet controlled artistic intent, one in which the aesthetic develops out of the simple operations of making the pot, carried out with an economy of effort and a great deal of experience and restraint.

The design of this jun ware bowl is based on a circular motif in which the round shape has been emphasized by the two concentric circles formed by the flared rim. The glaze has run from the two raised edges of this rim, revealing the white body beneath. In contrast to this almost geometrically perfect form, two imperfect, nonconcentric circles are painted in reddish-purple. Here the brush must have been applied in a syncopated rhythm of slowing speed and lowering toward the surface in order to form the oval shapes and then raising to a point and quickening, and once again lowering, to form the thin lines of uneven width. Most potters capable of wheel throwing would paint a banded decoration in which the wheel is turned beneath the brush, leaving a concentric line of constant thickness. However, this has none of the visual interest found in this jun ware, in which the circular symmetry of the shape of the double raised rim is emphasized by the double painted rings and doubling of solid reddish-purple ovals. Lest this be considered a coincidence, examination of the reverse side shows that the exterior of the rim continues as a single band and is accompanied by a single reddish-purple oval. Thus the eye is led to the visually active back.

Although there is no identifiable image or iconography in the jun ware bowl, it does evoke significant cultural ideas and associations. The visual contrast and tension between such opposing elements as the controlled geometric shape and the seemingly uncontrolled decoration, each of which isolates and emphasizes different aspects of the circular nature of the jun ware, are a statement of a Chinese outlook on life—one is practical, orderly, and often rigid in one's public life, embodying Confucian virtues, whereas in one's private life, there can be an appreciation of disorder and even a disregard of responsibility.

The glaze was applied by firmly gripping the bowl by its foot and dipping it into a thick glaze slurry. Thumb and finger marks can be seen on opposite sides of the foot. Excess glaze was wiped off and the purple and red decoration was applied on the glazed ware with a brush saturated with a water-based paint containing a copper colorant. The application was heavier at the beginning of the brush stroke and concentrated drops in the center of the plate dried to form local high concentrations of copper. During firing these areas of copper were reduced to metallic copper and the surrounding areas are seen as green spots.

After drying, the ware was placed on a clay plaque inside a refractory sagger for firing in a horseshoe kiln, as shown in Figure 4.2. This kiln had a single, small, firing chamber about three meters across with two separate fireboxes in front. Three flues at the back of the kiln that led to chimneys could be separately adjusted to control and direct the draft across the kiln in order to achieve a distribution and uniformity of temperature. The kiln was built into the sandy clay ground rather than constructed of bricks. The earth wall on the interior of the kiln was fired to a dense, strong monolithic structure, and was in turn supported and insulated by the surronding, more loosely packed earth. The kiln did not have a wall, often called a bag wall, to separate the firebox from the ware; instead a row of saggers was set so the flames and hot gasses would pass through and up over them and then through the other loaded saggers. The saggers were set close together where an increase in the flow of flames and hot gasses was required and widely spaced to slow the draft, in order to provide efficient heat transfer from the gas to the ware and achieve the desired temperature patterns that long experience had shown to be most effective.

Such kilns, insulated by the surrounding soil and densely packed with saggers and ware, have a large thermal mass. They take a long time to heat, and even longer to cool. A country brick kiln of this same general style typically is fired on a ten-day schedule in which three days are required to reach temperature and seven days to cool. An indication of the long time at temperature and the slow cooling is the formation of cristobalite crystals on the surface of the quartz particles in the glaze. Cristobalite is a high-temperature form of silica that takes a long time to form. A view of the surface of a quartz grain overgrown with cristobalite is shown in Figure 4.3. The quartz grain in Figure 4.3a cannot be seen beneath the cristobalite, but we found a cross-sectional view of a quartz grain sur-rounded by cristobalite at the edge of a broken chip of glaze in a characteristic pattern sometimes referred to as a "horse's tooth" pattern (Figure 4.3b). As we shall learn, the long, slow cooling is absolutely essential for the development of the jun opalescence and translucency. Modern techniques using a faster firing cycle cannot replicate the qualities of jun glazes. Ming Dynasty replications employed a somewhat faster firing than the Song originals; the products are inferior to the originals but better than most modern replications.

The development of the appearance of the jun ware depends critically on slow cooling. In the center of Plate IXb is a glaze sample that was heated to the firing temperature and then quickly cooled. The result is a clear, transparent, bluish-green glaze not at all like the jun glaze shown on the left. In contrast, if the glaze is fired to the same temperature and cooled too slowly, an opaque white glaze results, as illustrated on the right side of Plate IXb. This opaque white appearance is found in some ancient jun glazes, but it does not characterize the best products of the Song Dynasty Henan potters. The stoneware body used for jun ware containing about 2 percent iron oxide was compounded of a mixture of locally available clays

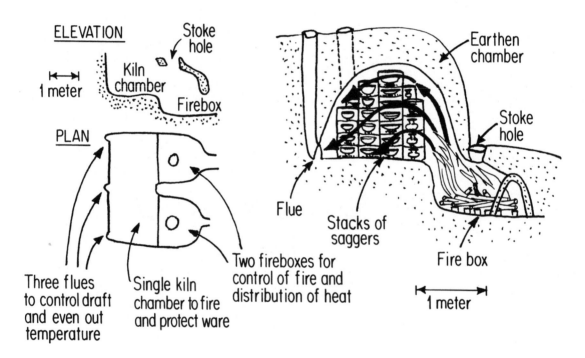

Figure 4.2. Plan and elevation from an excavated jun ware kiln shown next to a schematic reconstruction of what this kiln might have looked like had the arched roof been intact. A single firing chamber is fed with two fireboxes. The draft goes across the kiln loaded with saggers and ware to the back where three flues are connected to chimneys. The multiple fireboxes and flues provide optimal control of the temperature distribution in the kiln.

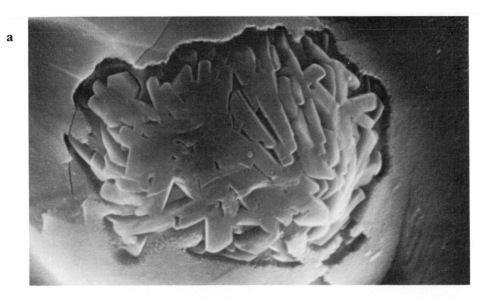

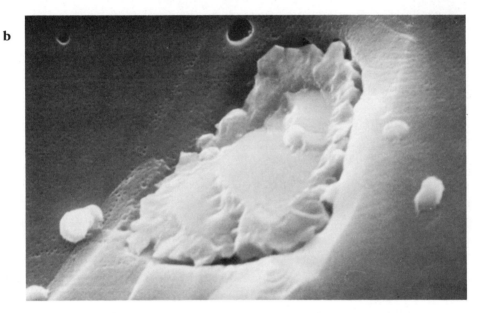

Figure 4.3. Two views of cristobalite, a high-temperature form of silica that has grown at the surface of quartz grains in the glaze. The presence of cristobalite is an indication of the long heating and very slow cooling necessary to produce the jewel-like effects in jun ware. (a) The top view shows cristobalite that has completely covered a partially dissolved quartz grain. (b) In a fractured edge of the glaze was found a broken quartz particle surrounded by cristobalite in a characteristic reticulated or so-called horse's-tooth pattern.

mixed with a powdered feldspathic-quartz rock. The glaze was made from the same rock, but with a smaller amount of clay. Lime was added to the glaze, together with some plant ash, which probably provided a small amount of calcium phosphate. Incompletely burned lime and phosphates served as a source of bubbles in the fired glaze.

Iron oxide, the most common impurity in raw materials used to make ceramics and glass, is necessary to the color of the jun ware body and glaze. Specks of residual black iron oxide (Fe_3O_4) give the body its gray color and can be seen with a magnifying glass on a fractured surface of the body. The blue color of the glaze and the development of opalescence are also derived from the iron content. The iron in the jun ware body and glaze is responsible for the gray color of the body and the blue glaze because the ware was fired with a reducing atmosphere in the kiln. To achieve the high temperature required, above 1250°C, and the temperature uniformity desired, a long, hot flame resulting from an excess of fuel for the air being sucked in by the draft was used. This reducing atmosphere provided the excess carbon monoxide necessary for the reduction of iron oxide to give the blue and gray colors.

As shown in Figure 4.4 and Plate IXa, a white layer of anorthite crystals between the body and glaze acts as a white ground to scatter and reflect light back into the glaze. During the long firing, some of the body constituents dissolve in the glaze at the interface between the body and glaze, resulting in a layer at the interface that is different from the overall composition of the glaze. The higher clay content of the body gives an increased amount of alumina and potassia at the interface, and from this local composition, just as in local areas high in potassia and alumina in the Longquan celadon glazes, anorthite crystals form. These are needlelike in shape, but because of the long firing, they have grown larger, into a mass of lathlike crystals. The anorthite crystals form a white layer between the glaze and body, which grows out into the glaze and which acts as a rough white ground to scatter and reflect the light back into the translucent jun glaze. This layer of anorthite gives the glaze a more brilliant jewel-like appearance. Sometimes this reaction layer has been mistaken for a white slip applied beneath the glaze, but that is not the case; the layer is a chemical reaction zone.

The basis of the translucence in jun glazes is the formation of an emulsion of two different liquids in the glaze, much like an oil–vinegar salad dressing. Each of the two constituents is clear, but the emulsion scatters light, which bends as it passes from one constituent to the other. In a glaze, just as with a mixture of water and oil in a frying pan, two liquids may stay in solution as long as they are heated, but separate when cooled. This is the case with jun glazes. Because glasses and glazes with high silica content are viscous at high temperatures, a long time at high temperature is required for emulsion formation. Figure 4.5 shows the emulsion in a jun ware glaze. The droplets are very small, about 800Å (Ångstroms) in diameter. One of the technological secrets of jun glazes is the formation of an emulsion of two different liquids in what is technically termed a liquid–liquid phase separation.

We have investigated the limits of composition and temperature for this emulsion formation. By analyzing small chips from six jun shards and many similar compositions melted in the laboratory, we have found that emulsion formation requires a temperature at or below 1200°C. By heating and cooling these compositions and noting whether an emulsion formed, the limits of composition that produce emulsions were determined as shown in Figure 4.6. Most jun glazes contain about 70 percent silica; in plotting the three other major constituents (alumina, calcia, and potassia), we find that the compositions of jun glazes lie in the calcia-rich corner and cluster just at the edge of the region of emulsion formation. Celadon glazes cluster outside the region of easy emulsion formation. As the temperature is increased above 1200°C, the region of emulsion formation decreases, and the jun compositions form a clear glaze. If rapidly cooled, the glaze gives the result shown in Plate IXb. Only during slow cooling below 1200°C is an emulsion formed that gives rise to the characteristic opalescence and color.

In addition to the blue opalescence, there are white cloudy areas that contribute to the overall translucence and texture of the glaze, as seen in Plate VIII. A micrograph of these white areas is shown in Figure 4.7 in which there are regions covered with rounded white crystals of wollastonite. These particles grow in high-calcium regions of the glaze, and have a particle size in the micrometer range that is nearly equal to the wavelength of light. They bend and scatter the incoming light to form the white cloudlike regions of jun glazes. If the glaze has been cooled too slowly, an overabundance of these wollastonite crystals makes the glaze opaque.

The interplay of white cloudlike crystals, bubbles, and blue opalescence just at the limit of visual resolution gives rise to the special depth and texture of jun glazes. This microstructure is not the result of accident, but is obtained by milling techniques used by generations of potters. This milling produces a particle size of the added lime that is in the 100-μm (0.1-mm) range. The change in composition across the glaze thickness can be measured just as for the Longquan celadons, and the same sort of variation is found for the jun as for the celadon glazes (Figure 3.9). Variation

Figure 4.4. A cross section of the jun glaze and body shows
   the growth of anorthite crystals from the body into the
   glaze to form a white layer that serves as a reflective
   ground for the glaze. This white ground has a rough
   surface that scatters the light, thus adding to the soft,
   diffuse appearance of the jun glaze (800X).

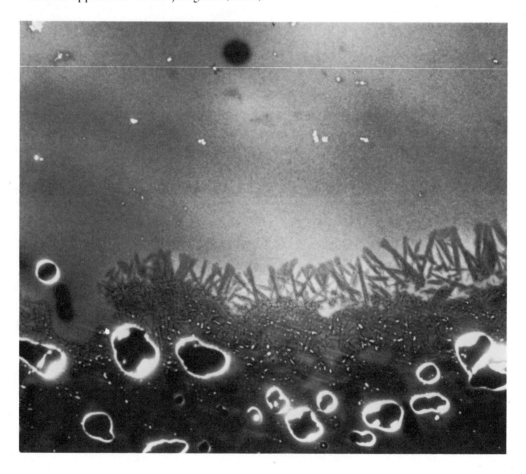

Figure 4.5. The blue opalescence is caused by an emulsion that forms on a very fine scale as shown in this view at 80,000X with the transmission electron microscope. Individual droplets are about 800 Å (0.0008 mm) in diameter.

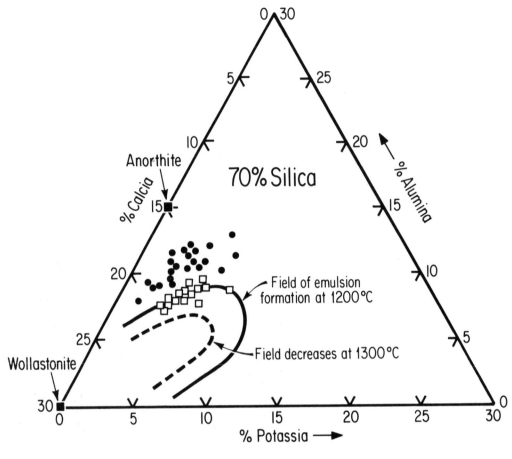

□ Jun Glaze Compositions
● Celadon Glaze Compositions

Figure 4.6. Jun and celadon glaze compositions occur in the calcia-rich corner of the phase diagram. The silica content of this diagram is 70 percent, and ratios of the three other major constituents are plotted. The jun compositions lie along the edge of the shaded region of emulsion formation, which occurs at 1200°C. There is a smaller region of emulsion formation at 1300°C; jun glazes fired at this temperature would be transparent. As more alumina is dissolved into the glaze from the body, the composition of the jun glazes is shifted upward toward the celadon region of composition.

in the ratio between calcia and alumina concentrations gives rise to local regions rich in lime, which favor the formation of white wollastonite particles. These regions of wollastonite growth occur as striations or cord in the glaze, corresponding to the white cloudy areas. Along the rim and on the inside vertical surfaces of the bowl, the glaze layer is thinner and has reacted with the body to dissolve enough additional alumina to remove it from the region of emulsion formation and toward that of celadon compositions. As a result these areas are clear and glossy without the opalescence characteristic of jun wares.

The purplish-red areas that accentuate the cloudy blue are formed by painting a solution containing copper onto the glazed but unfired pot. This

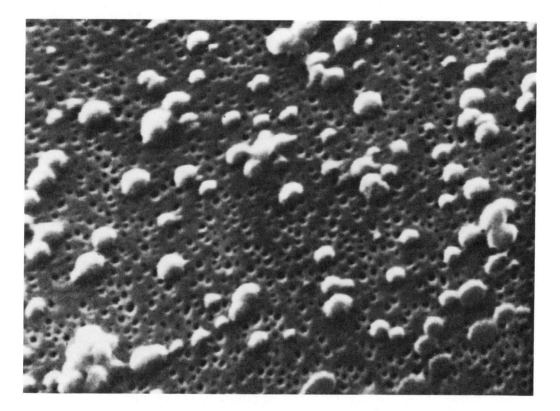

Figure 4.7. The white cloud effect is caused by regions of white spherical crystals of wollastonite with the emulsion shown in Figure 4.4 interspersed between the crystals. This micrograph was taken with a scanning electron microscope of a sample etched in a bath of hydrofluoric acid for about ten seconds. This etch preferentially removed the droplet phase of the emulsion. (Also see Figure 1.5.)

method of applying the copper color has been confirmed by determining the copper concentration across the thickness of the glaze as shown in Figure 4.8. The copper concentration is highest at the surface, indicating that the material was painted on and the solution soaked down through the porous glaze before firing. The opalescent purple color results from the formation of tiny particles of metallic copper. In some areas of the glaze that appear as an almost opaque brick red, there are particles of cuprous oxide. Along the edges of the concentrated copper, a mixture of the copper red, iron blue, and opalescence gives rise to a range of purplish

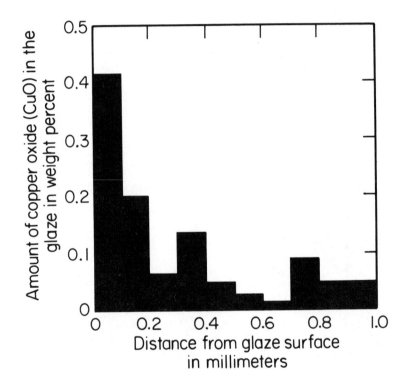

Figure 4.8. The amount of copper in the glaze is considerably larger on the surface than in the interior, thus showing that the copper colorant was painted on the surface of the unfired glaze. On the left can be read the amount of copper in weight percent of the glaze, as if all the copper were present as copper oxide. Along the bottom is the distance from the surface, with the outer surface shown at left and the interface with the glaze at right. The glaze thickness is about 1.0 mm.

hues. In a few spots, drops of the copper solution have dried to form a copper concentration high enough to result in the formation of a metallic aggregate. The remaining copper in solution in this high-lime, high-alumina glaze is green. It is an indication of the inventiveness of the Henan potters that these were the first Chinese wares decorated with copper red.

In summary, the depth, translucency, brightness, opalescence, and blue color of the jun ware were attributable to a composition that created an emulsion during cooling. This, in combination with the bubble structure formed by phosphate and carbonate decomposition and the recrystallization of small wollastonite crystals, resulted in a texture, depth, and variety that are truly remarkable. They also depended on a slow cooling rate that allowed the emulsion and wollastonite particles to form. Too rapid a cooling would lead to a clear, transparent glaze such as is obtained with the same composition using European techniques. Too slow a cooling resulted in the opaque glaze seen on some objects. The texture of the glaze is also critically dependent on the grinding and mixing of the raw materials. Large areas too high in calcium form a runny, opaque glaze—the dense white streaks that are present on some of the less successful ware. Excessive reaction time leads to the solution of alumina from the body and regions of transparent glaze characteristic of the thin glaze layers on rims of the Song Dynasty ware and present in excess on much of the later Yuan and Ming Dynasty production.

Jun ware is a remarkable technological and aesthetic achievement of northern Chinese ceramics of the Song Dynasty. A confluence of several factors, only some of which were under the control of the potters, was necessary. To maintain this complex technology required that the composition of jun glazes be held just at the borderline area necessary to obtain the best quality of blue emulsion and white clouds of wollastonite precipitation without developing excessive opaque white streaks. Proper control of the grinding and mixing of constituents was needed as too little, or too much, would not produce the desired result. High firing followed by slow cooling extending over several days required the development of kiln designs based on the neolithic kilns found at Pan-po, and perfected through countless generations of artisans.

Abundant raw materials with the proper amount of iron and other constituents reinforced the depth of the ceramic tradition out of which jun wares grew. The importance of this craft tradition cannot be underestimated, when combined with the aesthetic and technological acuity to recognize, learn to control, and refine the visual effects that make jun ware one of the finest examples of ceramic art and technology.

RECOMMENDED READING

Articles by Chang Fukang, Li Jiazhi, and P. Vandiver in *Ceramics and Civilization*, Vol. 1, W. D. Kingery (ed.), American Ceramic Society, Columbus, Ohio (1985).

Blunden, Caroline, and Mark Elvin, *Cultural Atlas of China*, Facts on File, New York (1983).

Sato, Masahiko, *Chinese Ceramics: A Short History*, Weatherhill, New York (1978), pp. 117 ff. General overview of Chinese ceramics with a chapter on the problems associated with jun chronology.

REFERENCES

1. Tregear, Mary, *Sung Ceramics*, Thames and Hudson, London (1982). Recent art historical description of jun and other wares.

2. Zhuo Zhen Xi, et al., "New Discoveries from the Reconnaissance and Excavation of the Yao Zhou Kilns," *Kaogu yu Wenwu (Archaeological Antiquities)*, vol. 3, pp. 58 ff. (1980). Description of kilns for jun ware production.

3. David, Percival, *A Catalogue of Chinese Pottery and Porcelain in the Collection of Sir Percival David*, Stourton Press, London (1934). Presentation of jun and other wares in an excellent Western collection.

4. Hobson, R. L., *Chinese Pottery and Porcelain*, Dover Reprint, New York (1976), of Cassell Co., London 1915 edition. Early art historical description of jun ware.

5. Medley, Margaret, *Yuan Porcelain and Stoneware*, Faber and Faber, London (1974). Short description of jun production.

6. Franchet, Louis, "On the Development of Copper Red in a Reducing Atmosphere," *Trans. Brit. Ceram. Soc.*, vol. 7 (1907), pp. 71–79. Early technical description of copper red glazes.

7. Heatherington, A. L., *Chinese Ceramic Glazes*, p.p. I. Perkins, South Pasadena, Calif., 2nd revised edition (1948). Early description of the role of copper in red glazes.

8. Chen Xian-qui, Huang Rui-fu, Chen Shi-ping, Chou Xue-lin, and Ruan Mei-ling, "The Structural Characteristics of Henan Antique Jun (Chun) Ware Sherds and the Evidences of Their Two Kinds of Phase Separation," *Jour. Chinese Silicate Soc.*, vol. 9, 245–254 (1981). A technical description of jun microstructure.

9. Kingery, W. D., P. B. Vandiver, I.-W. Huang, and Y.-M. Chaing, "Liquid–Liquid Immiscibility in the Quaternary System K_2O-Al_2O_3-CaO-SiO_2," *Jour. Noncrystalline Solids*, vol. 54, pp. 163–171 (1983). A technical description of the liquid–liquid phase separation underlying the blue jun effect.

10. Kingery, W. D., and P. B. Vandiver, "Song Dynasty Jun (Chun) Ware Glazes," *Bulletin of the American Ceramic Society*, vol. 62, no. 1, pp. 1269–1279. Intensive analysis of one jun shard for microstructure and microcomposition as the basis for understanding jun technology.

11. T'ao Shuo, Book 2, Folio 5.

CHAPTER *5*

AN ISLAMIC LUSTERWARE
FROM KASHAN

*T*he lusterware plate illustrated in Plate X and Figure 5.1 is a beautiful example of the application of new ways of making and decorating ceramics that developed and spread through the Islamic world from the ninth through the thirteenth century when Islamic art, crafts, science, and technology flourished. When this plate was made at Kashan, Persia, in 1208 A.D., methods of fabricating quartz-based white bodies and tin-opacified glazes, and the difficult technique of luster painting, had been virtually perfected—new techniques that enhanced the importance of painting as a primary ingredient of ceramic art. The visual effect of Kashan lusterware is based on its rich, opulent gold and white surface, delicate workmanship, and intricate painting, as illustrated in Plate XI. From a distance one has the impression of concentric circles and bands, alternating in white and gold, in the center of which is a large gold and white medallion. The outside border is painted with a repetitive floral pattern, while the inner golden and white bands contain a poem written in a cursive calligraphic style. The poem continues around the inner white band and the gold frieze of the scalloped vertical wall, requiring not only that the plate be rotated to read it, but also that it be tipped and rocked back and forth to reveal the characters. This movement of the plate causes flickering reflections in the golden surface, adding to the feeling of the plate's richness.

The circular shape of the plate, the vertical scalloped wall, and the

111

bands and friezes of decoration bound the central medallion and serve to focus the viewer's attention on the central painting of a hunter on horseback, a young man of authority. The design featuring a beaming round face surrounded by a halo looming out of a background in which the horse, ducks, and arabesques of foliage, dots, and spirals are all intertwined is thoroughly Persian. The painting is delicate, but complex, almost mazelike, and it is difficult to delineate the individual parts. Much of the surface of the rider and horse is filled in with patterns and dots, and much of the background has been scratched through with little arabesques so that there is a complex ambiance between what is object and what is ground. The same interplay of positive and negative spaces and surfaces is found in the bands of calligraphy. The aesthetic appeal on many different levels is characteristic of the best Islamic art.

Two of the three elements from which this ware was created—tin-opacified glaze and luster painting—seem to have originated during the ninth century at the cultivated and luxurious court of the Abbasid Caliphate at Baghdad. By the ninth century, the Islamic world extended from Spain to India and encompassed all of the Near East. There was extensive trade and the white glazed Tang porcelain from China must have inspired the first tin-opacified glazed earthenware to be made for the caliph's court. Simple lead glazes had been widely used since the first century, but they remained the exception rather than the rule until the ninth century, when glazed wares became quite common. White tin-opacified glaze was only one type among many. The earliest painting using copper and silver metallic lusters on pottery also seems to have developed in Baghdad, based almost certainly on the earlier use of silver and copper stains for glass, already practiced during the eighth century in Cairo.

With the decline of the Abbasid and emergence of the Fatamid reign at Cairo in the tenth century, there was a renaissance of the arts and expanded production of luxury wares in Egypt. It was there that artisans developed a method for producing a white ceramic body nearly equivalent to the Chinese porcelain. Neither the raw materials for Chinese porcelain nor kilns capable of attaining the high temperature required (1250–1300°C) were available in the Islamic world. The technical solution to making a similar product using local raw materials and available kilns was an adaptation of the earlier Egyptian faience composition described in Chapter 2. The major constitutent was pure quartz, which has a good whiteness in its powdered form. Selected white quartz pebbles were crushed, finely ground, and mixed with about 10 percent of an alkaline glass frit and 10–20 percent of a fine, highly plastic, white montmorillonite clay, which makes

Figure 5.1. The Islamic world was a great source of inspiration and technology in ceramics, marked by the development of techniques for producing luxury wares, such as this luster-painted, tin-glazed quartz-frit-clay plate made in Kashan and dated 1208 A.D. By the beginning of the thirteenth century when this plate was made, methods of fabricating quartz-based white bodies, tin-opacified glazes, and luster painting had been perfected. The inscription encircling the 35.3-cm-diameter plate reads: "Oh heart, do you see any sign of joy in life and do you see anything streaming from my eyes but jewels? I am happy in the hope of living for a fleeting moment but people are but what you see." "In Rajab in the year six hundred and four [January 1208]". Some small areas have been heavily restored. (Courtesy of the Board of Trustees of the Victoria and Albert Museum, C51.1952, Kelekinn Collection, no. 136.) (See Plate X.)

the body suitable for throwing or molding. (If this clay were used by itself or for a large part of the body, its drying shrinkage would be excessive; in combination with the frit and quartz, a quite usable composition results.) To increase the dry strength of ware to be thinned by turning, about 1 percent of a natural gum was often added to the body. For the alkaline frit, selected desert plants were collected and calcined. After ignition to eliminate the volatile constituents, a typical composition of the residual ash was as shown in the following table.

Constituent	Weight, %	Constituent	Weight, %
Sodium oxide	45	Silica	5
Potassium oxide	10	Alumina	2
Lime	20	Phosphorous oxide	2
Magnesia	15	Iron oxide	1

The principal alkali was soda, Na_2O, but important constituents were the lime and magnesia necessary to make a sufficiently hard insoluble glass. Potash by itself is soluble in water, so that it cannot be used as a body constituent or it would effloresce to the surface, causing defects. A mixture consisting of about half calcined plant ash and half crushed quartz pebbles was melted together to form a glass to be used as a constituent of both the glaze and the body.

During the middle of the eleventh century, one of the most creative periods in ceramic history began under the Seljuk Turks in northwest Persia. Coming from central Asia, the Seljuks vitalized the culture and encouraged the development of trade and liberal pursuits. Important pottery centers developed at Rayy and Kashan and the round faces of Seljuk huntsmen such as shown on Plate X appear again and again in twelfth and early thirteenth century pottery decoration. Kashan was especially noted for its tiles decorated with luster painting. It was fully developed as a pottery center toward the end of the twelfth century, and was noted for the hard white body, technical quality, delicate workmanship, and intricate decoration of its wares. The Kashan plate illustrated in Plate X was made by forming over a porous fired earthenware mold. The well-mixed body was rolled out on a flat surface to give a "pancake" shape that was a bit larger than the mold. It was placed over the surface of the dampened mold, and then pressed firmly against the surface to obtain a uniform thickness. The edges were pressed down over the sides of the mold and trimmed.

Some circumferential cracks remain on the outer edge surface from the sharp deformation necessary to form the edges. When sufficiently dry to hold its shape, but before shrinkage tightened it onto the mold, it was gently released from the mold and allowed to dry. After drying the edges were smoothed with a wet cloth and a glaze coating was applied by pouring the glaze slip over the body for a uniform glaze thickness.

After the glaze had dried, a drop of cobalt blue glaze and a drop of a lighter copper blue glaze were placed at the edges of the plate to impart a bit of individuality, color, and interest. Many experts believe that these colored drops were the result of accidental glaze drips in the kiln, but we think they were intentional. The plate was made by master potters and painters as an important object and was fired in a saggar, and the drips seem to be more planned than accident. The piece was set in a saggar on a layer of coarse sand (to allow shrinkage without cracking) and fired to a temperature of about 1050°C. At this temperature the body matures and the glaze flows over the surface. In the body the clay and alkaline frit react with the ground quartz particles to form concave lenses of viscous alkaline silicate between the particles. These viscous liquid lenses wet the particles and draw them together by capillary action, leading to firing shrinkage and a consolidation of the body. When the liquid cools, it solidifies as a glass with the resulting microstructure illustrated in Figure 5.2. The small amount of iron present is dissolved in the glass and becomes nearly colorless so that the body is hard, white "frit porcelain." The hardness of the ware depends on the amount of clay and frit added, the time and temperature of firing, and the fineness of the crushed quartz. This particular body is harder than most modern quartz-clay bodies made in Iran, which have almost no added frit (being chiefly clay plus ground quartz), and than tile bodies using coarser quartz grains, such as the Iznik tile described in Chapter 6. However, it is less hard and translucent than the seventeenth century "Gombroon" ware fired for longer times at a higher temperature.

Our understanding of the processes used to make this ware is enlightened by a description written 100 years later, in 1301, by Abūl Qāsim, and by observations made by Hans Wulff in Persia of similar processes still being used in 1937–1941. Abūl Qāsim and Wulff describe making a frit with potash and quartz, preparing the body from crushed quartz, frit, and clay, and making a lead-tin calcine for the glaze. We have extended these descriptions by using the capabilities of electron microprobe analysis separately to determine the overall body composition and the composition of the bonding phase in the body illustrated in Figure 5.2, and of the glaze. These results are shown in Table 5.1.

The glaze contains tiny particles of tin oxide as an opacifier, which makes the glaze translucent and white (Figure 5.3). Tin oxide can be produced by heating molten tin in air. However, if tin is heated alone, the result is a gray powder. When a mixture of three parts of lead to one part of tin is melted, the oxide formed on the molten metal is a white mixture of lead oxide and tin oxide. This is the reason that lead always accompanies tin in the preparation of tin-glazed pottery. The glaze composition shown in Table 5.1 was made by milling together about five parts of the alkaline silicate frit made from desert potash and crushed quartz with one part of the lead oxide–tin oxide mixture, straining the resulting suspension through a cloth, and then evaporating off the excess water to form a slurry of the proper consistency for use. Our analyses indicate that the body was made from a mixture of about seven parts of crushed quartz pebbles, one part of the alkaline glass frit, and two parts of a white montmorillonite clay. These proportions differ a bit from the formula given by Abūl Qāsim, but

TABLE *5.1*

Chemical Composition of Lusterware Frit Porcelain Body and Glaze. Compositions were determined by Electron Microprobe Microchemical Analysis.

	Alkaline Glaze	Body	Bonding Phase in Body
Silica	59.2	86.9	66.4
Alumina	1.6	6.6	16.8
Iron oxide	0.4	0.3	0.75
Magnesia	3.2	0.6	1.5
Lime	4.7	0.5	1.2
Sodium oxide	10.4	3.0	7.6
Potassium oxide	2.7	1.8	4.6
Chlorine	—	0.1	0.2
Sulfur dioxide	—	0.2	0.4
Lead oxide	12.0	—	—
Tin oxide	4.0	—	—

Figure 5.2. In the microstructure of Persian quartz-frit porcelain we see grains of crushed quartz, somewhat rounded by solution during the firing process, held together with silicate glass derived from the frit and clay components of the body formulation. The body is white because the small amount of iron present has been completely dissolved in the glass.

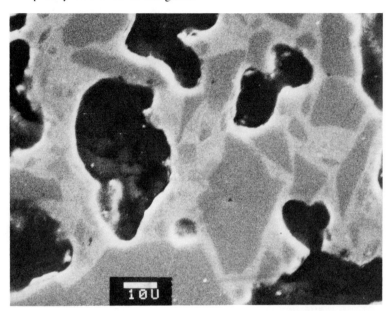

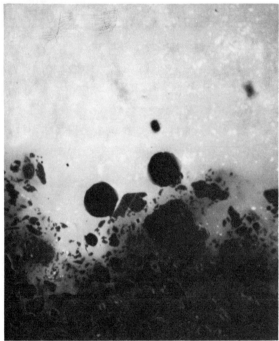

Figure 5.3. The alkaline-lead glaze fired simultaneously with the body in a single firing process penetrates into and becomes well bonded to the ware. Addition of 4 percent tin oxide provides the particles in suspension that give the desired white translucence.

that is to be expected. Master potters varied their compositions to suit their purposes.

Overglaze lusters are formed by painting a metal-containing compound on the surface of a glaze and firing to a red heat in a mildly reducing atmosphere; the metal first diffuses into the glaze and then, at a higher temperature, is reduced to form metallic particles. Essential requirements for success are (1) a compound of silver or copper that will wet and flow over the surface and allow exchange with and diffusion into the glaze, (2) a fine particulate nonreactive carrier powder to hold the metallic constituent in place, and (3) control of the kiln atmosphere to allow precipitation of metal particles after their penetration into the glaze. Minor constituents such as lead and bismuth, which are frequently found in silver ores, can play an important role in aiding the reduction process. Modern formulations frequently use chlorides or resinates as the metal compound, and it has been shown that the classical addition of vinegar as an aid to disperse the calcined clay or ocher is not absolutely essential. Vinegar is specified in Abūl Qāsim's Persian recipe as well as in those from Spain and Italy. In addition to its role in giving a paintable suspension, vinegar reacts with copper and silver on heating to form acetates. It thus plays an active role in uniformly distributing the metal before it decomposes and deposits the metal oxide at a temperature of about 240°C.

The color of lusters is a complex function of precipitate particle composition, size, and concentration. In heavy concentrations copper lusters give a darker reddish gold and a coppery sheen. Silver lusters are more yellow in color and form a silvery sheen when heavily applied. Mixtures of copper and silver form lower-melting-point liquids that spread more easily. Silver is more easily reduced than copper, and favors a more yellow golden color; most golden lusters are mixtures of silver and copper. Chemical analysis with the electron microscope shows that the luster of Plate X is mainly silver. It was made by crushing and milling together a silver ore and a fine-particle-size ocher or calcined clay, which was sieved through a fine cloth, mixed with vinegar and some gum (as a binding agent), and then finely ground by a mortar and pestle to form a smooth suspension. The design was painted in a thin layer, into which the scrolls were scratched on the golden luster while the paint layer was still damp. Magnified details of the painting are shown in Plate XIIa.

The darker spots of concentrated luster seen in Plate XII result from a greater concentration of silver at the contact points of the mineral aggregates with the surface. At these points the silver is concentrated during the initial spreading at low temperatures. After diffusion into the surface during slow heating, reduction to precipitate metal particles occurs at a dull red heat in a reducing atmosphere. A uniform dispersion of very fine particles of silver results as shown in Figure 5.4. The individual particles are about 200 Å (0.02 μm, or 0.00002 mm) in diameter. Viewed only in reflected light, they would be silver in color; viewed only in transmitted light, they would be yellow. For particles at the glaze surface, some of the light is reflected and some is refracted back from the tin-opacified glaze below the particle layer, as shown in Figure 5.5. This combination is responsible for the reflective metallic golden color.

Good-quality yellow-gold lusters are rather difficult to produce. Underfiring or too short a firing results in a pale, nonreflecting luster with poor durability because insufficient and undersized metal particles form. Overfiring can result in a dull appearance, sometimes with the ocher pow-

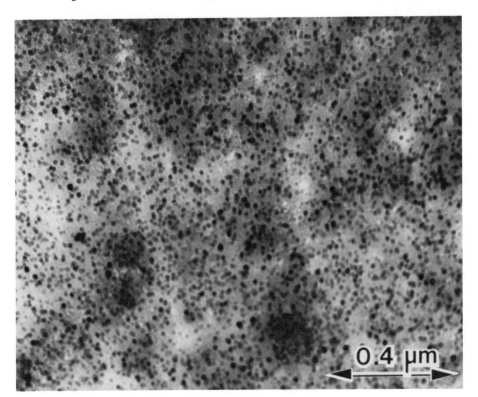

Figure 5.4. Transmission electron microscopy at very high magnification (80,000X) shows the individual silver particles dispersed at and under the top surface of the glaze. These are responsible for the golden metallic luster. (Micrograph courtesy of Y. Moriyoshi.)

der sticking to the glaze. Copper lusters, particularly heavily reduced ones, are easier to produce, but have a darker reddish sheen. In addition, copper diffusion into the glaze around the edges of the painted design almost always results in some formation of red colloidal copper (red flashing, Plate XIIb) and prevents the attainment of clean, sharp edges on the painting.

The large Kashan lusterware plate we have illustrated achieves its visual impact not only because of the white body, which was made of a material quite difficult to mold and shape, or the ivorylike depth of the semiopaque glaze, but also because of the skilled application of the gold-colored luster painting. This painting has the appearance of metal because light is reflected from fine metallic particles near the surface of the glaze; the golden color results from light scattered through these particles from the tin-opacified glaze. The intricate painting of what is clearly an authoritative and powerful figure with its surrounding poetic inscription seems to have been specially made as a commission or gift and was clearly meant to be an important possession. It represents an outstanding example of one of the high points of ceramic art and craftmanship.

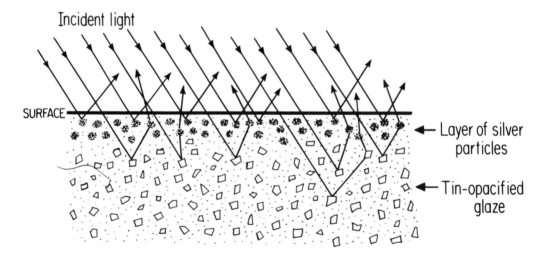

Figure 5.5. Metallic reflection from the surface layer of silver particles takes on a golden color when it is reinforced with light scattered back through the layer from the tin-opacified glaze beneath.

RECOMMENDED READING

Caiger-Smith, Alan, *Lustre-ware*, Faber & Faber, London (1985). This book describes in detail both the history and the manufacture of lusterwares based on the author's extensive research and personal experience.

Caiger-Smith, Alan, *Tin-Glaze Pottery*, Faber & Faber, London (1973). This is one of the best books on the art, history, and technology of tin-glazed wares, including those from Persia. Caiger-Smith produces lusterware tin-glazed pottery himself, and shares his knowledge.

Lane, Arthur, *Early Islamic Pottery*, Faber & Faber, London (1947). This classic description of the early development of pottery in the Islamic world remains widely accepted.

REFERENCES

1. Allan, J. W. "Abūl Qāsim's Treatise," *Iran*, *11* (1973) Translation of the twelfth century text describing the preparation of quartz-clay-frit bodies and glazes.

2. Allan, J. W., L. R. Llewellyn, and F. Schweizer, "The History of So-called Egyptian faience in Islamic Persia: Investigations into Abūl Qāsim's Treatise," *Archeometry*, vol. 15, no. 2, pp. 165–173 (1979). Overall chemical composition of twelfth century samples are compared with compositions given in text.

3. Wulff, Hans E., *The Traditional Crafts of Persia*, M.I.T. Press, Cambridge, Mass. (1966). A thoughtful description of many crafts including frit porcelain, as they existed in 1936–1942 Iran.

4. Franchet, L., *La Fabrication Industrielle des Emaux et Couleurs Cera-miques*, Paris (1911). Formulas for ceramic colors and overglaze colors are explained. Experiments describing luster formation are described.

5. Watson, Oliver, "Persian Lustre-Painted Pottery—The Rayy and Kashan Styles," *Transactions of the Oriental Ceramic Society*, *40* (1973/75). A discussion of the provenience of Islamic lusterware.

6. Philon, Helen, *Early Islamic Ceramics*, Southby Parke-Bernet (1980). Interpretation of historical questions related to Islamic ceramics in the light of recent archaeological research.

CHAPTER 6

AN IZNIK TILE

*T*he brilliantly colored tile illustrated in Plate XIII and Figure 6.1 was made at Iznik, Turkey, during the classic period of Iznik ceramics in the last half of the sixteenth century. The white body is decorated with an underglaze of bright cobalt blue, copper turquoise, and vivid "sealing-wax" red outlined in black under a brilliant lead-alkali-silicate glaze, resulting in a wonderful jewel-like quality. The design, related to those seen on other Ottoman handicrafts, was the work of court painters at Istanbul and was executed at Iznik with technical mastery and complete assurance. The freedom and exuberance of this period, which have seldom been equaled in ceramic history, coincided with the greatest strength and self-confidence of the vast and powerful Ottoman Empire at the end of the reign of Süleyman the Magnificent (1520–1566).

The Ottoman Empire had its start with the breakdown of the Seljuk state in the thirteenth century and it swiftly expanded its terrtories, growing in wealth and power. Istanbul was occupied in 1453; Egypt was conquered in 1517; Hungary was entered in 1526. Süleyman's father, Selim I, unified central power and eliminated possible dissidence by putting to death his brothers, their seven sons, and four of his own sons, leaving Süleyman as his sole heir. Süleyman's reign marked the golden age of Ottoman history. Payroll registers show that at the end of his reign 636 artists and artisans were working at the palace in Istanbul in a court institution called the Ehli Hiref, begun during the reign of Bayezid II (1481–1512). Within the Ehli Hiref, the nakkashave, or painting studio, created designs used by the tile workshops in Iznik.

Figure 6.1. During the middle half of the sixteenth century, the Ottoman Empire of Süleyman the Magnificent was at its peak and there was a great building program in Constantinople. More than 300 workshops at Iznik turned out technically excellent tile that combined bright, clear colors under a brilliant lead-alkali glaze with wonderful interlocking symmetries executed with sensitivity and skill. (This 33-cm by 33-cm tile is on display at the Musée National de Céramique at Sèvres, no. 18.024, donated by M. de la Charbonne. The upper-left-hand corner has been repaired and repainted.) (Courtesy of the Musée National de Cérameque, Sèvres. (See Plate XIII.)

The central design in the tile shown in Plate XIII and Figure 6.1, three balls with an inner ball to create a cresent (cintemani) accompanied by a pair of wavy lines called cloud bands, was widely used in decorations in the classical period. Although the basic motif can be traced to Buddhist traditions, in Ottoman art the balls were associated with leopard spots and the wavy lines with tiger stripes symbolizing power, but they were also used in a purely decorative manner. Blossoms such as the carnation and tulips were also predominant decorative elements in classical Ottoman art. The overall design is quite complex, with a stylized floral element as part of the cintemani and smaller groups of balls within the larger ones. This complexity extends to the symmetries, which begin with a twofold mirror reflection down the middle of the tile, continue onto the threefold symmetry of the central balls, and then to the fourfold symmetry of the wavy cloud bands surrounding the central spherical elements. This complex "simplicity" and the opulent jewel-like color are typical of the best Islamic art of the sixteenth century.

Iznik, which became the center of the ceramic industry in the classical period, had been founded by the Romans (called Nicaea then, site of a church council in 325 A.D.), and grew in importance after Constantinople became the capital of the Empire. Iznik lies about 60 miles from Istanbul on the main road to Damascus. It had an early history of earthenware pottery manufacture, but quite suddenly entered a new phase at about 1500—producing ware with a white quartz-clay-frit body and underglaze decoration. It is suggested that potters may have come from Edirne, where these techniques were used earlier, to Iznik, which was closer to the capital, and had plentiful fresh water and wood for fuel, along with a very fine whitish clay and fine white sand.

In any event the first wares were decorated with cobalt blue on a white ground, then copper turquoise was added to the palette, followed by manganese purple. Beginning about 1550 and lasting through 1700 or so, bright iron reds were added to the palette and both pottery and brilliant, colorful wall tiles were manufactured in large quantitites. A detail showing the colors used is presented in Plate XIVb. The earliest use of the full palette, including red, was to decorate the Süleymaniye mosque built in Istanbul by the architect Agha Sinan between 1550 and 1557. A single tile does not do justice to the visual impact of a series of tiles used for architectural ornamentation. Tiles were often made up into wall panels of about the same size and proportions as a carpet, with each panel surrounded by a decorative border and fitted into an overall pattern for the room or hallway so lavishly covered. When viewed from a distance, as shown in Plate XIVa and Figure 6.2, the overall color of a panel is seen as blue, and the intricate pattern more as a texture with turquoise, blue, and black the predominant colors.

For architectural purposes large numbers of tile are needed, and economy requires that the bulk of the thick tile body be made from inexpensive easily prepared materials; the interior of the tile shown in Plate XIII has a yellowish-gray tone attributable to iron impurity in the sand. The fine white surface was obtained by adding a thin slip layer made from more carefully selected pure raw materials. The overall structure of the underlying body, quartz-clay-frit slip layer, and glaze is illustrated in Figure 6.3. At a higher magnification, Figure 6.4, we can see how the angular quartz particles are held together with a sort of glue consisting of a fused mixture of clay and frit. The mixture for the body consists of about 80 percent crushed and milled sand combined with about 20 percent of the heterogeneous glass phase that bonds the quartz particles together. We have carried out microchemical analysis of the bonding material with an electron microprobe and found that there are local areas high in clay, others high in dolomite, some that contain lead oxide, and some with none, in what is basically a clay-frit mixture, with the exact nature of the mixture depending on the availability of raw materials. The variability of the tile body contrasts with the more carefully prepared Kashan lusterware plate illustrated in Chapter 5.

In addition to fine white sand, and the local very fine, nearly white clay, the principal ingredients used to form the ware were a premelted alkaline-silicate frit and lead oxide. The alkaline-silicate frit was achieved by melting a mixture of about half potash, made from calcining desert plants, and half fine sand. After cooling as a glass, the material was finely ground before use. Our analysis of the lead-alkali-silicate glaze shows it to be 63 percent silica, 13.7 percent lead oxide, 16.8 percent soda, 1.3 percent potassia, 1.2 percent lime, 1.1 percent chlorine, and less than 1 percent each of alumina, magnesia, and iron oxide. This composition corresponds to a mixture of five or six parts of the alkaline frit with one part of lead oxide.

The first step in making the tile was to mix the body ingredients—about eight parts fine sand, one part fine clay, and one part alkaline-silicate frit or leftover glaze. These ingredients were milled together and then wedged to provide a workable mix. A suitably sized lump of this body was thrown into a wooden mold and beaten into the corners to be sure the mold was densely packed, then smoothed off and emptied from the mold. After drying, the tile was held by the sides and the face dipped into a slurry.

Figure 6.2. Seen from a distance, a panel of the Iznik tile gives an impression of overall blueness. The brighter colors become apparent on closer examination. This panel indicates the complex symmetries within the overall simple design. It is on display at the Victoria and Albert Museum, London. (See Plate XIV.)

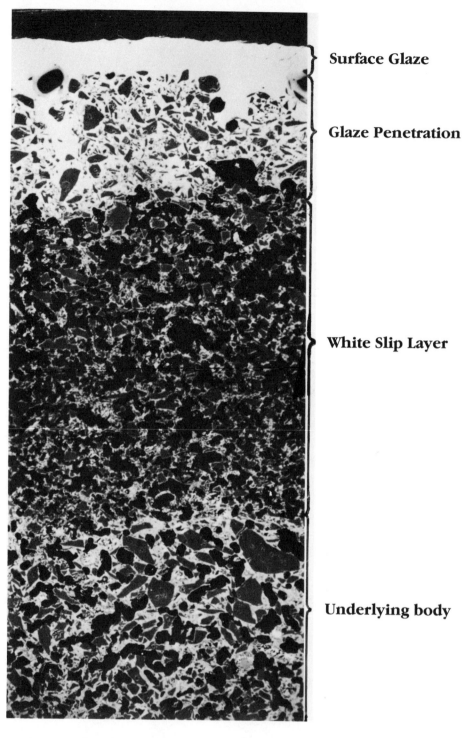

Surface Glaze

Glaze Penetration

White Slip Layer

Underlying body

Figure 6.3. Cross section of a tile illustrates the opaque yellowish body covered by a layer of white frit porcelain and glaze. The microstructure of the body is a coarse mixture of ground sand bonded with a clay-frit mixture. The white slip layer is more carefully prepared from fine-particle-size crushed quartz. The lead-alkaline glaze wets and penetrates into the slip layer (100X).

The slurry was made of finely crushed and ground quartz pebbles, selected to be free of iron, mixed with about 10 percent white clay and 10 percent glass frit. Careful selection of raw materials, fine milling, and sieving of the slurry assured a fine white surface. After the slip was wiped off the edges, the tiles were dried thoroughly and were ready to paint.

The central accomplishment of the Iznik tilemaker was the painted pattern of bright colors with sharp outlines immersed in a brilliant glaze. Their special quality results from the use of underglaze painting covered with a lead-alkali silicate glaze; a cross section is shown in Plate XVb. The glaze consists of a mixture of five or six parts of alkaline frit milled together with one part of lead oxide made by melting lead and scraping the oxide off the surface. This formulation imparts a turquoise color to areas containing copper as the colorant. Other samples we have analyzed were made with only two parts of alkaline frit for each part of lead oxide. This higher lead content gives a green color to areas containing copper as a colorant. In general less lead (bluer turquoise) was used in earlier periods and rather more lead (greener) in the later periods.

Five different colors were employed in painting, they were prepared as an intimate mixture of colorant and glaze frit by wet grinding with a mortar and pestle. The colorant for turquoise is copper oxide, that for blue is cobalt oxide, and that for the black lines is an iron chromite spinel mineral. The colorant for red is Armenian bole, a mixture of red iron oxide and quartz.

The pattern was outlined by use of a stencil with small holes corresponding to the pattern through which charcoal was dusted onto the unfired tile to provide guidelines for the painting. The outlines were then painted on with the black pigment, which consisted of finely ground mineral chromite particles in a water-based paint bonded with gum. Then the colored areas were filled in with cobalt blue, copper turquoise, or iron red, as illustrated in Plates XIV and XV. The black chromite pigment is a very hard mineral that does not grind easily and this results in the larger size of the individual pigment particles (Plate XV). The copper turquoise and cobalt blue colorants go into solution in the glaze (as opposed to the black pigment particles and the red iron oxide). This results in a tendency for these colors to form diffuse halos at the edge of the color (Plate XV).

The bright red color of the Iznik tiles is attributable to the fine particle size of the iron oxide, which is intermingled with quartz particles and bonded together with the alkali silicate frit. The high concentration of pigment and quartz particles prevents the thick painting of the iron red from flowing out during firing, and often leads to a lens-shaped relief of

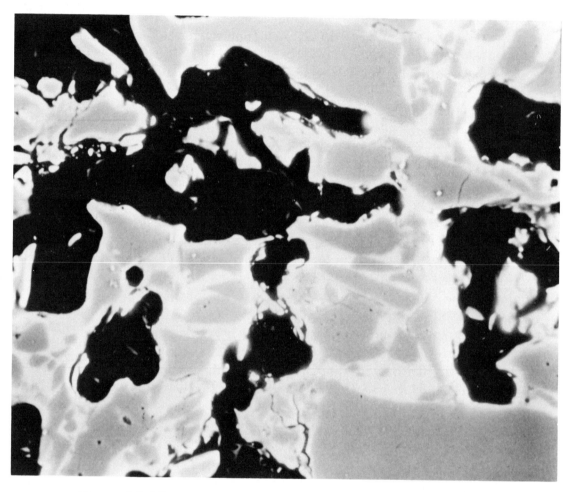

Figure 6.4. Microstructure of the Iznik tile illustrates the angular quartz grains bonded together
with a glassy matrix containing a heterogeneous
mixture of finer crystals (1000X).

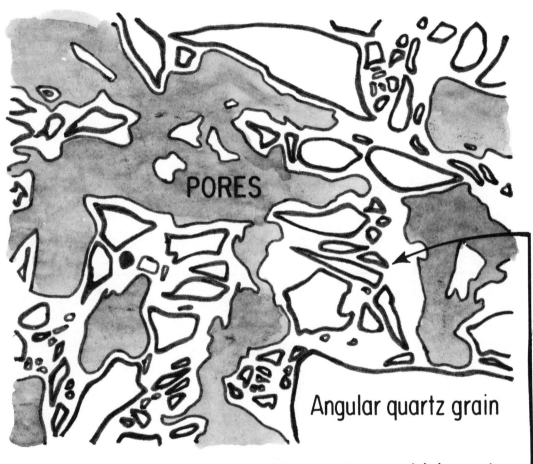

PORES

Angular quartz grain

Glassy phase which coats
and coheres quartz grain

the glaze layer over the red pigment. The glaze penetrates into the upper boundary of the red pigment and acts as a lense to enhance the optical effect, as shown in Plate XV. The characteristics of the iron oxide particles are shown at high magnification in Figure 6.5; they are of similar particle size but are present in a much higher concentration than in the coral red of the K'ang Hsi porcelain plate described in Chapter 8.

Once the underglaze painting had dried, glaze was applied to the tile by pouring a slurry over the surface from a small container to give a uniform thickness. After wiping the excess glaze off the edges and drying, the glaze was fired in a muffle kiln, protected from flue gases, to a temperature of about 900°C.

The earliest Iznik tiles had blue-on-white decorations with design elements related to the Chinese Ming Dynasty porcelains being imported. However, the technology at Iznik allowed the use of a wide palette of

Figure 6.5. Electron micrograph of the porous red colorant shows it to be a mixture of quartz particles bonded together with a frit in which fine red hematite particles are dispersed.

pigments stable at the Islamic firing temperature to attain bright colors for underglaze painting covered with a lead-alkali-silicate glaze, which affords a brilliance not attainable with the high-temperature lime-alkali glazes used for the Chinese porcelain. This development revolutionized the production of tile; designs were no longer made by fitting together separate colored pieces like a puzzle, and more complex designs could be used. Molded tiles with patterns in relief all but ceased production. The good control of colors greatly improved the uniformity, and therefore the setting, of tiles, allowing large quantities to be used for architectural decoration.

The dazzling jewel-like colors of the white-bodied Iznik ware resulted from a combination of the traditional quartz-clay-frit Islamic luxury-ware paste with bright colors painted under the brilliant lead-alkali glaze. Careful preparation of the materials, particularly the white slip layer and pigments, was required in concert with imaginative designs and skilled execution. The result was truly remarkable, affording a whole new mode of decoration for pottery and architectural use.

RECOMMENDED READING

Lane, A., *Later Islamic Pottery*, 2nd ed., Faber and Faber, London (1971). This classic art historical description of sixteenth century and later wares presents the development of Iznik tile in a historical perspective.

Petsopoulos, Y. (ed.), *Tulips, Arabesques and Turbans*, Abbeville Press, New York (1982). Includes descriptions of different Islamic arts including an excellent chapter on the aesthetics, symmetries, and decoration of Islamic ceramics by John Carswell.

Wulff, Hans E. *The Traditional Crafts of Persia*, M.I.T. Press, Cambridge, Mass. (1966). Wulff relates his first-hand observations of tilemakers in Persia in the period just before World War II. The craft methods that Wulff observed are closely related to methods used in the sixteenth century.

REFERENCES

1. Atil, Esin, *Ceramics from the World of Islam*, Smithsonian Institution Press, Washington, D.C. (1973). Catalog of the Freer collection of Islamic ceramics, which updates Lane's publications and provides thermoluminescent dates for many wares.

2. Atil, Esin, translation, *The Anatolian Civilizations III*, Turkish Ministry of Cultural Tourism (1983). Catalog of Topkapi Palace Museum Exhibition with a short history of Ottoman art, including ceramics. Many objects photographed and described.

3. Raby, Julian, "Diyarbakir: A Rival to Iznik" *Istanbuler Mitteilungen*, 27, 28, pp. 429–459, plates 146–162 (1977–1978). A discussion of the panel from the Victoria and Albert Museum, which suggests the outer tiles are the same as those made in Diyarbakir. However, there are differences in color, quality, and glaze texture, which lead us to believe that the inner tiles were made at Iznik.

CHAPTER 7

A MEDICI PORCELAIN BOTTLE

As the first porcelain manufactured in Europe, Medici porcelain occupies an important place in the history of European ceramics. Because of its relationship to Near Eastern techniques, which preceded it, and to later soft-paste porcelain, this porcelain has played an important role in the history of ceramic technology.

Italian merchants carried on a vigorous trade with Egypt, Syria, and Turkey during the fifteenth and sixteenth centuries, and imported both translucent blue-and-white Chinese Ming porcelain and blue-and-white Persian frit porcelain, called Levantine porcelain, a descendant of the Kashan lusterware described in Chapter 5. In his work *Les Origines de la Porcelaine en Europe*, Baron Davillier[1] describes several European collections and gives many documentary sources. The techniques being used for Italian production of tin-glazed earthenware maiolica were well established at this time and described in some detail by Piccolpasso in 1557. Early in the sixteenth century, there were documentary references to "counterfeit porcelain" being made in Venice and Ferrara. While no samples are known to exist, efforts to replicate the imported Chinese and Persian wares seem to have been widespread.

The first success for which samples are extant was achieved in Florence under the patronage of the Grand Duke Francesco I de Medici, son of Cosimo I. Francesco took charge of the affairs of Tuscany as regent in

1564, two years after his mother's death had left Cosimo bereaved. Like his father, Francesco took an interest in the practical arts. He was a keen student of chemistry, and active in stimulating the glass, pottery, metals, tapestry-weaving, and crystal-cutting industries of Florence. Francesco was quiet and withdrawn, often melancholy, and frequently retreated to his laboratory where his experiments with alchemy and melting natural crystals were something of an obsession. He succeeded to the crown in 1574, and one year later Andrea Gussoni, the Venetian ambassador to Florence, wrote that the method of making "Indian porcelain" had been rediscovered, that ten years had been devoted to the effort, and that a "Levantine" had pointed the road to success. In 1587 Grand Duke Francesco died. Without his continuing patronage, porcelain manufacture in Europe ended for a time, not to be revived until the production of soft-paste porcelain at St. Cloud in 1695, more than 100 years later (Chapter 10). Medici porcelain is rare and valuable—fewer than 60 pieces are known. In 1973 a 5 ½-inch-diameter bowl described as "small and misshapen" was sold at auction in New York for $180,000—the highest price paid for any European ceramic to that time.

The square porcelain bottle illustrated in Plate XVI and Figure 7.1 is on display at the Musée National de Céramique at Sèvres, France. It bears the royal arms of Philip II of Spain, is dated 1581, and is known to be a gift to Philip from the Grand Duke Francesco in 1582. (One of the basic tenets of Francesco's foreign policy was to remain in the good graces of Philip.) It is attributed to Pier Maria of Faenza and is marked on the bottom with the dome of Florence. The bottle is 25 cm (10 inches) tall; the back has been restored.

The blue-and-white underglaze decoration is similar in feeling to Chinese and Islamic blue and white, but the shape upon which it is applied and the decorative motifs are European. The importance of the coat-of-arms design is emphasized by its large size, which extends to the edges of the front panel of the bottle, covering most its surface. Below the coat of arms is a small smiling head of a jester and design elements of foliage in full flower. Above the coat of arms is the crown as a symbol of power, together with two crosslike shapes as symbols of piety and morality. The design motifs of the Medici bottle thus embody in a concrete, self-conscious, and self-confident way the robust, open, optimistic spirit of the late Renaissance. The world is well ordered and what is presently unknown is ultimately knowable, the working mechanisms of authority are unquestioned, and one's place in the social and economic order is established. Not only is the Medici bottle important historically and technologically, but,

Figure 7.1. The first success in European efforts to produce ware equivalent to Persian and Chinese porcelain was achieved under the patronage of Grand Duke Francesco I de Medici in Florence. This square Medici porcelain bottle, made in 1581, was formed in a two-piece plaster mold. The underglaze design was painted with manganese lines that were filled in with cobalt blue and then overglazed with a slightly translucent lead glaze. (Courtesy of the Musée National de Céramique, Sèvres, France, Inv. MNC.5778, donated by Don Michelin.) (See Plate XVI.)

although based on Islamic forebears, it also sets a standard for European decorative art, demanding sculpted shapes and opulent painted surfaces along with an inherent visual statement of the object's function and expected use.

Close examination shows that the bottle was made by rolling out thin slabs of the body and shaping them in a two-piece plaster mold. Along the sides where the two halves were joined together there is an excess thickness, and on one side incipient cracks have developed from differences in drying shrinkage. There are variations in the cross section and the bottle is not precisely square, but rhombohedral, the long axis being between the corners, which were joined during molding. In addition the walls are not perfectly flat, but have buckled a bit inward at the top and outward toward the bottom. These defects were initiated with strains introduced when the damp bottle was taken from the mold and joined to the base; they were accentuated by deformation during firing. Close examination of Medici porcelain on exhibit at the Victoria and Albert Museum in London, at the Musée National de Céramique at Sèvres, and at the Metropolitan Museum of Art in New York shows that in nearly every example of Medici porcelain some distortion occurred during firing.

Refiring tests done on a tiny fragment from the Museo Internazionale delle Ceramiche di Faenza indicated that the body was fired at a temperature near 1100°C. Italian potters of the time fired their ware at 950°–1000°C; to achieve 1100° in their uninsulated kilns would have required large amounts of fuel, and may even have buckled the kiln walls. The manufacture of Medici porcelain was not easy—Francesco's support was surely required.

After the first firing, the design was outlined on the bisque in a black manganese pigment and then filled in with blue cobalt oxide. These materials were well known to the potters of the time, but normally were used on a white clay engobe or underglaze tin-oxide surface. After painting, the glaze was applied by pouring a glaze slurry over the bottle and allowing it to run off one corner. As a result, the glaze along the bottom is thicker than at the top. The glaze was wiped off the foot and the second firing took place at a temperature of 900–950°C, a common practice at the time. The glaze ends about 1 mm from the base and has not run. Actually the glaze is a bit underfired, with numerous fine bubbles remaining, a characteristic of Medici porcelain. Plate XVI and Figure 7.2 show details of the painting, illustrating the application of the outline, the filling in of the blue, and the associated bubble structure, which is typical of many samples of this ware. The glaze contains unmelted particles of feldspar and quartz,

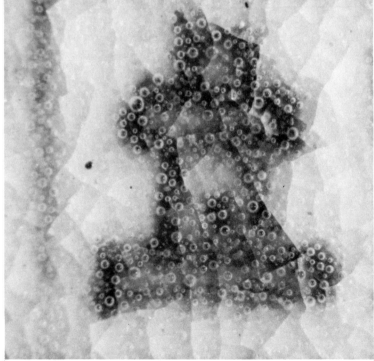

Figure 7.2. Close-up views of the Medici porcelain bottle illustrate the underglaze drawing outlined in manganese black pigment and then filled in with cobalt blue. The many bubbles in the overglaze lead glaze are typical and contribute to the translucency. The upper figure is magnified twice, the lower figure ten times. (See Plate XVII.)

and also numerous fine precipitates of calcium phosphate. Not enough to make the glaze opaque, the suspended particles impart a softness and translucency, as illustrated in the microstructures shown in Figure 7.3. Where the glaze is thicker, as on the left-hand side of Plate XVI and Figure 7.1, the blue color of the underglaze painting appears lighter and more diffuse because a thicker layer of translucent glaze lies above the painting. The residual quartz and feldspar particles, variations in the lead content, and the variable glaze thickness indicate a rather careless technique, but we should remember that the usual practice for using a lead glaze on majolica was to employ a much thinner layer, in which these imperfections would be unnoticed and entirely acceptable. The glaze composition is 57.3 weight percent silica, 5.7 alumina, 3.0 lime, 6.2 soda, 4.0 potassia, 22.0 lead oxide, no tin oxide, and less than 1 percent each of iron oxide, magnesia, and titania.

The pottery technology used for manufacturing majolica ware in Italy during the sixteenth century is described in some detail by Piccolpasso[2] in his work, *The Three Books of the Potter's Art*, written in 1557. To make glazes it was common practice to react soluble alkalies with silica by a sintering process in which three parts of ground sand and one part of calcined wine dregs were mixed, placed in a clay container, and baked under the kiln while firing a load of pottery. Some variations included salt as an ingredient, and Piccolpasso reports that in Venice it was common to use calcined Levantine plant ash imported from the Near East. The sintered product (marzacotta) was a hard mixture consisting in large part of an alkali silica glass, but also including calcined lead oxide, a calcined lead oxide/tin oxide mixture (usually three parts of lead to one of tin, but sometimes as much as seven to one), crushed sand, flint pebbles, and salt.

The principal ingredient of calcined wine lees is potassium carbonate; they also contain appreciable amounts of lime and silica and lesser amounts of magnesia, but little soda. Our analysis of the glaze composition indicates that it would have been made by milling together calcined wine lees, sand, lead oxide, and salt. Piccolpasso and the Baldelli Boni manuscript both give this general type of recipe. The exact composition of several of the ingredients varies from time to time, so, as Piccolpasso suggested in 1557, the recipe would be varied accordingly. In other words, if one batch of wine lees were found to be weak in fluxing power, more than the usual amount would be added. The milled ingredients would have been sintered, then crushed and milled. The excess water was decanted from the glaze material to give a slurry ready for pouring over the ware.

One aspect of our analysis that was puzzling was the high alumina content we found, more than 5 percent. This amount of alumina is needed to give good glaze properties, but it is not an obvious constituent of any of the materials used. To check this point, we obtained several samples of sixteenth century majolica from the Faenza Museum collection and found that about 5 percent alumina was also typical of majolica lead glazes made at the time. It probably resulted from the use of a sand containing clay or mica, or perhaps a clay-bonded or mica-bonded sandstone for the "sand" constituent—but also may suggest the separate addition of clay to assist glaze suspension (not mentioned in documentary sources). We do not know for sure.

The chemical composition of the body, determined on a millimeter-size sample by electron microprobe analysis, is 77.6 weight percent silica, 9.5 alumina, 2.5 lime, 3.4 soda, 5.4 potassia, no tin oxide, and less than 1 percent each of iron oxide, magnesia, lead oxide, and titania. We emphasize that there is no tin oxide present because this finding is in direct contradiction to one of the documentary formulas that has been widely quoted, and is incorrect. The body is a composition in which a glazemaker's sinter (marzacotta) made of sand, salt, and calcined wine lees was milled and mixed with fine sand and 15–25 percent of a white clay. The resultant microstructure (Figure 7.4) is a compact, translucent body consisting of fine-particle-size quartz grains embedded in a glass phase in which there are even finer pyroxene crystals (mostly calcium silicate and calcium-magnesium silicate, but also containing some sodium, aluminum, and titanium in solid solution), which contribute to the whiteness of the body. The porosity is appreciable—closed pores with a typical size of about 10 μm.

If we compare the Medici microstructure with the later Vincennes soft-paste porcelain illustrated in Chapter 10, we see that they are very similar. However, the Vincennes silica is present as cristobalite, formed during sintering, whereas the Medici silica is mostly quartz added to the body after sintering. Even more important, the Medici composition contains much more alumina, which, together with the alkalies present, affords a composition that becomes completely molten over a small range of temperature during firing; that is, it has a "short firing range." This is illustrated in the phase diagram of Figure 7.5. The combination of this short firing range and the necessity for firing at the upper limit of available kiln temperatures explains why all the ware was more or less warped during firing. The amount lost in firing must have been staggering.

After the death of Grand Duke Francesco, his brother Cardinal Ferdinando took his place, but had little enthusiasm for supporting this expensive and not wholly successful manufacture. In view of the inherent

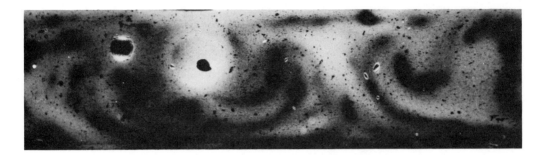

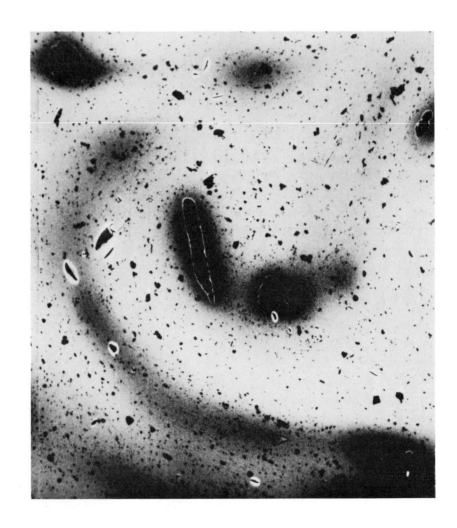

Figure 7.3. Electron micrographs of polished glaze cross sections show striae of light lead-rich and dark lead-poor silica-rich regions. Large quartz and feldspar particles and fine calcium phosphate particles show up as black with a dark surrounding ring of partial solution in the lead glaze. [(a) at 200X; (b) at 400X.] An etched surface of the intersection of body and glaze (c) shows glaze reacting with the surface of the body, part of a pore, fine needlelike particles of calcium phosphate, and a few feldspar or quartz grains (etched for 30 seconds, in 8 percent hydrofluoric acid, 1500X).

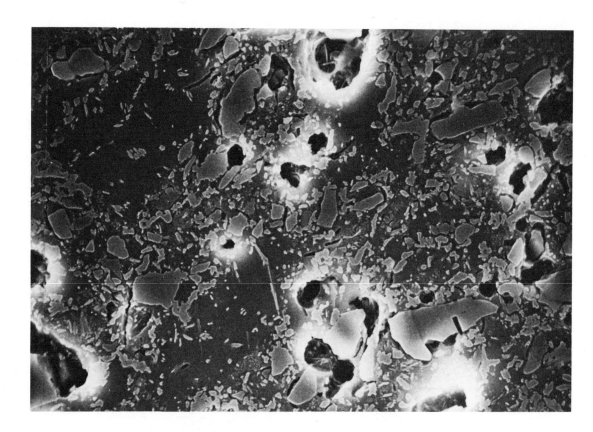

Figure 7.4. Scanning electron micrograph of lightly etched (ten seconds, 1 percent hydrofluoric acid) Medici body shows that the microstructure consists mostly of approximately 0.01-mm quartz grains and 0.1–1-μm (0.0001–0.001-mm) silicate particles distributed in a glass matrix. Porosity is also present, with a size range of 0.002–0.010 mm (1000X).

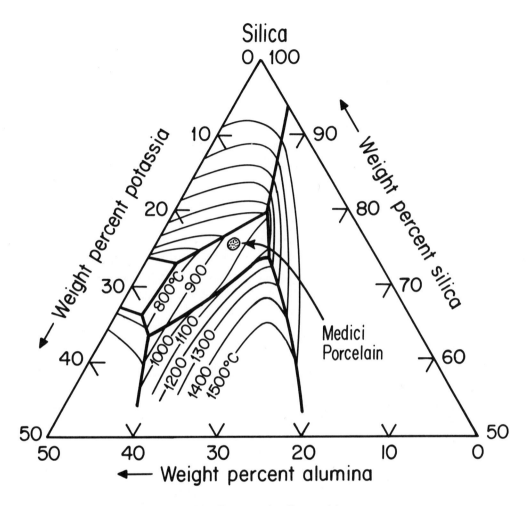

Figure 7.5. On this diagram the lines with temperatures indicated show the temperature at which a composition is wholly liquid. When these are close together, as on the right side of the diagram (where triaxial clay-quartz-feldspar whitewares are found), the onset of melting is gradual. In the central part of the diagram, where the composition of Medici porcelain is shown, the surface contour of complete melting is flat and the onset of melting is rapid, resulting in a narrow range of acceptable firing temperatures. The lime content of Medici porcelain does not change the shape of this "liquidus" surface very much, but raises the temperatures by about 150°C.

difficulties in forming and firing this composition, the pieces actually made must be regarded as successful tests rather than an established technology, and it is not surprising that production lapsed without Francesco's continuing support.

Both documentary sources and the experimentally determined composition indicate that the concept of a high-silica body with a glazelike bond and limited clay content came from the Near East. The Near Eastern potters, however, used a melted frit (which was also a glaze constituent) whereas the sinter for Medici porcelain was based on Italian majolica techniques that were completely different from the methods employed in the Near East. To be successful, this combination of foreign composition and local method required application of the emerging chemical science with its concepts of systematic experimentation and of pushing the current methods to their limits to achieve new results. It would seem to be no accident that the earliest successful porcelain manufacture was achieved at the court of Francesco de Medici. Here there was the proper combination of trade contacts with the Near East, a deep interest in chemical and high-temperature experimentation, and the practical skills of a group of highly capable craftsmen.

Overall one must admire Grand Duke Francesco I and his Florentine artisans for their perseverance in working with a body composition that was difficult to shape, required a high firing temperature, and had such a short firing range that their efforts must have resulted in heavy kiln losses.

RECOMMENDED READING

Kingery, W. D., and P. B. Vandiver, "Medici Porcelain," *Faenza*, no. 4 (1984). This article contains details of the analyses performed on a Medici shard and several sixteenth century majolica shards from the Faenza collection.

Lane, Arthur, *Italian Porcelain*, Faber and Faber, London (1947). Lane gives an excellent historical perspective on the development of porcelain in Italy.

REFERENCES

1. Davillier, M. le Baron, *Les Origines de la Porcelaine en Europe*, Librarie de l'Art, Paris and London (1882).

2. Piccolpasso, Cipriano, *The Three Books of the Potter's Art* (1557), R. Lightbown and A. Caiger-Smith translation, Scolar Press, London (1980). Piccolpasso's classic work is the first European book describing pottery techniques. He gives many details of formulations and methods used in the sixteenth century, and the translators' notes provide an excellent and authoritative commentary.

3. Biavati, E., "Studio Tecneco Chimico Ceramico Porcellana dei Medici," *Faenza*, fasc. V, p. 73 (1973).

4. Liverani, G., *Catalogoi delle Porcellane dei Medici*, Piccola Biblioteca de Museo delle Ceramiche de Faenza, Faenza, Lega (1936).

CHAPTER 8

A K'ANG HSI FAMILLE VERTE *PORCELAIN PLATE*

T he plate shown as Plate XVIII and Figure 8.1 was made at the imperial kilns of Ching-te-Chen for the Emperor K'ang Hsi's 60th birthday in 1713. In the four cartouches along the narrow flattened rim are the Chinese characters for "long life without limit," an imperial birthday greeting. The geometric border pattern in two shades of iron red serves to frame the inner landscape, and also incorporates the birthday wish in the medallions at four cardinal points. The composition has the same elements of aerial perspective and balanced asymmetry one finds in the finest landscape painting (Plate XIX). The strong, hard, dense white porcelain plate with its good ring and skillfully executed overglaze painting provides an example of the outstanding quality that was achieved within a factory production system.

China had been in a state of turmoil during the last stages of the Ming Dynasty and during the early part of the Manchu or Ch'ing (Qing) Dynasty, which began in 1644. These troubled times were only brought to an end with K'ang Hsi, the second Ch'ing emperor during whose long, tranquil reign (1662–1722) art, music, poetry, and literature were cultivated. In 1675, during the Wu San-kuei rebellion, a large part of Ching-te-Chen (Jingdezhen), the porcelain manufacturing center of China, was destroyed. Efforts to establish porcelain manufacture at the imperial residence in Peking were not successful; and the emperor requested sugges-

Figure 8.1. The strong, hard, dense white porcelain developed in China forms a classical ground for the skillfully executed overglaze painting of the K'ang Hsi *famille verte* porcelain plate believed to have been made at Ching-te-Chen for the emperor's 60th birthday in 1713. (On display at the Percival David Foundation of Chinese Art, London.) The four cartouches along the rim contain the Chinese characters for "long life without limit." The popular appeal of this ware and the description of its manufacture in the letters of Père d'Entrecolles had an enormous influence on the development of European porcelain and the emergent industrial revolution. (Courtesy of the Percival David Foundation of Chinese Art.) (See Plate XVIII.)

tions from an imperial commission, which recommended rebuilding Ching-te-Chen. Ts'ang Ying-hsuan, a master of the potter's art, was appointed superintendent of the imperial porcelain factories at Ching-te-Chen in 1683. His successes were such that he was sometimes regarded as being in league with the supernatural. Porcelain was once again produced at the Ching-te-Chen imperial kilns, and extensive commercial production was revived for both domestic markets and export. The population of this porcelain city was reported to be a "million souls," and there were said to be 3000 furnaces processing ware for export—estimates that were probably exaggerated. Great amounts of porcelain were exported to Europe. The leadership of Ts'ang Ying-hsuan, and the emperor's personal interest, inspired a renaissance in ceramic technology. The technical excellence of the porcelain made at Ching-te-Chen in the early eighteenth century has not been improved upon. Some connoisseurs, perhaps overwhelmed by the technical excellence and high rate of production, have tried to downgrate the artistic merit of this period.

Father François Xavier d'Entrecolles went to China in 1698 as a Jesuit missionary to the province of Kiangsi, where he remained until 1722 when he became superior of the French residence in Peking. In 1712, and again in 1722, Père d'Entrecolles wrote letters to France describing porcelain manufacture at Ching-te-Chen. These were published many times and had a good deal of influence on the developing porcelain industry in Europe. He also sent samples of the "kaolin" clay and the "petuntze" china stone, which were studied by the French chemist, Reaumur. Père d'Entrecolles' description of worker specialization in which as many as 70 different people would participate in making a single piece was particularly important. (Wedgwood, who read these reports, is given credit for introducing this factory system into England.) While his discussions of processes and materials are sometimes a bit garbled, his first-hand description of Ching-te-Chen and its porcelain production at the height of the K'ang Hsi reign were avidly studied in Europe at the time, and remain as important sources in the history of porcelain manufacture.

During the reign of K'ang-Hsi, a wide variety of wares were manufactured—white porcelains, blue-and-white ware, blue-ground ware, peach bloom, underglaze reds, and others. A major development was the perfection of enamels for painting on white porcelain, including the *famille verte* palette of traditional enamels. Named for the often prominent apple green, this palette also included a variety of blues, reds, purples, grays, and browns, most of which were transparent or translucent. Toward the end of the K'ang Hsi period, the *famille rose* palette was introduced. This featured the prominent use of a colloidal gold pigment, but even more important, an opaque white that allowed the formation of a variety of pastels. Referred to as "foreign colors" since they originated in Europe, they became prominent in the reign of Ch'ien Lung. Another innovation during the K'ang Hsi reign was the use of soapstone (talc) as a partial replacement for kaolin in ware sometimes referred to as "Chinese soft paste," but completely different from the European soft-paste frit porcelain described in Chapter 10. (Père d'Entrecolles reported this utilization of soapstone and his letters may have contributed to its use for a time at Worcester.)

The dense, white, hard translucent body has a good ring when the plate is held on the fingertips and tapped. The composition consists of carefully selected china stone (*petuntze*—a fine mixture of quartz, feldspar, and mica), which first was broken into small pieces with a hammer and then ground to a fine powder in a trip-hammer mill operated by a water-wheel. After grinding, the powdered stone was suspended in water, thoroughly mixed, and the coarse material was allowed to settle and the fine-particle-size portion placed in another settling tank. The "mud" from this tank was transferred to a drying platform and then formed into small blocks in a wooden mold for transport to the factory. The other ingredient was kaolin, a white clay. At the factory the two ingredients were again purified by settling and equal parts of the suspension thoroughly mixed together, partially dried, and then wedged in preparation for forming. By careful material selection, the iron content was kept low. The elaborate process of milling and slaking achieved a fine-particle-size body that gave sufficient plasticity without addition of the less pure ball clays that are included in most modern Western formulations. Still, the body is much less plastic and forgiving than the sort of body used for wheelthrowing by modern potters. Père d'Entrecolles makes clear that ware using the relatively "short" porcelain body (i.e., one in which only a limited range of water content gives suitable plasticity) was thrown quickly and then, after partial drying, molded and turned to its final shape.

Molds were extensively used for bowls and plates, as well as for complex figures. The molds were made with a yellow plastic clay, which was kneaded, strongly beaten (wedged) with a sort of wooden mallet to remove inhomogeneities, formed into shape, and then, when dry, turned on the wheel. After forming, molds were heated at a temperature to sinter and strengthen them, but not eliminate porosity. (Plaster of Paris molds used in Europe at this time were not known in China.)

The plate shown in Plate XVIII and Figure 8.1 would have been shaped by forming the upper surface on a fired earthenware mold of sufficient porosity to absorb some moisture from the plastic body. The final shape of the bottom of the plate and foot rim were formed by trimming the partially dry piece with a template contoured to give the same profile to each plate. (An automated version of this process is known as "jiggering.") After forming, finishing, and drying, the plate was dipped into a glaze slurry consisting of a mixture of selected glaze stone plus a mixture of lime and ash made by calcining lumps of limestone interspersed with ferns, which added an ash-contributing alkali and a certain amount of phosphate to the burned lime. The resultant glaze is a classical lime-alkali-alumino-silicate composition. After dipping, the foot was carefully wiped and the sample was set on a bed of sand in an enclosed saggar for firing. A typical body composition we have determined is 69.7 weight percent silica, 24.5 alumina, 0.2 lime, 2.8 potassia, and 3.0 soda. The glaze has less alumina, which indicates only a small clay addition, and more lime, that is, 69.6 weight percent silica, 15.1 alumina, 10.1 lime, 3.3 potassia, and 2.1 soda.

Wood was used as fuel in an oval cross-draft kiln as shown in Figure 8.2, in which long flames reached from the firebox at the front over and around the saggars, with a substantial draft developed from the chimney in the rear. Père d'Entrecolles describes the K'ang Hsi kiln as being 12 feet high, nearly 24 feet long, and well insulated. The sides were buttressed with a sand-clay soil that had good thermal insulation. The arch, with its insulation, was thick enough that one could walk on it during firing and not be bothered by the heat. This good insulation made it possible to reach temperatures in the range of 1200–1300°C with only one firebox as a source of heat, a remarkable achievement for a kiln of this size. Stacks of saggars full of glazed ware were placed on a bed of quartz gravel. There are temperature variations both from bottom to top and from front to back, and ware was so distributed that those requiring the highest temperature were toward the front and those demanding a lower temperature were toward the rear. The bottom two saggars in each pile were left empty because of the low temperature at the bottom of the kiln. Celadon and underglaze red wares were placed near the middle where the temperature is moderate and the atmosphere is reducing; glaze compositions were adjusted to be softer at the lower temperatures toward the rear. Sight holes in the door and along the top were used for observing temperatures as indicated by the color and glow and for drawing test samples from the kiln. These holes could be left open or closed to help control the draft. In these kilns a temperature of 1300°C could be reached, sufficient to densify the body, giving a microstructure consisting of rounded, partly dissolved

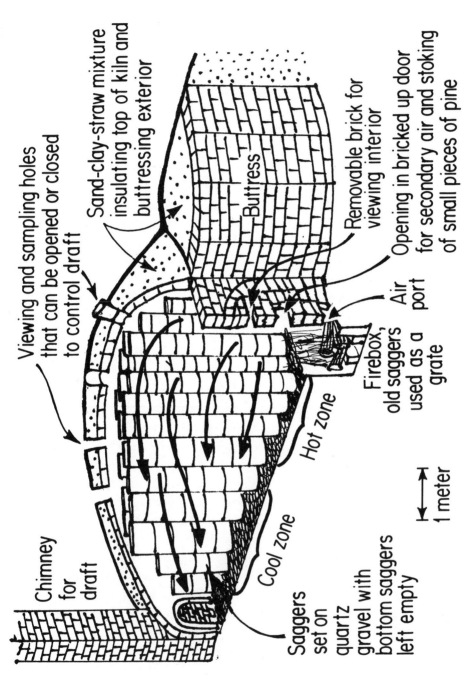

Figure 8.2. The Ching-te-Chen-type kiln was egg-shaped with one fire-box at the larger end and a chimney at the rear. Over a period of time, the size increased from about 10 feet long for the earliest kiln to some 24 feet in length during the K'ang Hsi period.

quartz particles in a matrix of silicate glass in which fine particles of mullite are dispersed (Figure 8.3). The iron content is low and entirely dissolved in the liquid silicate matrix, resulting in a white or slightly bluish body color.

Ching-te-Chen was a city of specialists. For commercial production, one factory mined the raw materials, and another ground them and formed them into blocks. Another factory mixed these materials with water, re-purified them, and prepared them in a plastic form. Other skilled workers formed the ware, using molds prepared by still other specialists. After drying, the ware was glazed and then sent to the kilns, which were in-dependently operated. Separate specialists manufactured the saggars. After the ware was fired, specialist artisans, the painters, applied the overglaze decoration, which was fired on the surface in low-temperature muffle kilns. Père d'Entrecolles tells us that the task of painting was divided among a large number of workers. "One makes only the first colored circle that one sees next to the edge of the porcelain; another traces flowers that a third one paints; this one does water and mountains; that one birds and other animals." The skill of the painting is illustrated in Figure 8.4. The painting was done with fine brushes in which the line width of the rim decoration and design is only a tenth of a millimeter. Colors were filled in with a watercolor technique, flowing a thin layer of enamel on the surface. Ob-taining a precise result is more difficult than with watercolors, of course, because the porcelain glaze is a nonabsorbent ground. In addition, the color of the paint did not match the final color, which appeared after the porcelain was subjected to the low-temperature enamel firing. The painter had to envision the end result while proceeding with the painting.

The preparation of the colors shows the same care and technical ex-cellence as with the underlying body and glaze. Père d'Entrecolles describes how pigments for the various colors were prepared and then mixed with white lead and crushed quartz pebbles. The paint was then finely ground with a mortar and pestle, some animal glue added as a binder, and the paste diluted with water to the desired painting consistency. Pigment prep-aration is a tricky operation and requires careful attention to detail. Père d'Entrecolles describes how the coral red pigment was made from ferrous sulfate (which must be very pure—technical grade 99.8 percent $FeSO_4$ gives a muddy color) placed in a crucible with another crucible cemented on top that had a small hole for the gases to escape. The heating had to be stopped just as the color of the emerging fumes changed from black to a "fine delicate cloud" (about 600°C). The best quality red was a fine powder deposited on the upper crucible—fine particles of the high-purity

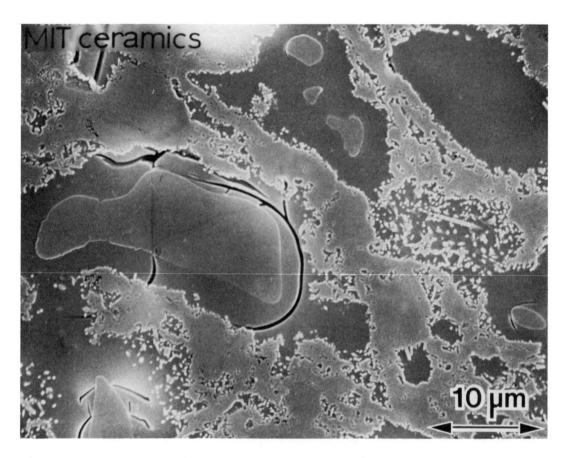

Figure 8.3. K'ang Hsi porcelain is dense, hard, and translucent. The microstructure consists of partly dissolved rounded quartz particles in a matrix of silicate glass, which also contains fine mullite crystals. (Scanning electron micrograph of lightly etched sample—1 percent hydrofluoric acid for ten seconds—1000X.)

hematite form of iron oxide. As the calcination temperature was increased, the same chemical composition became a darker brownish red as shown in Plate XXIIb; if the atmosphere was oxygen-deficient (i.e., reducing in nature), the oxide transformed to the magnetite form of iron oxide, a black color. Electron microscopy of a K'ang Hsi coral red enamel (Figure 8.5) shows the very fine (0.1 μm; 0.0001 mm) uniform hematite iron-oxide pigment particles suspended in the low-melting lead-silicate glass.

Using electron microbeam techniques, we have analyzed several enamels on a K'ang Hsi sample. We find from our analyses that the basic formula used was about 28 weight percent quartz and 72 percent white lead ($PbCO_3.Pb(OH)_2$), which corresponds reasonably well to the 25 percent quartz/75 percent white lead formula reported by Père d'Entrecolles. As expected, we find that the blues contain cobalt, the purples manganese, and the greens copper; when substantial colorant was added, 6 percent copper for a dark green, the amount of lead was decreased to maintain a nearly constant silica content, about 30 weight percent, so that the different colors melted at the same temperature. The black enamel has manganese oxide particles as the major pigment. However, enamel formulas are actually more complex and sophisticated than this overall view suggests. On this one piece, three different green enamels were used, two of which have iron and one of which has manganese as an added colorant, as shown in Table 8.1.

In addition, the dark-green copper enamel contained a mill addition of widely separated quartz particles in the size range of 2–20 μm to provide better translucence and depth of color, as shown in Figure 8.6. The cobalt-blue enamel contains some copper and iron impurities and was formulated with less lead, higher silica, and a potassia addition, which combine to help avoid any green hue from the copper and iron content. (Père

TABLE 8.1

Composition (Weight Percent) of Three Green Enamels Used on One Piece

Color	Copper Oxide	Iron Oxide	Manganese Oxide
Dark green*	6.0	0.34	0.15
Apple green	2.1	1.1	0.0
Olive green	3.1	1.0	0.0

*Blue-green in thin layers.

Figure 8.4. Enlarged views of some of the details reveal the precision of the painting. The line widths of the figure outlines are about a tenth of a millimeter, which is very fine to accommodate later painting; the colors are filled in with a variety of washes in a technique similar to that used with watercolors. (See Plate XX.)

d'Entrecolles lists saltpeter, potassium nitrate, along with powdered flint and white lead as glaze ingredients.) The coral-red pigment contains 4.8 percent alumina; this was added to brighten the color. It is clear that there was extensive research at Ching-te-Chen on methods of color preparation. These differences in enamel composition are shown in Table 8.2.

During K'ang Hsi's reign, the combination of expert craftsmanship with lifelong specialization, imperial interest, and the direction of Ts'ang Ying-hsuan as the superintendent of the imperial kilns led to Ching-te-Chen porcelain having a truly remarkable technical virtuosity. The birthday plate we have studied has a strong, hard, white translucent body with a good ring that provides a wonderful ground for the skillfully executed overglaze painting. Analysis of the composition and microstructure of the

Figure 8.5. High-magnification scanning electron microscopy illustrates the very fine (0.1m; 0.0001 mm) hematite (Fe_2O_3) pigment particles that give the K'ang Hsi coral-red color when suspended in the low-melting lead-silicate glass.

overglaze enamels demonstrates that the same high levels of technical sophistication and care were used in their preparation. When we consider
that the Ching-te-Chen potters were also producing a wide range of monochrome glazes, underglaze blues and reds, and glazes with just a trace of
cobalt to give "clare de lune,"—wares for the palace, for domestic use, and
for export—we have to be impressed, even a bit overwhelmed. Not only
the ware itself, but also the craft specialization used in its manufacture,
well described in the letters of Père d'Entrecolles, served as a source of
inspiration for the factories of Europe during the rest of the eighteenth
century.

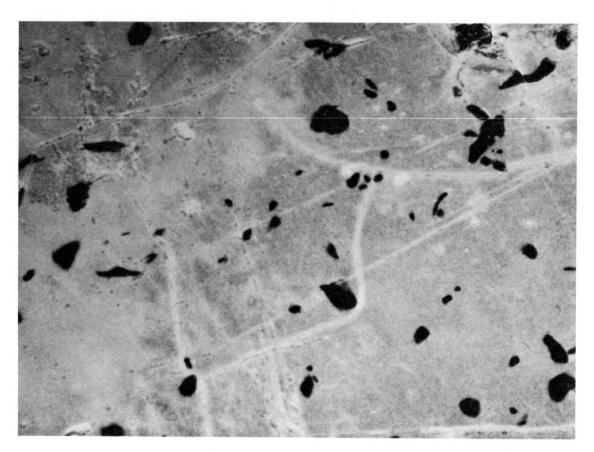

Figure 8.6. Quartz particles were added to the copper-green glaze
to provide translucence. Scanning electron microscopy of lightly
etched sample (1 percent hydrofluoric acid, ten seconds) 350X.

TABLE *8.2*

Principal Constituents Present in K'ang Hsi Enamels (Weight Percent)

	Color					
Element	Dark Green	Olive Green	Green	Light Purple	Blue	Coral Red
Silica	32.3	29.0	31.5	29.0	42.2	23.9
Lead oxide	58.7	66.2	62.7	69.5	47.8	41.4
Alumina	1.0	0.6	1.0	0.8	0.4	4.8
Lime plus magnesia	0.7	0.2	0.4	0.1	0.9	2.5
Soda plus potassia	0.7	0.2	0.2	0.3	6.7	0.6
Copper oxide	6.0	2.1	3.1	0.1	0.1	0.1
Iron oxide	0.3	1.1	1.0	0.1	0.3	22.8
Cobalt oxide	—	—	—	—	0.2	—
Manganese oxide	—	—	—	0.23	—	—

RECOMMENDED READING

Medley, Margaret, *The Chinese Potter*, Charles Scribner's Sons, New York (1976). An excellent discussion of the history of Chinese wares and the methods of production.

Tichane, R., *Ching-te-Chen*, New York State Institute for Glaze Research, Painted Post, N.Y. (1983). This description of the history and manufacturing methods of Ching-te-Chen also contains English translations of the 1712 and 1722 letters of Père d'Entrecolles; *The Twenty Illustrations of the Manufacture of Porcelain*, by Tang Ying; *A Trip to Ching-te-Chen*, by F. Scherzer; *Studies on Chinese Porcelain*, by Georges Vogt; and *Researches in the Composition of Chinese Porcelain*, by J. J. Ebelman and L. A. Salvatat.

REFERENCES

1. Bushnell, Stephen Q., *Description of Chinese Pottery and Porcelain*, a translation of the T'ao Shuo, Oxford University Press, London (1910 and 1977). Includes a description of porcelain manufacture by T'ang Ying as well as the traditional Chinese classification of wares.

2. Wirgin, Jan, "K'ang-Hsi Porcelain," *Bull. of the Museum of Far-Eastern Antiquities*, vol. 46, pp. 65–90 (1974) (Stockholm). A description of wares produced during the reign of K'ang Hsi.

3. Sayer, G. R., (translator), *Ching-te-Chen t'ao-lu, or the Potteries of China* (1951); *T'ao Ya or Pottery Refinements* (1959), Routledge and Kegan Paul, London. Translations of several Chinese sources describing wares and techniques of manufacture.

4. Sung Ying-Hsing, *T'ien-Kung K'ai-Wu: Chinese Technology in the Seventeenth Century*, translated by E-Tu Zen Sun and Shiou-Chuan Sun, Pennsylvania State University Press, University Park, Pa. (1964). A treatise written in 1637 that describes many Chinese crafts and industries, including ceramics. Wood block prints of important activities are included.

CHAPTER 9

A BÖTTGER PORCELAIN

T he tea caddy illustrated in Plate XX and Figure 9.1 is an early result of the successful research efforts of Johann Friedrich Böttger, Count Ehrenfried Walther von Tschirnhaus, and Gottfried Pabst von Ohain to find a European equivalent to Chinese white porcelain. This achievement was one of the most exciting results of the scientific revolution in Europe. Böttger recorded in his notes the successful firing of a white translucent product at his Venusbastai laboratory in Dresden on January 15, 1708. This remarkable accomplishment of the discipline of experimental science was supported by a royal patron interested in the development of porcelain as a "necessary" luxury product.

The shape and design of the Böttger porcelain discussed here were copied from the Chinese; the caddy was first made in red stoneware in imitation of the Chinese I-Hsing ware. Indeed, the output of the first decade of production at Meissen consisted chiefly of Chinese imitations and designs based on silver prototypes. There are even examples of direct copies of I-Hsing ware in which a mold was taken from the Chinese original. The copy is an exact replica, although reduced in size by about 10 percent as a result of shrinkage during drying and firing. The Meissen tradition of complex molding and overglaze painting, for both utilitarian vessels and figures, did not develop until the 1730s when recognized artists began to work with ceramic factories. This tradition of collaboration thereafter characterized the best of European ceramic production and established ceramics as a fine art.

The example shown in Plate XX and Figure 9.1 was inspired by a classical Chinese shape and Chinese design motifs of a flowering tree and a bird, perhaps a phoenix. The molded six-sided tea caddy displays two different designs on alternating panels. The relief is quite low, requiring the viewer look closely at the panels to discern the details of the design; in so doing one becomes intrigued by the ceramic itself and its translucent porcelain. In fact, the shape, design, and purpose of this piece are close enough to one's expectation of Chinese porcelain that the Meissen example might well be mistaken for a Chinese product. To be appreciated, the alternating panels of design require that the object be held and turned to see how many different designs are present and to determine their symmetry. The caddy is an interesting shape to handle, with its curves, angles, and a small cylinder offset at the top. It satisfies one's tactile and visual interest while arousing one's curiosity as to its origin. What was the nature of the technical effort required to arrive at this long-sought goal—the production of European translucent porcelain?

During the fifteenth and sixteenth centuries, blue-and-white Ming Dynasty porcelain was being imported to Europe in limited quantities. After the Portugese reached the port of Canton in 1517, and with the establishment of the Dutch East Indies Company in 1602, and that company's development of a base on Taiwan in 1624 to compete with the

Figure 9.1. The first successful European hard-porcelain production was achieved at Meissen in 1708 by a research team under the direction of Johann Friederich Böttger. An example is this molded tea caddy from the period 1713–1718. The body was a mixture of white clay and calcined alabaster; the required firing temperature was above 1350°C, a level never before achieved in Europe. (Courtesy collection of the Metropolitan Museum of Art, New York.) (See Plate XXI.)

Portugese at Macao, Chinese imports were greatly increased. Following a lull during the turbulent last years of the Ming Dynasty in the mid-seventeenth century, imports sharply increased again with the revival of full production at Ching-te-Chen under the Ching emperor K'ang Hsi (1662–1722). Along with the traditional blue underglaze, polychrome-overglaze-decorated wares such as described in Chapter 7 were being exported from Ching-te-Chen. Two other types of Chinese ware that also appeared on the European market were white figurines and vessels with relief decoration made at De hua in Fujian (Fou-Kian) called *blanc-de-chine*, and red-brown relief-decorated stoneware vessels, particularly tea sets produced at I-Hsing (Jiaxing) near Shanghai.

Although porcelain was beginning to be used for utilitarian purposes (coffee, chocolate, and tea were becoming more common), mostly it was displayed in cabinets to be viewed as exotica from the mysterious East, alongside mineral samples and natural curiosities, paintings, and silverware. At the same time, along with the centralization of authority and the establishment of autocratic rule after the model of Louis XIV in France, chemistry and physics experiments were exploring new phenomena, there was new exploitation of natural resources, and new manufacturing methods were being developed. The best European ware being made in imitation of the Chinese imports was the clearly inferior blue-on-white Delft ware faience. In this environment various claims for making porcelain were put forth and royal warrants were issued, but the only actual production was of soft-paste ware that began at St. Cloud around 1695, as discussed in the next chapter.

In Saxony, official court policy, as with other monarchs of the time, was to encourage and support art, science, manufacturing, and trade—but Augustus the Strong, Elector from 1694 to 1735, had a special interest in porcelain; his personal collection was the largest in Europe. His active patronage of the Saxon porcelain research effort and beginning of manufacture was essential to its success.

Another important participant in the European invention of porcelain was Count Ehrenfried Walther von Tschirnhaus (1651–1708), scion of an ancient Bohemian family, who had studied mathematics and physics at Leiden. After an extended scientific tour of Europe in 1674–1679, he carried out numerous experiments on materials behavior using high temperatures achieved by focusing sunlight in a solar furnace. This research was sufficiently appreciated that he was made a member of the French Royal Academy in 1683. He carried out studies of Saxon mineral resources with mining superintendent Pabst and was responsible for establishing three glass houses, together with the grinding and polishing capability to produce burning lenses more than a meter in diameter. With these he reached higher temperatures than had previously been attained in Europe and conducted experiments aimed at beginning porcelain development by 1694, when he wrote to his famous mathematician friend, Leibnitz, in Berlin that he had "no more than a little piece of artificial porcelain." He reported to the French Academy of Science in 1699 on research showing that while pure sand and lime were separately infusible, they could be melted in his solar furnace when combined. The lowest melting temperature of a lime–sand mixture is 1436°C, so the burning-lens furnace must have reached at least this temperature, much higher than could be achieved in an ordinary furnace. In 1701 von Tschirnhaus visited the ceramic factories at St. Cloud and Delft.

The principal researcher, Johann Friedrich Böttger (1682–1719), had been the assistant to a well-known apothecary in Berlin, where he claimed to have transformed mercury into gold; he gave what was apparently a convincing demonstration of this in 1701. When widespread reports of this achievement led Frederick I to demand proof, Böttger found it expedient to flee to Wittenburg in Saxony and enter the university. Requested to return the young man, Augustus instead sent him, under guard, to Dresden. Here he worked under the direction of Gottfried Pabst von Ohain, a well-known chemist and metallurgist who was Saxony's superintendent of mining. Böttger seems to have been performing effective chemical and metallurgical tests for Pabst as well as continuing experiments aimed at uncovering the alchemical secrets of making gold. Locals referred to the brick building where he worked as the "House of Gold."

In September 1705 Augustus changed Böttger's assignment, sending him to work at a laboratory in Albrechtsburg at Meissen. A team of five assistants trained in mining and metallurgy was provided in 1706 and von Tschirnhaus and Pabst von Ohain came frequently to consult. The objectives of this research were kept as a closely held secret, but the facts make it clear that Böttger was in the porcelain-discovery business and that the research team already felt it was on the road to success. One of the first helpers was Paul Wildenstein[3], a Freiberg miner, who reported on this period to an investigating commission in 1736. He recalled:

In 1706, I came to Meissen to the Baron Böttger, to the secret laboratory, and we were shut in there for 18 weeks. Even the windows had been walled up to half of their height, and Herr von Tzschirnhaussen [sic] from Dresden was often with us as well as the mining councillor Pabst from Freyberg. We had a laboratory with 24 kilns, and the baron and Tzschirnhaussen had already made specimens of red porcelain in the shape of small slabs and marbled slab stones.

Just when things were going well and the group was realizing that clay could be made fusible with a calcerous flux, the Swedes invaded Saxony. On September 5, 1706, Böttger was taken as a prisoner to a safe haven at the fortress on the Konigstein, where he stayed for a year.

On September 22, 1707, Böttger was returned to a new laboratory that von Tschirnhaus had been busy setting up in the cellars of the Jungfernbastei at Dresden. There, according to Wildenstein[3]:

Herr von Tzschirnhaussen, too, was giving instructions, and they began to research. Among other things, specimens of red porcelain were made, as well as white. Köhler and I had to stand nearly every day by the large burning-glass to test the minerals. There I ruined my eyes, so that I now can perceive very little at a distance.

Things moved forward at a rapid rate. Upon hearing the good news, Augustus advanced long overdue funds in November 1707, and on January 6, 1708, Dr. Bartholomai, personal physician to Böttger and the prince, was sworn in as arcanist to learn the secrets of manufacturing both red stoneware and white porcelain. On January 12, 1708, the king approved the pay of workers in von Tschirnhaus' basement laboratory. Among the personal papers of Böttger, notes have been found indicating that a successful firing to achieve a white translucent ware was carried out on January 15, 1708. Few details are available, but clearly in the frantic period November–December 1707, research had advanced to a point where success was certain.

Utilizing the principle of mixing a refractory material with a lower melting one, or with a small amount of an active "flux," a variety of mixtures were tested, with potential products ranging from marbled bodies to artificial gems such as lapus lazuli and jasper, to red and brown stoneware and white porcelain. In anticipation of jewel production, facetting and polishing equipment was set up by von Tschirnhaus. In addition to this program, a delftware factory was initiated at Dresden Neustadt in February 1708, with a formal decree of foundation dated June 4, 1708. This facility had the furnaces necessary to produce both stone and marble bodies as well as delftware. Hollander Christolph Ruhle and his son-in-law Gerhard van Malcem were the first master fashioners and decorators. The court potter, Fisher, was called into service, and Dr. Bartholomai, very active as an arcanist and mixer of the secret "recipes" during this period, listed a modeler, a glass cutter, and a potter as among the workers. The actual wares produced were first a dense red-and-brown stoneware formed in ceramic shapes that could be cut and polished, and then the white, translucent porcelain.

As modern research directors well know, achieving a successful result in the laboratory is one thing and putting it into production quite another. It was more than a year later, on March 28, 1709, that Böttger announced to the king the discovery of porcelain, and a commission was established to consider such questions as the quality of the ware, the availability of materials, the reliability of production, and estimated costs. It was not until November 1709 that glazed white porcelain samples were submitted to this commission. Finally, on January 24, 1710, Augustus announced to the world the founding of European porcelain manufacture and samples were exhibited at the Leipzig Easter Fair that year. In June 1710 space was acquired for manufacturing at the Albrechtsburg in Meissen, with the councillor of mines and finance, Michael Nehmitz, as director. In these first years, there were many commission studies, changes in direction and directors, problems with production, personality clashes; all was chaos. During October of 1711, Jacob Irminger, court silversmith, visited the works, and by June 1712 was artistic director. The first production was almost entirely Chinese imitations and designs based on those of silverware.

Little is known about the details of experiments studying the response of different soils and soil mixtures under the high temperatures developed by von Tschirnhaus' lenses. A mixture of one part red "English earth" from a pharmacy and two parts of a local low-melting calcerous loam is said to have led to successful stoneware. In any event the first commercial product was brown-and-red stoneware made with red clay from Zwickau added to clay from Plauen, ware that remained in the Meissen catalog through 1735. This European version of the Chinese I-Hsing ware (some was made in molds taken from I-Hsing samples) was fine grained, hard, and dense, and was referred to by Böttger as "jasper porcelain." Much of it was cut, engraved, and polished using jewelry techniques. Upon replicating a clay-iron oxide-lime mixture equivalent to Böttger's formula, we learned that the color developed was sensitive to the firing temperature, becoming less red and darker as the temperature increased, corresponding to a gradual reduction of the amount of oxygen in the hematite structure at the higher temperatures. By comparing the color of our samples with Böttger's production, we inferred a firing temperature of 1200–1300°C. This is in accord with descriptions of the stoneware as being fired in the same saggars and kilns as the white porcelain, but at a lower temperature.

Successful manufacture of white porcelain was first achieved with white Colditz clay and calcined alabaster (calcium sulfate) from Nordhausen, but soon a white kaolin from Aue (Schnorr earth) was being used. The six-sided tea caddy (Figure 9.1) is typically Oriental in shape and design, and was made in both stoneware and white Böttger porcelain. There are two different alternating panel designs, one with a flying bird and the other with a bird perched on a flowering vine (Figure 9.2). The model from which the plaster-of-Paris mold was made was probably done in hammered copper by Jacob Irminger. The jar's side panels were formed in a three-piece plaster mold and then the separately molded cylindrical top and flat bottom were added when the pieces were leather hard. After the piece was dried and dipped in glaze, the glaze was wiped off the bottom, which was

Figure 9.2. There are two panel designs on the hexagonal Böttger porcelain tea caddy. The models for these were formed in copper by Jacob Irminger.

then sanded perfectly flat before firing. The lime-alkali glaze has not run, but crawled slightly from the exposed base. Schulle and Ullrich[5] recently analyzed Böttger porcelain, with the results shown in Table 9.1. That composition is illustrated on the lime-alumina-silica phase-equilibrium diagram in Figure 9.3. If no alkali at all were present, a firing temperature of 1400°C would have been required, a level never before approached in European practice. With the alkali content reported in Table 9.1, the necessary firing temperature was a bit above 1350°C, a temperature well above prior European practice. One of Böttger's early helpers, Paul Wildenstein,[3] described their efforts:

We couldn't manage to make a strong fire in the new kiln; all our toil was fruitless and the fire remained weak. While it was burning, we had to make the fire walls sometimes higher, sometimes lower, but it was no use until we finally discovered the fault in the casing. The coals wouldn't burn all the way down, so we had to pull them out every thirty minutes. . . . Our hair was scorched and the floor had grown so hot that our feet were covered with large blisters.

While most descriptions of the invention of European porcelain focus on composition, there were three principal secrets of Böttger's success: (1) the concept of partially fluxing a white clay with lime; (2), the experimental testing of suitable compositions with von Tschirnhaus' burning lenses; and (3) achieving the high kiln temperature necessary for satisfactory firing. The microstructure of Böttger porcelain was reported by Schulle and Ullrich to consist of mullite crystals in a lime silicate glass (Figure 9.4a). A replica of this composition, made in our laboratory (Figure 9.4b), also shows mullite and a glass as the principal phases present, as required by the phase-equilibrium diagram (Figure 9.3). As Böttger porcelain does not

TABLE *9.1*

Chemical Composition of Böttger's Porcelain and the Later Meissen Porcelain Using Feldspar As a Flux (Schulle and Ullrich[3].)

	Böttger Porcelain (1715)	*Meissen Porcelain (1731)*
Silica, SiO_2	62	60
Alumina, Al_2O_3	33	35
Potassia, K_2O	0.1	4.0
Soda, Na_2O	0.2	0.8
Lime, CaO	4.8	0.3
Other	0.9	0.9

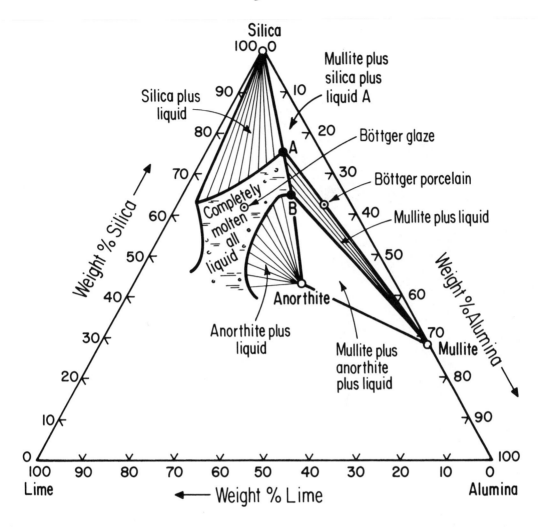

Figure 9.3. The composition of Böttger porcelain is shown on a 1400°C section through the lime-alumina-silica phase diagram, indicating a mixture of mullite and glass. The presence of about 0.3 percent alkali lowers the temperature required from the 1400°C shown here to near 1350°C.

Figure 9.4. Microstructure of a Böttger porcelain. (a) A sample from 1715 heavily etched (12 minutes in 2 percent hydrofluoric acid) shows mullite needles in a glass matrix that has been etched away (1500X). (Courtesy of W. Schulle and B. Ullrich.) (b) Replica prepared in authors' laboratory that has been polished and lightly etched (ten seconds, 1 percent hydrofluoric acid) that also shows mullite crystals in a glass matrix (2000X).

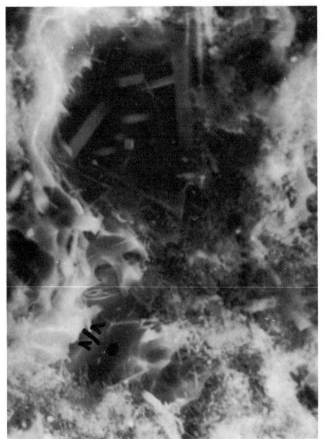

A

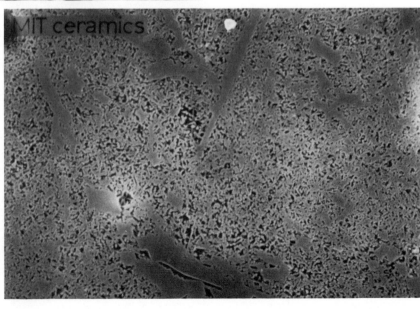

B

contain much of the quartz phase found in Chinese porcelain, and was not based on a mixture of feldspar, quartz, and kaolin, it should properly be referred to as an entirely new composition, which produced an effective white porcelain at a very high firing temperature.

Wildenstein[3] described a visit of Augustus the Strong to Böttger's Jungfernbastai laboratory to view a firing:

His Majesty arrived with the Prince of Fürstenberg, but when they entered the laboratory and felt the terrible fire, they would rather have turned back. Since, however, the baron—looking like a sooty charcoal-burner—was so close to him, His Majesty entered and urged the prince to come in, too. The baron told us to stop firing for a while and to open the kiln, and during this time the prince said several times, "Oh, Jesus." The king, however, laughed and said to him that it was in no way to be compared to Purgatory! The kiln was opened, and all was bathed in white heat so that nothing could be seen. [*Note*: color temperatures are 1300°C, dull white; 1400°C, bright white.] The king looked in and said to the prince, "Look, Egon, they say that porcelain is in there!" The prince said he couldn't see anything either but finally the kiln grew red, since it was open, so they could see the porcelain. I had to draw out a specimen, which was a saggar containing a small teapot.

A tubful of water stood nearby, so that the glowing iron could be extinguished. The baron immediately seized the tongs, drew the teapot out, and threw it into the water. Suddenly a loud bang was heard, and the king said, "Oh, it's smashed." but the baron replied, "No, Your Majesty, it must stand this test." He then rolled up his sleeves and took it out of the tub. It indeed proved to be intact.

We were a bit doubtful about this story, but students in our laboratory repeated the experiment with the same result! The microstructure of Böttger porcelain, consisting of mullite crystals in a high-lime glass with little or no quartz (Figure 9.4), gives it an extraordinary resistance to thermal shock. As indicated by the analysis of a 1731 sample (Table 9.1), the Meissen formula was modified to use feldspar as a flux in place of lime after Böttger's death in 1719. The indicator of feldspar as a flux is the increased amount of potassium and lower lime content of the 1731 sample. The addition of feldspar allowed a somewhat lower firing temperature, roughly equivalent to K'ang Hsi porcelain (Chapter 7). Even so, the quartz content of Meissen porcelain remained lower than that of the Chinese ware and most other European hard porcelain, as shown by the microstructure of a 1731 sample, which is virtually identical to the earlier Böttger ware (Figure 9.5).

When we examined three samples of Böttger porcelain fluorescing under ultraviolet illumination (black light), we were surprised to find that while the bodies all showed a typical cream-colored fluorescence, the glazes were quite different on the different pieces (Plate XXI). Some of the glazes exhibited a purple fluorescence that results from the use of feldspar (studies are now in progress with quantitative electron microprobe analysis to extend this result). That is, glazes were made with feldspar as a flux prior to the time it was introduced as a body constituent. This early experience with feldspar as a glaze flux surely explains its rapid introduction into the ceramic itself soon after Böttger's death.

The Böttger kiln was horizontal with a semicircular cross section; it was 1.2–1.5 meters high, 0.9 meter wide, and about 3 meters long, with fireboxes at one end and a chimney at the other. The temperature achieved with this type of kiln depends on the draft drawing in sufficient combustion air to one or more well-designed fireboxes. Some air must flow over the fuel, resulting in partial combustion and generating combustible vapors. Additional combustion air must enter under the grate and be preheated before combustion takes place in a long flame where the hot air and hot vaporized fuel react to give a high flame temperature. European kiln insulation was not nearly as good as in Chinese porcelain kilns, so a more

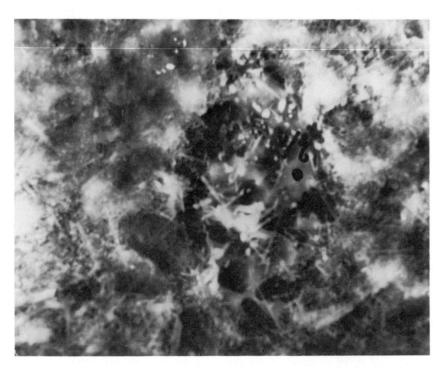

Figure 9.5. Microstructure of Meissen porcelain from 1731 illustrating mullite needles in alkali-alumino-silicate glass. Heavily etched (12 minutes in 2 percent hydrofluoric acid). (2500X.) (Courtesy of W. Schulle and B. Ullrich.)

rapid rate of heat generation—that is, multiple fireboxes—was required for attaining the highest temperatures. Kiln master S. Stöltzel took the Meissen kiln design to Vienna in 1719, and a kiln of this type was still in use at Vienna as late as 1812. It had three fireboxes, each of which had preheated combustion air entering under the grate. This same basic horizontal-gas-flow design was used for German salt-glazed stoneware production at the time and is similar to the later German Kassel kiln type and the English Newcommon type, and is related to the much larger K'ang Hsi Chinese porcelain kilns at Ching-te-Chen described in Chapter 7.

Brongniart[4] and others have pointed out that pushing to achieve the high temperatures necessary for porcelain production with the Böttger-type kiln resulted in sharp temperature variations along the length of the kiln, as was also true of the much larger Ching-te-Chen kilns. The first and last rows of saggars had to be left empty, and the higher temperature near the firebox and lower temperature near the chimney required that different compositions of body and glaze be used in different sections of the kiln. This seems to be confirmed by the different glaze compositions indicated in Plate XXI. It was only in the latter part of the eighteenth century when hard porcelain manufacture began at Limoges, that cylindrical updraft kilns with several fireboxes around the circumference became the norm. According to Brongniart,[4] the first of these was a small cylindrical furnace with four fireboxes made by M. Parent in 1769. Not until the nineteenth century did the downdraft versions of this general design come into use, that provided a much more uniform and easily controlled temperature distribution.

In Vienna Claudius Innocentius du Paquier had been experimenting with porcelain manufacture without much success. In 1717 he obtained the services of Cristoph Konrad Hunger, a gold worker from Meissen, but was not completely successful in his efforts until Meissen kiln master Samuel Stöltzel came to Vienna in 1719. In a way this worked out well for Meissen, because Stölzell returned in 1720, bringing with him Johann Gregor Horoldt, who became Meissen's most important painter. Manufacture of hard porcelain remained the exclusive preserve of Meissen and Vienna until midcentury, when Johann Jakob Ringer is said to have taken the secret to Höchst (1746), Nymphenburg (1747), Fürstenberg (1747), and Berlin (1751), among others. By 1783 twenty-three factories in Germany were producing hard porcelain.

The tea caddy we have illustrated has a Chinese-based shape and design typical of early Böttger porcelain. Its production was the result of a process of research, development, production startup, and associated industrial espionage so modern in form as to be astonishing. This achievement was undoubtedly one of the outstanding accomplishments of early European experimental science and engineering.

Père d'Entrecolle's[5] letters of 1712 and 1722, which describe porcelain manufacture in China, were widely distributed, and samples of Chinese raw materials were given to the famous French chemist Reaumur for analysis. In 1727 and 1729, Reaumur[6] published his findings that one of the ingredients, kaolin, was infusible; whereas the other, petuntse, fused readily in his furnace, and he formulated the theory that Chinese porcelain consisted of a mixture of an infusible earth with a fusible constituent. As is most often the case, porcelain manufacturers had applied the same considerations in making ware long before publication of the scientific explanations.

RECOMMENDED READING

Ducret, S., *German Porcelain and Faience*, Diana Imber translation, Universe Books, New York (1962). Ducret gives only a short history of Böttger and Meissen, but also includes the histories and extensive illustrations of eighteenth century German porcelain from some 25 factories.

Goder, Willi, Klaus Hoffman, Ingelore Menzhausen, Eberman Neubert, Werner Pfuhl, Friederich Rirchel, Wolfgang Schulle, Rolf Sonnemann, Eberhard Wachtler, Hannes Walter, and Otfried Wagenbreth, *Böttger: die erfindung des Europäischen Porzellans*, W. Kolhammer, Stuttgart (1982); French translation, *Meissen, la decouverte de la porcelaine Europeenne en Saxe*, Pygmalion, Gerard Watelet, Paris (1984). Extensive explication and history of Böttger porcelain and subsequent Meissen production written by a number of specialists from different points of view.

Walcha, Otto, *Meissen Porcelain*, Helmut Reibig translation, G. P. Putnam's Sons, New York (1981). Authoritative history of Böttger and Meissen in English translation is based in large part on archival studies at Meissen.

REFERENCES

1. Lister, D. Martin, *A Journey to Paris in the Year 1698*, London (1699).

2. Schulle, W., and B. Ullrich, "Ergebnisse Gefügeanalytische Untersuchungen an Böttger porzellan," *Silicattechnik*, vol. 33, pp. 44–47 (1982).

3. Wildenstein, Paul, "Manufactury Commission Report" (WA 1 A 24a/312 ff). Cited in Walcha, *Meissen Porcelain*, p. 440 (1980), and by Engelhardt in *Johann Friedrich Böttger—Inventor of Saxon Porcelain* (1837).

4. Brongniart, Alexandre, *Traite des Arts Céramiques*, two volumes, 2nd ed., Paris (1854).

5. d'Entrecolles, Pere, 1712 and 1722 letters published in translation in R. Tichane, *Ching-te-Chen*, pp. 51–128, New York State Institute for Glaze Research, Painted Post, N.Y. (1983).

6. de Reaumur, R. A. F., "Idée Generales des Differentes Manières dont on Peut Faire la Porcelaine, et Quelle Sont les Véritables Matièrres de Celles de Chine," *Mem. Acad. Sci.*, pp. 185–204 (1727); "Second Memoire sur la Porcelaine, on Suite de Principes qui Doivent Conduire dans la Composition des Porcelaines de Differens Genres," *Mem. Acad. Sci.*, pp. 325–344 (1729).

CHAPTER 10

A BOUCHER SOFT-PASTE UNGLAZED BISQUE SCULPTURE—LA DANSEUSE

*T*he sculpture illustrated in Plate XXII and Figure 10.1, made at Vincennes in 1752 after a design of François Boucher, is one of the first series of unglazed bisquit figures to be made in soft-paste porcelain. It resulted from the collaboration of a highly regarded painter with what was to become the royal manufacture at Sevres and is an early example of the conscious use of ceramics as an art medium. François Boucher, an established artist and member of the Academie des Beaux Arts, produced a drawing for *La Danseuse*, which was modeled by an unknown sculptor, perhaps Pierre Blondeau, at the factory of Vincennes. Another painter, Jean-Jacques Bachelier, had come to Vincennes from the Academie des Beaux Arts in 1749 and was made the factory's artistic director in 1751. In a memoir written in 1781, Bachelier claims credit for the idea of producing unglazed bisquit sculpture similar to marble and for doing a series of pastorals by Boucher. It has also been suggested that Boucher did the pastorals at the request of Madame de Pompadour, one of his patrons, who had a financial interest in the porcelain manufacture at Vincennes. It was at about this time that she had commissioned Boucher and the sculptor Falconnet to do similar figures in stone for her chateau at Crecy.

Prior to the production of the Boucher figures, ceramic figures were

179

Figure 10.1. *La Danseuse,* modeled at Vincennes in 1752 after a design by François Boucher, was one of the first series of unglazed bisquit figures made in soft-paste porcelain. Earlier glazed figures were not as precisely molded. "La Danseuse" represents the attainment of full technical competence in the production of French soft-paste porcelain, together with the introduction of recognized artists as participants in French ceramic manufacture. The bonnet has been restored. (Courtesy of the National Musée de Céramique, Sèvres, France, no. 20-069.) (See also Plate XXIII.)

usually glazed and did not have either the precise form expected of sculpture or the appearance of accepted sculpture materials such as white marble. *La Danseuse* is an unglazed bisquit figure made of soft-paste porcelain, and is delicate yet precise in form with the white, grainy translucent appearance of marble. And it is shaped as though in marble, complete with the supportive elements at its base of that would have been necessary to support the upper part of such a statue in stone. By the standards of most Baroque and Rococo art, *La Danseuse* is quite simple in composition; the frontal view of a young girl is emphasized by the symmetry of her arms and costume, the bonnet that frames her face, and the horizontal detail of her bodice, all of which are balanced over her forward right foot. The action of the figure resides in the forward leaning stance of the dancer combined with the arc made by the motion of the left foot, and is carried upward in the drapery of the skirt and around to the head. Although one's first impression of the statue is of a straightforward, simple piece, it actually epitomizes many of the design and compositional devices common to Rococo sculpture, in which action is emphasized at the expense of a central area of focus.

The soft-paste porcelain of which *La Danseuse* was made was the first commercial European equivalent to the Chinese white translucent porcelains that were imported into Europe in large quantities during the seventeenth century. The invention of soft-paste porcelain in France is often attributed to Edme Poterat and his son, Louis Poterat of Rouen, who received a royal privilege to manufacture porcelain in 1673, but no verified sample of their porcelain is known. The first certain production was at St. Cloud, perhaps of porcelain invented by Pierre Chicaneau as early as 1677, but undoubtedly produced by his widow and her new husband, Henri Trou, beginning about 1695.

An Englishman, Dr. Martin Lister, visited the St. Cloud factory in 1698 and was told that the first success had been achieved three years earlier after 25 years of experimentation. Lister reported, "I did not expect to have found it in perfection, but imagined this might have arrived at the *Gomroon ware*, which is, indeed, little else but a complete vitrification; but I found it far otherwise, and very surprising, and which I account part of the felicity of the age to equal, if not surpass, the Chinese in their finest art."[3] Production of similar ware began at Chantilly in 1725 under the patronage of Louis Henri de Bourbon, Duc de Conde. After having worked at St. Cloud and then at Chantilly, the DuBois brothers received the support of Marquis Orry de Fulvy, brother of the Comptroller General of Finances, to establish a manufactury at Vincennes. Their initial results were not very successful, but François Gravant was able to supply the factory with an exceptionally white and translucent body material in the early 1740s. Orry de Fulvy died in 1751, and there were financial difficulties. Louis XV, under the influence of the art-loving Madame Pompadour, renewed the privilege of the manufacture and arranged that a well-known chemist, Jean Hellot, president of the Academy of Sciences, should record the factory's manufacturing secrets and processes. In 1753 the king became a principal shareholder, and in 1756 the factory was transferred to a new building at Sèvres, where it remains in operation. Hellot's notes, which have been preserved in the Sèvres archives, provide detailed information as to the methods and formulas being used in 1752.

While there is no documentary evidence as to exactly how soft-paste porcelain ware was invented, it certainly is derived from the tradition of Near Eastern quartz-frit-clay compositions combined with methods used for faience manufacture in a way similar to the earlier Medici porcelain described in Chapter 7. In 1698 Dr. Lister was told that at St. Cloud they "made a thing not unlike frit for glass to be wrought up with the clay." By the middle of the eighteenth century, the process of manufacturing soft-paste porcelain used in the several factories near Paris was a fully developed and well-controlled ceramic technology. Hellot describes how soda ash, sea salt, potassium nitrate, silica, and lime (or gypsum) were milled together and heated for 30 hours or more at the back of the firebox under the hearth of the kiln to form a white opaque product. This process reacted the alkali and quartz to produce an alkali silicate glass containing residual quartz, which was mostly transformed into other crystalline forms of silica, tridymite, and cristobalite. This sintering technique is the same as that used to make majolica and faience glazes and glaze colors since the tenth century, and was also used for the Medici porcelain manufactured between 1575 and 1587. After 1750, calcined alum, a hydrated potassium aluminum surface, was added to the batch as a further source of potassia and alumina.

The glass formed in this sintering process had a high alkali content, and since sometimes not all of the alkali reacted to form insoluble glass, the sinter was washed with boiling water to remove any residual soluble alkalies. (Soluble alkalies would migrate to the surface during drying, causing defects in the bisque firing.) The sinter was then milled wet with the addition of 16.5 percent white limestone and 8.3 percent of a washed, decanted, calcareous marl clay from Argenteuil. This clay contains particles that are very fine in size, and it has been described as "very precious" because of its great plasticity. After settling, decanting the clear liquid, partially drying, and wedging, the body was stored for some months in wooden barrels, where the fermentation of organic constituents increased its plasticity and made it ready for use. The body could be molded as is, but for throwing and turning, a solution of black soap and parchment glue was added to give it the necessary green strength. Because of its relatively low green strength, thrown ware requiring final turning was trimmed in the bone-dry rather than leather-hard state.

La Danseuse, the bisque sculpture shown in Plate XXII and Figure 10.1, was assembled from eight individually molded parts. The details of the assembled figure were then modeled and incised. There are differences in the finished pieces produced from such molds because of the possible variations in joining and finishing. Four eighteenth century examples of *La Danseuse* are known; they differ in the design of the pitcher or watering can, details of dress, and tilt of the head. The example illustrated here is on display at the Museé National de Ceramique at Sèvres. *La Danseuse* was one of several figures designed about 1750 by painter Boucher,[6] and produced at the Vincennes factory in 1752. (The Vincennes factory became Sèvres when it moved to its present site in 1753–1756.) The technique involved, as noted, having a sculptor make models of the drawings. Then a plaster mold from the sculpted clay model was used to make a master piece mold, from which working molds were cast for production. Since each piece of the mold had to be lifted cleanly, without any undercuts preventing release, the figure was skillfully divided into parts, and eight working molds, each with several sectional parts, were used to produce *La Danseuse*. A late eighteenth century mold for this figure remains, in worn but usable condition, at the Manufacture Nationale de Sèvres.

For each of the eight sections of the figure, a thin slab of the plastic body was first rolled out over a wet leather surface. The thickness of the slab was controlled by rods placed beneath the outer edges of the roller. After removing excess water and smoothing with a metal rib, it was pressed into the dampened plaster mold, first with a sponge, and then with the fingers. The thickness was built up with bits of clay as necessary, guided by a needlelike tool to gauge thickness. The front and back of the torso were formed separately, partially dried, and the edges trimmed. The halves then were roughened by incising a crosshatch pattern, coated with a layer of slip, pressed together, and allowed to set for about half an hour before removal from the mold. Figure 10.2 shows the torso halves just before being pressed together. The head with two sections of the working mold removed is shown in Figure 10.3.

The figure was assembled from the eight separate molded pieces, each of which has a linear drying shrinkage of about 3–4 percent. Any difference in drying rate between the parts would cause differential shrinkage and thus cracks to develop at the joins. Slow drying and an attempt to equalize the water content of the parts were achieved by aging the separately molded pieces for many hours in a humidity-controlled cabinet. Then the separate pieces were pressed and worked together, and joined with slip, using the same technique as illustrated in Figure 10.2. Joining of the arms, which are attached at both ends, presented a particularly difficult problem. The feet were molded with an inset that fits into the base; cracks are more likely to occur between the leg and dress than at the foot because of the larger contact area and greater amount of slip used. After joining the parts together, the entire piece was again placed in a humidity-controlled cabinet and kept there between finishing operations. Even with the considerable care exercised, close examination of eighteenth century figures reveals, almost without exception, small cracks at some of the joins. In Figure 10.1 a crack between two molded parts can be seen where the foot joins the base. There are also many cracks on the internal surfaces.

A radiograph of the piece (Figure 10.4) illustrates some aspects of its construction and some of the difficulties of producing a complex sculpture. The process of forming the torso by pressing 6–10-mm-thick layers (thickness shown at A) in the upper and bottom halves of the mold and joining them leaves two voids in the torso; there is a similar void in the head (B). To obtain better bonding of the head to the torso, a hole was cored into the torso (C), which allowed some of the bonding slip to penetrate and solidify, fixing the lateral position of the head more firmly on the shoulders. The arms were molded as solid pieces in separate molds; two internal elongated bubbles are seen at D. Since the plastic body was rolled out to form a slab at low pressure, residual internal porosity occurred throughout at regions of locally lower density, E, as is typical of ware formed by modeling or molding at low pressure.

Differential drying shrinkage cracks occur where the arms are joined to the body, but also in the head and where the tree trunk is joined, as seen in the radiograph at F. These defects are very common and result from nonuniform water content and subsequent differential drying shrinkage. They are seen in almost all eighteenth century ware. (In modern production of complex sculpture, superficial cracks such as these are often filled with dental cement.)

After assembly a great deal of forming and finishing remained to be done in the damp state to remove mold lines and incise and model the final sculpture under the watchful eyes of the sculptor. Once finished and dried, problems of distortion during firing existed since there was another 9–12 percent linear firing shrinkage with which to contend. The finished figure was designed to lean forward, but for firing, a wedge-shaped support of the same composition as the unfired body was placed under the base to tip the figure back to a vertical position. Even so, the figure shown in Figure 10.1 leans further forward after firing than it did originally. For more complicated sculptures, posts of the same composition as the body were used for support to prevent slumping or distortion during firing. These supports were separated from the sculpture itself with a mixture of finely ground quartz and gum arabic; this cements the assembly together in the dry state, but can be brushed off after firing when the kiln is opened. An elaborate support system is necessary for such sculptures. The ware was fired for periods of up to 90 hours at temperatures of about 1050°C.

During firing a marblelike surface and translucency developed, which were enhanced by polishing the surface with a sandstone abrasive. The resulting texture has a fine-scale roughness that scatters the reflected light,

Figure 10.2. N. Depierre, chief molder at the Manufacture Nationale de Sèvres in 1984. With slip applied to the halves of the torso of *La Danseuse*, he is ready to press them together to form a single hollow piece—one of eight separately molded parts of the figure.

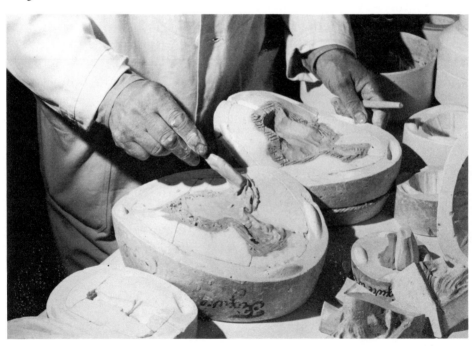

as shown in Figure 10.5, to give a soft diffuse reflectivity rather than the mirrorlike specular reflection that would make the piece look greasy or glossy. Actual determination of the surface roughness in the laboratory with a special instrument shows that it is very similar to the texture of frosted glass.

Many attempts must have been made to produce dense, white porcelain using a melted glaze frit together with a white clay, and most must have suffered from the short firing range described for the Medici porcelain in Chapter 7. The success of the French soft-paste formulation resulted from the high lime content and the low alumina content achieved by using only 8 to 10 percent clay; this was made possible by the excellent plasticity of the limey clays of Argenteuil. A typical composition is 73 percent silica, 15.5 lime, 3.2 sodium oxide, 3.5 potassium oxide, 1.5 magnesia, and only 0.6 iron oxide and 2.1 percent alumina. We can represent this composition on the phase diagram of Figure 10.6, which shows that the constituents present at a firing temperature of 1050°C are the cristobalite form of silica,

Figure 10.3. The head of *La Danseuse* is molded as a single piece in a sectional mold made of eight separate parts carefully fitted together. The mold illustrated is of late eighteenth century manufacture.

Figure 10.4. Radiograph of *La Danseuse* illustrates the wall thickness *A*, the hollow torso and head *B*, the cored hole at the neck to provide support for the head *C*, bubbles in the molded arms *D*, porosity in the molded clay *E*, and cracks at joins resulting from differential drying shrinkage *F*. (Courtesy of F. Drilhon, Laboratoire de Recherche des Musées de France, Musée de Louvre, Paris, France.)

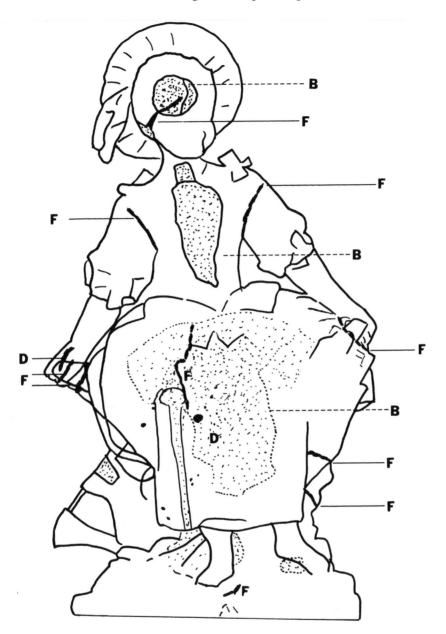

Figure 10.4. Radiograph of *La Danseuse* illustrates the wall thickness, the hollow torso and head *B*, the cored hole of the neck to provide support for the head, bubbles in the molded arms *D*, porosity in the molded clay *E*, and cracks at joins resulting from differential drying shrinkage *F*. (Courtesy of F. Drilhon, Laboratoire de Recherche des Musées de France, Musée de Louvre, Paris, France.)

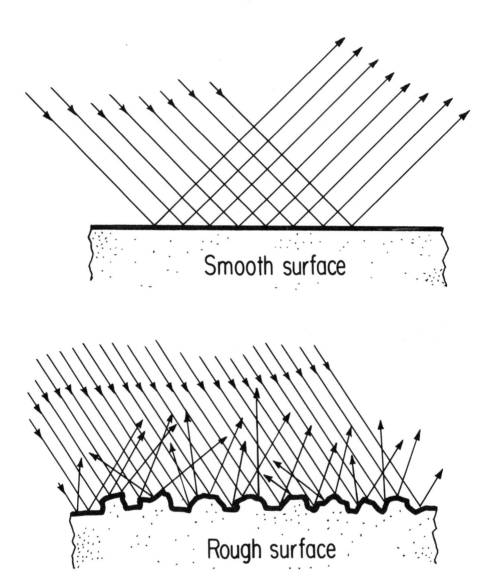

Figure 10.5. The surface roughness of bisque porcelain is more similar to that of frosted glass than to a smooth glass surface. This gives a diffuse soft reflectance from the surface rather than a greasy or glossy look.

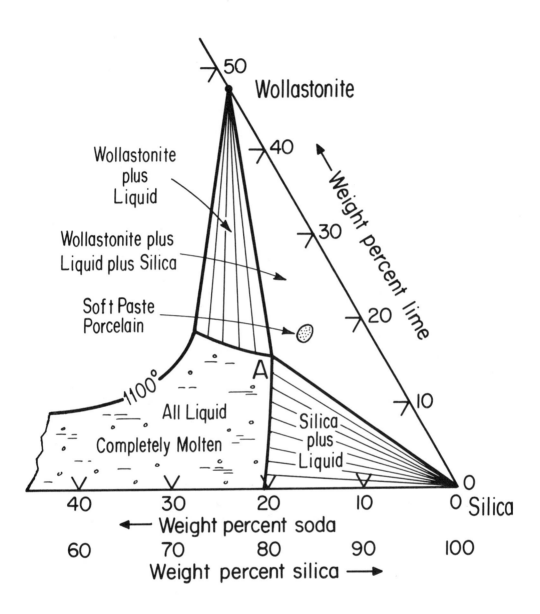

Figure 10.6. Phase diagram for the Na_2O-CaO-SiO_2 system illustrating the isothermal section at 1100°C and the location of a typical French soft-paste porcelain, which at equilibrium is a mixture of cristobalite, wollastonite, and liquid A. As the temperature increases, the amount of liquid increases, but its viscosity also increases, leading to an increased allowable firing range.

wollastonite (calcium silicate), and a viscous siliceous liquid. If the temperature is increased or lowered a bit, the amount of liquid increases, but its composition changes to include more lime and less soda, tending to make it more viscous. As a result the composition is much friendlier with regard to variations in firing temperature than had been its predecessors. Also, in the intervening century, the precision of temperature control in the range 1050–1100°C had been much improved.

The resulting microstructure shown as Figure 10.7 consists of cristobalite grains, some of which have an inner residual core of quartz, together with fine-grained blocky wollastonite particles immersed in a silicate glass matrix. It is a structure that is quite analogous to the quartz-mullite-glass microstructure of the K'ang-Hsi porcelain described in Chapter 8. Light passing through the body is scattered most strongly by the small grains present that are closest in size to the wavelength of light. How effective they are depends on the refractive index of the particle and how close that value is to the value of the glass matrix. If these values are very close, the mixture will be almost transparent; if they are far apart, the mixture will be opaque. For the soft-paste microstructure, the relative values for wollastonite and glass are closer than the values for mullite and glass. As a result soft-paste porcelain is even more translucent than its hard-paste porcelain counterpart.

When the quartz changes into cristobalite during firing, the resulting cristobalite grains consist of a number of crystals. Fracture tends to occur through and around these polycrystalline grains rather than through the glass matrix. The fracture surface of soft-paste ware thus tends to be less smooth than that of hard-paste ware, and it has a lower strength and a greater susceptibility to break when subjected to sudden temperature changes. The better strength of the hard-paste variety may have been part of the reason that the manufacture of soft-paste porcelain at Sèvres was abandoned in 1804, although the technical director at the time, Alexandre Brongniart,[8] wrote, "The modeling of the old artificial soft-paste porcelain was very complicated as well as unhealthy; because the paste did not have sufficient plasticity to be roughly shaped on the wheel, it was always formed on a mold and turned when dry, and the resulting vitreous alkaline dust was dangerous to the pulmonary organs."[8]

Even though soft-paste porcelain is difficult to form and is not as strong as the hard-paste type, it has a whiteness, translucence, and surface texture that made it an ideal material for unglazed bisquit sculpture. *La Danseuse* represents the beginning of the eighteenth century tradition of outstanding artists working with porcelain as an art medium.

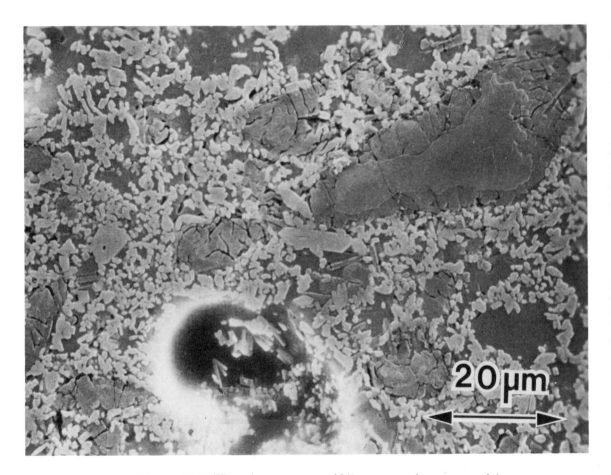

Figure 10.7. The microstructure of Vincennes soft-paste porcelain shows extensive cristobalite development. Some of the cristobalite grains have remnant quartz cores. Wollastonite precipitates from the glass phase during long firing. A typical microstructure consists of about 15 percent cristobalite, 30 percent wollastonite, and 55 percent glass (1000X).

RECOMMENDED READING

Brongniart, Alexandre, *Traité des Arts Céramiques*, Dessain and Joira (1977) (facsimile of 1877 edition). Brongniart was a well-known geologist before he was appointed a technical director of the Sèvres manufacture. His treatise covers the whole range of late eighteenth and early nineteenth century methods.

Kingery, W. D. (ed.), *Ceramics and Civilization—I*, American Ceramic Society, Columbus, Ohio (1985). This book contains "Steps in the Manufacture of the Soft-Paste Porcelain of Vincennes According to the Books of Hellot" by A. d'Albis, and also "Eighteenth Century French Soft-Paste Porcelain" by W. D. Kingery and D. Smith, the definitive works on the composition and manufacture of soft-paste porcelain.

REFERENCES

1. d'Albis, Antoine, *Faience et Pate Tendre*, Dessain et Tolra, Paris (1979).

2. Preaud, Tamara, and Antoinette Fay Halle, Catalogue de l'Exposition "Porcelains de Vincennes," Edition des Musees Nationaux (1977).

3. Lister, Martin, *A Journey to Paris in the Year 1698*, London, 1699, pp. 138 ff.

4. Auscher, E. S., *A History and Description of French Porcelain*, William Burton translation, Cassell & Co., Ltd., London, 1905.

5. Granger, M. A., "La Porcelaine Tendre," *Soc. d'Encouragement pour l'Industrie Nationale*, no. G13, pp. 1–55 (1913).

6. Savill, R., "François Boucher and the Porcelains of Vincennes and Sevres," *Apollo, CXV*, no. 241, pp. 162–170 (1982).

7. Bachelier, J. J., *Memoire Historique*, Paris (1781).

8. Brongniart, Alexander, *Op. Cit.*

CHAPTER *11*

A WEDGWOOD JASPERWARE

The attractive chocolate pot shown in Plate XXIV and Figure 11.1 was made about 1790 of a truly innovative new composition developed by Josiah Wedgwood in 1774 and first produced in 1775. The overall shape of the pitcher is that of a teardrop in which a ground line is provided for the figures supported by vertical stripes that give visual depth to the bas relief and roundness to the form. The scene was designed by a well-known artist, Lady Elizabeth Templeton. The pot was produced in a modern factory whose purpose was to manufacture high-quality ceramics at a profit. The Wedgwood jasperware is included primarily to illustrate the successful transition of ceramics from being mostly objects of interest to royal collectors to products for the general public, as a result of the development of factory-produced fine ornamental wares. And nothing was more influential in bringing this about than the genius of Wedgwood.

The eighteenth century was a period of remarkable and intense development in ceramics. At the beginning of the century, potteries were a craft institution. The development of soft-paste porcelain at St. Cloud and its subsequent manufacture at Vincennes and Sèvres transformed the situation in France; discovery of the secret of hard porcelain by Böttger at Meissen changed the nature of ceramic manufacture in Germany; in England, building on the careful body preparation methods and salt-glazing techniques introduced by the Dutch Eler brothers in the late seventeenth century, Staffordshire potters developed a high-quality white, semivitreous, salt-glazed ware based on plastic ball clay mixed with a substantial fraction of white ground flint. The growing field of experimental science was both

Figure 11.1. One of the most remarkable innovators of the eighteenth century was Josiah Wedgwood, inventor of "jasperware," which began production in 1774. This chocolate pitcher from about 1790 was made of cobalt-blue jasper dip with applique bas-relief decoration based on a design by Lady Elizabeth Templeton, and modeled by William Hackwood. The tip of the spout has been repaired. (Courtesy of the Collection of the Metropolitan Museum of Art, New York.) (See Plate XXIV.)

learning from and contributing to ceramics development. When Père d'Entrecolles sent back samples of Chinese raw materials to France, chemist Rene Antoine Farchault de Reaumur was assigned the task of analysis. By 1751, when there was a royal interest in the manufacture at Vincennes, it seemed entirely appropriate for Louis XV to send Jean Hellot, president of the Royal Academy of Sciences, to evaluate and record the secrets of porcelain manufacture. When kaolin was discovered in France, it was quite normal to have academicians and famous chemists Macquer and d'Arcet assigned to work out techniques for manufacturing hard-paste porcelain. By the end of the eighteenth century, ceramics had come to be viewed as a product of chemical science. At the same time, the ceramic industry played an influential role in the industrial revolution and development of factory systems in England and on the Continent. The adaptablity of the industry in utilizing new techniques such as transfer printing was a com-

Figure 11.2. This design by Lady Templeton, who created designs for Wedgwood in the period 1783–1789, was modeled by William Hackwood. He worked for Wedgwood from 1769 to 1832, beginning at the age of 12.

plete change from the workshop mentality that existed at the beginning of the century.

A leader in this revolution was Josiah Wedgwood, born in 1730, the last child of a family of 12. The Wedgwood family had been potters in Staffordshire for four generations; his father died when Josiah was nine years old, and it was only natural that he should leave school and work for his brother Thomas in the potteries. Later, in 1744, he was formally apprenticed to Thomas for five years, and continued to work for him until 1752. After a brief partnership with Harrison and Alders of Stoke, he entered into a new partnership with one of the outstanding potters of the Staffordshire area, Thomas Wieldon. During his apprenticeship Josiah had contracted smallpox and suffered a permanently disabled leg, it eventually was amputated, in 1768. This may have been an advantage, as it made it easier for him to continue his self-education and his interest in experimentation. By the time he went into partnership with Wieldon, he had developed enough experimental competence that it was part of their agreement that Wedgwood should not be required to disclose his secret formulas. During that partnership Wedgwood began, and maintained throughout his life, a record book in which he kept details of numerous experiments to improve both bodies and glazes.

Wedgwood left Wieldon and went into business for himself in 1759, with a cousin, Thomas, working with him as a paid potter. The earliest production was mostly salt-glazed stoneware, but fine green and yellow glazes and a clear glaze were developed, along with a body composition containing a fraction of white clay and finely ground flint that withstood sudden alterations of heat and cold and could be manufactured easily. This cheap and attractive creamware, much of which was decorated with transfer printing by Sandler and Green in Liverpool, became the foundation of Wedgwood's success. With it he established both a domestic and profitable export trade in dinnerware.

Soon after he began his own business, Wedgwood met Thomas Bentley, who was then a member of a firm that became Wedgwood's Liverpool agents. Bentley was a confirmed neoclassicist and influenced Wedgwood in that direction. In 1767 Bentley and Wedgwood became partners in the manufacture of ornamental wares, and a new factory was opened in June 1769. Much of the first production was an improved unglazed black stoneware, already being produced in Staffordshire, which Wedgwood called "basalte." To decorate the Basalte ware, Wedgwood invented smooth, durable matte glazes, which he referred to as encaustic painting, done in imitation of antique Greek and Italian wares. A tan-colored unglazed bisquit stoneware prepared from Staffordshire clays was referred to as "cane ware." These wares were sometimes cut and often polished in the manner of semiprecious jewelry.

Wedgwood continued to work on experiments aimed at developing new compositions he hoped could be colored in imitation of gemstones, and would take a polish as well. He also experimented with hard porcelain, but the use of Cornish clay and Cornwall stone for that application had already been patented in England. By 1773 he had developed a fine white terra-cotta body that contained a small fraction of barium carbonate. During the next year, he carried out dozens of experiments using a substantial fraction of this material; it occasionally gave excellent results but was highly variable and impossible to control. The exact chemistry of barium-containing minerals was uncertain, but he tested a form a barium sulfate, called *cawk*, which was abundant in Derbyshire where it occurred along with lead deposits. By September 1774 he had developed a new composition for the production of a porcelain-like, white, unglazed bisquit body based on a large fraction of barium sulfate. Shortly thereafter he found that this composition readily incorporated cobalt oxide to make an attractive blue. His enthusiasm and confidence in these initial results were such that in January he wrote to his partner Bentley, "The only difficulty I have is the mode of procuring and conveying incog the raw material. . . . I must have some before I proceed, and I dare not have it in the nearest way nor undisguised." Wedgwood kept his compositions in code in his experiment book (barium sulfate is 174), and various formulas were undoubtedly tried. In a February 6, 1776, letter to Bentley, he gives the preferred jasper composition as one part of flint, six parts of barium sulfate, three parts of potter's clay, and one-quarter part of gypsum. At that time his mixing was done in secret and the nature of this composition was closely guarded. The formula given, however, is in agreement with the analysis carried out by us.

Jasperware production was initiated in 1775 on a limited basis for cameos using mostly a blue body, but also sea green, dark blue, gray, lilac, and yellow. In the early months of production, it was found that the colored ground of the cameo tended to bleed into the white surface relief during firing; in addition, Wedgwood complained about the sharp increase in the cost of the cobalt oxide used as the blue pigment. The manufacturing method was changed to a process in which the basic shape was white jasperware, which was subsequently slip-coated in a colored jasper dip. This was found to give an increased range of subtle color and to avoid some of the previous problems with solid jasper bleeding. Our microchemical analysis of slip-coated blue jasperware made about 1790 indicates that the bleeding was controlled by having more clay and less barium sulfate in the pigmented dip than in the body. This led to somewhat lower translucency in the dip, which was acceptable but would not have done for a solid-colored body. Another motive for changing production to the jasper-dip process was probably to achieve more economical production. Jasperware could be better mass-produced with the ware made in a single white composition and then dipped in different colors as the market demanded. One of Wedgwood's marketing techniques was to display two different colors side by side to see which was more attractive to customers, and using this information as a basis for planning production. In addition, since smaller amounts of the colored material had to be mixed and milled, colors could be varied more easily while production of the white body continued uninterrupted.

For the chocolate pot illustrated in Plate XXIV and Figure 11.1, the basic shape was thrown in white jasperware, dried leather-hard, turned to final dimensions, and coated with the cobalt-containing blue slip when nearly dry. After the dip layer was applied and dried, the ridge under the figures was cut away and the lower part of the body, with its vertical fluted pattern, was done on an engine-turning lathe with an eccentric back-and-forth motion in synchronization with the rotation. Wedgwood had seen an engine-turning lathe at work in Matthew Fulton's factory for metals in 1763 and installed his own during that same year. Engine turning requires a great deal of skill and cooperative effort by the assistant, who turns the lathe while the turner hand-holds the cutting tool.

The design for the bas relief was drawn by Lady Elizabeth Templeton, from which William Hackworth modeled the form in clay. From the clay a "block" mold in plaster, which was a replica of the original subject, was first made and carefully reworked. "Working" molds in which the jasperware body was actually formed were made as the third step in the process. The plastic body was pressed into the working mold and then transferred to the surface of the pitcher as illustrated in Figure 11.2. This was first done only on flat surfaces because of difficulties with buckling and shrinkage. For successful application of such bas relief decoration, it is essential that the water content and subsequent shrinkage of the base layer and the applique be nearly identical to prevent cracks from developing. Close examination of this object and most similar ware shows a few small areas where there has been a slight separation. However, microscopic examination of a polished section indicates that the structure of the underlying body, the blue slip, and the sprigged decoration are extremely well bonded one to another; Figure 11.3.

As can be seen in Figure 11.3, there is a lesser amount of the white particles of barium sulfate and more porosity in the blue cobalt slip layer intermediate between the white body and white sprigged layer. Chemical analysis of a tiny sample with an electron microprobe confirmed the lower barium content and higher alumina and silicate value, corresponding to an increased clay content in the blue slip. The cobalt oxide concentration in the slip was only 0.36 percent, so it seems very unlikely that the cost of this ingredient was the main reason for going over to jasper dip. A changed dip composition to decrease bleeding and more efficient organization of mass production must have been more important considerations.

During firing at a temperature of about 1250°C, a portion of the barium sulfate reacts with the clay component to form a barium-aluminum-silicate matrix containing residual barium sulfate particles. The matrix is a mixture

Figure 11.3. Scanning electron micrograph of body-slip-applique shows extremely good bonding. The white areas are barium sulfate; the gray areas are regions of fine celsian, and barium silicate in glass; the black areas are pores (100X). The central layer of cobalt-blue slip was made with more clay and less barium sulfate than the upper applique and lower body.

of a glass with fine particles of barium-aluminum-silicate (celsian) and barium silicate (sanbornite), as illustrated in Figure 11.4. Experimental studies have shown that with the levels of clay used by Wedgwood, about half the barium sulfate remains unreacted. Other studies have shown that for the eighteenth century jasperware composition, a liquid phase forms and significant firing densification begin at a temperature in the range 1120–1230°C. If one compares the resulting microstructure with the K'ang Hsi porcelain discussed in Chapter 8 or the Boucher soft-paste porcelain described in Chapter 10, one notes striking similarities. In each case there is a substantial fraction of a refractory constituent (here barium sulfate), and fairly large particles of an inert constituent, in a matrix of very-fine-particle crystals concentrated in a viscous liquid silicate that solidifies as a glass. As with these other porcelains, the refractive indexes of the barium-rich constituents in jasperware are close enough to one another that good translucency results.

Wedgwood's experiments and his detailed experimental notes were a model for the experimental methods of the time, and he was intensely interested in contemporary scientific developments. Wedgwood had a lasting friendship with the chemist Joseph Priestly and became one of several contributors who provided annual grants to Priestly, making it possible for him to devote his time to chemical research. James Keir, another friend of Wedgwood, was the English translator of the French dictionary of chemistry by P. J. Macquer. This apparently was the inspiration for Wedgwood to begin the manufacture of mortars and pestles and special bits of chemical apparatus, which he provided to Priestly and others free of charge. Wedgewood became a member of the Royal Academy and frequently attended meetings of the Lunar Society of Birmingham, which included among its members Priestly, James Watt, Matthew Bolten, and Erasmus Darwin.

Like other potters of the period, Wedgwood withdrew small samples from the furnace during his firings to ascertain the state of the ware. He went further, however, and carried out extensive experiments to develop a reproducible (even though very nonlinear) "pyrometer," which consisted of small cylinders of a standard clay composition for which the shrinkage, after they were removed from the furnace, was measured on a special brass scale. He carried out extensive experiments in calibrating this scale and read a scientific paper on his "ceramic pyrometer" to the Royal Society in May 1782. In retrospect his calibration was woefully poor, but at the time, high-temperature thermometry was scarcely developed and Wedgwood's pyrometer remained the standard of comparison for more than 30 years.

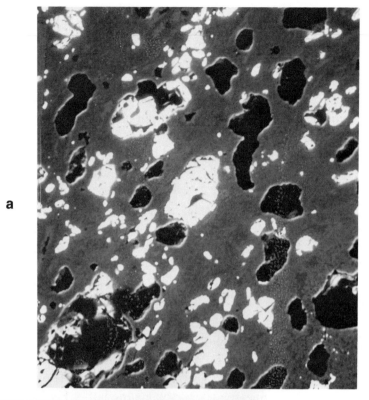

a

b

Figure 11.4. (A) The large white grains are unreacted barium sulphate; the black areas are pores
(400X). (B) the extremely fine-grained barium-
alumino-silicate matrix material seen at higher
magnification (4000X) is determined by x-ray
diffraction to be a mixture of submicrometer
crystallites of celsian (BaO-Al_2O_3-$2SiO_2$) and
sanbornite (BaO-$2SiO_2$) in a glass matrix.

The 1712 and 1722 letters of Père d'Entrecolles describing the Chinese manufacture of porcelain in the reign of K'ang Hsi were probably less helpful in formulating compositions than is generally believed. Nevertheless they were widely disseminated and described the method whereby specialists mined the material, and others milled and purified it. It was then supplied to special factories for the manufacture of the ware, with still other specialists operating the kilns, and separate shops where painters and enamelers decorated the products. These reports had a great influence on Wedgwood, who is generally given credit as the first European to organize a factory along similar lines. His method of dividing the manufacturing process into many separate parts, and allowing each worker to become expert in only one phase of production, was revolutionary at the time. His objective was to increase the performance of each worker in a particular area and thus reduce the requirement for overall skill. He also was concerned with trade secrets; each workshop at the Etruria factory had a separate entrance so that workers would not be exposed to more than a limited number of valuable secrets. It is said that a trap door beneath his study was the only entrance to a workroom where he experimented with new formulations. He was quick to take up new manufacturing techniques, such as the use of the engine lathe. He had wares painted at Chelsea and took advantage of the transfer printing method invented in Liverpool to have ware decorated there. (Transfer printing involves printing from an etched copper plate onto paper, and then transferring the design from the paper to the curved surface of the pottery.) These manufacturing innovations led to the production of uniformly high-quality ware at a minimal cost, resulting in quality and price advantages that made his product extremely competitive.

Along with the development of new compositions and manufacturing methods, Wedgwood and Bentley were extremely effective in their marketing techniques. A friend from Staffordshire, Deborah Chetwynd, had an appointment at court, and seems to have been instrumental in obtaining for Wedgwood his first royal commission. Queen Charlotte ordered a creamware tea and coffee service and a dinner set from Wedgwood in 1765 and allowed him to proclaim himself "potter to Her Majesty," a title prominently displayed above his London showroom. He described his cream-colored ware as Queensware thereafter. In 1773 Wedgwood received an order for a large service from Empress Catherine of Russia. The service consisted of 952 pieces of Queensware hand-painted in a purple enamel with 1244 different British scenes. The painting was done at the Chelsea studio and the ware was ready for the opening of Wedgwood and Bentley's new showroom in Soho, which took place in July 1774. It was on display for more than a month, and was visited by Queen Charlotte and others. Wedgwood's showroom had turned into a fashionable salon, which enormously enhanced the reputation of his wares. This thoroughly modern marketing technique of using endorsements by famous people is common today, but was novel and effective at the time. Wedgwood also displayed pieces of different colors together, thus allowing the customers' choices to determine his levels of production.

In the increasingly competitive entrepreneural economy of the eighteenth century, Wedgwood was one of the leading figures to have the foresight, and the willingness to expend the necessary effort, to promote the interest of the industry in general. In the early days of Staffordshire manufacture, transport of raw materials in and products out was accomplished with pack animals. Clearly, quantity production could not be achieved without better transportation. Wedgwood was instrumental in organizing a potters' association to push for adequate roads, and even more important, development of a canal system. Staffordshire potters agitated successfully in Parliament for the creation of the Mercy-Trent Canal, which opened in 1760 and ensured that Staffordshire would remain the center of English pottery production. Wedgwood was also instrumental in banding the Staffordshire potters together to eliminate patent barriers in the use of Cornwall clay and Cornish stone. These efforts were successful, and Wedgwood subsequently proposed that an industrial association of potters be set up to sponsor research on the development of new compositions and to study the use of china clay and Cornish stone in pottery. This was the first attempt to form such an association for joint research. A bill of organization was prepared, but discord developed over the method of payment and the association never materialized. Wedgwood was not upset by this, since at the time he was well along in his efforts to develop his new jasperware. In November 1775 he wrote to Bentley that "our experimental work expired in embryo last night. We could not settle the question whether the partners in company should pay separately or jointly . . . I shall now begin with the materials [i.e., jasperware] in earnest. I scarcely thought myself at liberty do do so whilst the partnership plan was in agitation."

In addition to earthenware and clay-based stoneware, both of which were made by Wedgwood, the principal luxury ceramics of the time were tin-glazed earthenware, soft-paste porcelain from France, and hard-paste porcelains of China and Germany. The addition of barium sulfate-based jasperware as a unique new composition was a remarkable achievement in the application of experimental research by Wedgwood. In addition to his development of modern factory manufacturing methods that gave rise to inexpensive wares and marketing techniques far in advance of anyone else, Wedgwood was clearly the leader in transforming the manufacture of luxury ceramics from an artisan-centered activity to mass production for the general public. His employment of outstanding artists for the design work together with the skilled modeling done in his factory resulted in a uniformly high-quality ware that was quite remarkable.

It is clear that the eighteenth century fostered the best-quality jasperware—smooth of body and uniform in texture, the wares were not fused to the point of greasiness or gloss, but neither were they dry and chalky. The ornamentation and modeling are well defined and sharp; hand undercutting was used to bring out design details and the contrast between relief and ground. However, demand for this ware eventually outpaced production capabilities, and this, coupled with increased competition, was responsible for a slight decrease in quality in subsequent manufacture. The popularity of Wedgwood's jasperware attracted quick imitation throughout Europe, the most sincere form of flattery, by Wedgwood's competitors.

RECOMMENDED READING

Finer, Ann, and George Savage (eds.), *The Selected Letters of Josiah Wedgwood,* London (1965). Wedgwood's letters give a first-hand glimpse into the way this remarkable man approached his many interests and activities.

Metegard, Eliza, *The Life of Josiah Wedgwood,* 2 vols., London (1865–1866); W. Mankowitz, *Wedgwood,* 3rd ed., Barrie & Jenkins, London (1980). These are the standard biographies of Josiah Wedgwood, full of details about his life and his pottery.

Reilly, Robin, and Savage, George, *The Dictionary of Wedgwood,* Antique Collectors Club Ltd. (1980). This profusely illustrated volume contains complete information about Wedgwood pottery, from decorator Willaim Absolon to encaustic painter Antonio Zucchi.

REFERENCES

1. El Adley, T., D. M. Ibraham, and M. T. Hussein, "Effect of the Main Whiteware Constitents on the Dissociation of Barite," *Ceram. International,* vol. 7, pp. 22–25 (1981); "Barite as a Main Constituent in Whiteware Composition," *ibid.,* pp. 26–30.

2. Russell, R., Jr., C. Valencia, and H. W. Emrich, "Barite in Ceramic Whitewares," *J. Amer. Ceram. Soc.*, vol. 39, p. 73 (1956).

3. Church, A. H., *Josiah Wedgwood*, Seeley & Co., London (1903).

4. Bedford, John, *Wedgwood Jasper Ware*, Walker & Co., New York (1964).

PART ***III***

CERAMIC
TECHNOLOGY

*I*n Chapter 1 we gave a historical overview of the development of ceramic bodies, glazes, decorations, and processes, emphasizing the way in which technology influences visual impact. Each of the objects described in Part II provides a specific example of a specialized technology at work. In this section we present a more general discussion of a few important scientific concepts underlying the technology, along with a description of the basic processes of shaping, firing, glazing, and decorating. Our objective is not to provide calculations or equations, formulas or directions. Rather it is a visualization of why and how the characteristics and requirements of the materials available to a skilled artisan affect the way in which that person shapes, decorates, and fires the ware to attain a particular goal, and the way in which these materials and methods in concert limit or allow achievement of a particular visual effect.

It is important to realize that there is a symbiotic relationship between materials and methods in creating any ceramic masterpiece. Development of new materials almost always demands new methods; new methods most often require materials to be modified. We believe that full appreciation and interpretation of any master work must include an understanding of the relationships among materials, methods, and aesthetic impact. None of our discussion is beyond the understanding of curator, collector, student, or afficionado; none of it requires any special preparation.

CHAPTER 12

SOME UNDERLYING SCIENCE

T he goal of studying ceramic science is to understand why things work the way they do. Since we are concerned with a variety of different materials, processes, and visual characteristics of ceramic masterpieces, there is a corresponding endless variety of scientific principles that may be applicable. For instance, to understand colorants, the physiology of human vision, the quantum mechanics of electronic energy levels, the formation of chemical bonds, crystal symmetries, and a dozen other scientific topics are things we might want to know. The list is a bit overwhelming, and thus, rather than trying to be comprehensive, we have selected three critical themes on which to focus: structure, capillarity, and the processes that occur at high temperatures during firing.

STRUCTURE

In Chapter 1 we introduced the visible level of *macrostructure*, which we can see, touch, and feel; the level of *microstructure*, which we can make visible with modern microscopes; and the level of *atomic structure*, which we can only infer from spectroscopic and diffraction data. Each level of structure results from the materials and methods used to make the ceramic; each affects the ceramic's properties. In this section we concentrate on how these elements of structure affect appearance. First we consider the surface. The microstructure and macrostructure of the surface together determine whether it is smooth and glossy, granular and unreflective, rough and textured, or perhaps a velvet matte. A glossy, glazed surface is smooth and reflective; matte glazes have crystals that disturb the surface smoothness and result in a velvety texture. Larger grain sizes at the surface give a coarser texture and more roughness than smaller grain sizes.

Control of the internal microstructure is equally important. All light that strikes an object either must be reflected from it, transmitted through it, or absorbed within it, and usually is scattered and changes direction in the process. The sum of these processes forms the image we see, although the particular light we use—sunlight, fluorescent, incandescent, candle-light—also influences our perception, and is particularly critical for color matching and color science. We mostly view ceramics in reflected light that is a combination of mirrorlike reflection, in which light is reflected back in a single path from a smooth glossy surface, and diffuse scattered reflection, in which light interacts with a heterogeneous material and is scattered and reflected in many directions (see Figure 12.1a). If we hold porcelain in front of a light, we can also view it in diffuse transmission, as illustrated in Figure 12.1b. The amount of specular mirrorlike reflection from a flat ceramic surface is determined by the composition of the glaze. For an alkaline glaze or window glass, about 5 percent of the incident light is reflected; for a high-lead or high-barium glaze, the specular reflectance almost doubles and greatly increases the glaze brilliance. High specular reflection is also obtained by metallic surface layers, most often burnished gold or platinum, but also copper or silver lusters.

Only a small fraction of incident light is reflected at the surface. Most of it enters the glaze and is reflected back by the underlying body beneath a transparent glaze or scattered in all directions by particles of semiopaque or opaque glaze. For a clear glaze, visual effects are determined by the absorption of the glaze, the reflection of the underlying body, and any underglaze decoration. To obtain bright glaze colors, the underlying body should be white and have a good reflectivity.

For many glazes it is desirable to have good opacity or covering power, which requires that the light be diffusively reflected back to the surface before it reaches the underlying body; particles immersed in the glaze must scatter effectively and diffusely reflect the light. For other glazes the desire is that they be lightly opacified or translucent; particles immersed in the glaze should be fewer, or be less effective at scattering and diffusely reflecting the light.

The opacity given by pigment particles depends on their concentration, relative index of refraction, and size. For maximum light scattering and opacifying power, the particles should have a refractive index far different from that of the matrix material and a particle size close to the wavelength of light, that is, about half a micrometer—a fairly small size. A number of materials are compared with an alkaline glaze and a lead glaze medium in Table 12.1. We can see that bubbles of air would be extremely effective if they could be kept sufficiently small, which they cannot. Arsenic and antimony compounds such as lead antimonate (Naples yellow) and calcium antimonate (white) are very effective opacifiers that have been used since antiquity. The most commonly used material now is titania, which also is very effective but has only become available in the past 50 years. Tin oxide offers a good combination of effectiveness as an opacifier and insolubility in glazes; it forms the basis for a whole class of tin-opacified wares, and is probably the material of choice for most potters. Wollastonite and anorthite, which form in Song Dynasty glazes, are not so effective; they create a soft translucency rather than dense whiteness. This is the case for

TABLE *12.1*

Effectiveness of Particles in Rendering a Glaze Opaque Is Determined by the Relative Index of Refraction.*

		Relative Refractive Index	
Opacifier	*Refractive Index (n)*	Alkaline Glaze $(n = 1.5)$	Lead Glaze $(n = 1.65)$
Tin oxide	2.0	1.33	1.20
Air	1.0	1.50	1.65
Antimony oxide	2.1	1.40	1.27
Arsenic oxide	2.2	1.47	1.33
Lead antimonate	2.2	1.47	1.33
Lead arsenate	2.2	1.47	1.33
Calcium antimonate	2.2	1.47	1.33
Calcium phosphate	1.63	1.09	1.01
Sodium fluoride	1.34	1.12	1.23
Quartz	1.55	1.03	1.07
Cristobalite	1.48	1.01	1.11
Mullite	1.65	1.09	1.01
Anorthite	1.58	1.05	1.04
Wollastonite	1.61	1.08	1.02
Titanium oxide	2.58	1.72	1.56

*When value is close to 1.0 the glaze remains nearly transparent; when the value is high and the particles are small, the glaze is opaque.

undissolved quartz particles, too, which also suffer from being quite large. The combination of the surface reflectance and microstructure-controlled internal scattering leads to reflectance patterns that are a combination of specular and diffuse reflectance, such as shown in Figure 12.1.

For porcelains to be translucent, it is necessary that the scattering particles not be too effective—as is the case with mullite and quartz in the alkali glass matrix of hard porcelain, and with wollastonite and cristobalite in the alkaline glass matrix of soft-paste porcelain. In each instance the pore size is several micrometers in diameter and the pore concentration is low so they do not have much effect on translucency. In contrast earthenware bodies have a large amount of fine porosity in the submicrometer-particle range, which affords extremely effective light scattering and keeps the translucence low.

The color of the light reflected through the glaze surface by the body or by particles within the glaze depends on the presence of ions that absorb energy in the visible spectrum. (Ions are atoms that have an electrical charge because an outer electron has been lost or gained.) The principal ions responsible for color are transition elements such as titanium, vanadium, chromium, manganese, iron, cobalt, nickel, and copper. In the transition elements, it is the outer electrons that absorb light and these electrons are much affected by the surroundings. As a result copper in an alkaline glaze is blue, in a lead glaze is green, and in lead-alkali glazes is turquoise in color. Iron ions may have either two or three outer electrons, are usually surrounded by six negatively charged neighbors, and may have many different colors. In goethite ($FeOOH$), a yellow ocher, or when the iron is substituted for aluminum in iron-bearing clays, the resulting color is yellow. When iron is surrounded by oxygen ions in red ocher, (hematite, Fe_2O_3), the color is a deep red. Iron sulfides are black (FeS) or yellow-green (Fe_2S_3). Iron chlorides are yellow-green ($FeCl_2$), or black ($FeCl_3$). The mixed iron oxide, magnetite (Fe_3O_4), is a deep black. Its structure, called spinel, can accommodate a variety of different transition elements, is stable to quite high temperatures, and is insoluble in glazes, and so forms the basis for many colorant stains such as cobalt-aluminate spinel blue.

The coloring ions or colored pigments or opacifier particles are illustrated in Figure 12.1 as distributed throughout a continuous glass medium, as is also true of the crystalline grains in porcelain. The glass medium is a material that has been cooled in the liquid state without crystalizing and can be visualized as a completely solid liquid—its constituent ions are in a random arrangement, but are locked into position so that all fluidity has disappeared. Glasses are hard, transparent, solidify with smoothness, and

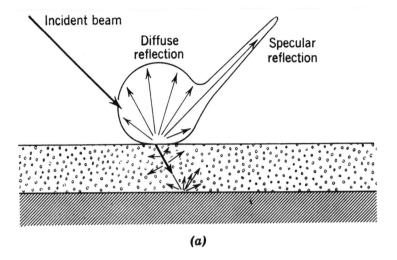

(a)

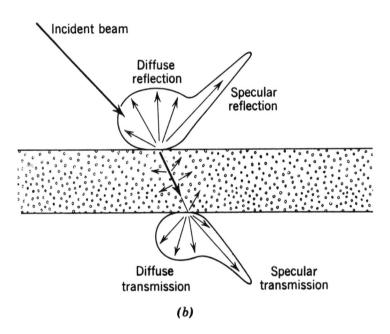

(b)

Figure 12.1. (a) Specular and diffuse reflections and transmission result from surface and internal reflections and light scattering of a glaze or enamel. A completely specular reflection is mirrorlike, while a completely diffuse reflection is velvetlike. (b) If a translucent porcelain is viewed in transmitted light, one is concerned with the diffuse and specular transmission.

fracture with a smooth or rippled surface. When they are heated, they become more fluid very gradually, changing from solid to butter to honey to a syrupy consistency as the temperature is raised. Glasses commonly occur in silicates, which are the principal constituent of ceramics. When liquid silicates have a relatively high silica (SiO_2) content—above 60 percent or so—they usually cool to form glasses. This occurs because the small silicon ion is always surrounded by four oxygen ions that join to other silicons to form a continuous random arrangement of atoms in the "rigid liquid" glass.

Glasses made from pure silica melt at much too high a temperature. As discovered by Count von Tschirnhaus with his burning lenses in 1698, the addition of lime, CaO, acts as a *flux* and lowers the melting point. Alkalies such as soda and potassia are even more effective in lowering the melting point. These fluxes serve as an added source of oxygen, so that there are too many oxygen atoms for all the silicon-oxygen units to be bonded at every corner—as a result, the network is weakened, becomes more open, and is liquified at a lower temperature (Figure 12.2). Too much alkali breaks up the network, and it becomes soluble in water. A good balance for most glasses is achieved with 60–70 percent silica, but a lesser amount can be used when combined with other oxides that act as glass formers, such as lead oxide, boron oxide, bismuth oxide, and phosphorous oxide.

As illustrated in Figure 12.2c, crystals are different from glasses. In crystals all the atoms line up like soldiers on parade and are stacked in ordered three-dimensional arrays. When they are heated, they remain in a regular array until they reach the melting point, when they quite suddenly "fall out" into a random arrangement. The nature of the crystalline arrangement is critical to the material's properties. Quartz, for example, is tightly packed, hard, and strong. In contrast the clay minerals are made up of regular layers and form as tiny platey particles able to slip and slide over one another readily. Just as a marching band can rearrange the pattern of its formation by each member taking only a step or two, alternate crystalline patterns can occur for the same composition in some special cases. One of these special materials is silica, of which the most common form is quartz. Upon heating there is a shift of atoms at 573°C to form a new structure, beta-quartz. This transformation is important for ceramics because the atoms are somewhat further apart in beta-quartz, so that the crystal expands on heating and contracts on cooling. In flint nodules expansion on heating causes stresses between the grains of quartz and makes it easy to grind calcined flint into a powder that is suitable as a constituent of fine white earthenware. The contraction on cooling of quartz in hard porcelain causes cracks in the surrounding glass matrix and is responsible for the typically smooth fracture surfaces observed. At a temperature above 900°C, quartz dissolved in an alkaline liquid may reprecipitate as an entirely different crystal structure, cristobalite. This is found in soft-paste porcelains.

The crystal structure and composition determine properties such as the index of refraction values in Table 12.1. As shown there the refractive indexes of the crystalline constituents of soft-paste porcelain—cristobalite and wollastonite—are closer in value to the glass matrix than the crystalline constituents in the microstructure of hard-paste porcelain—quartz and mullite. As a result there is less light scattering and soft-paste porcelain has a softer translucency than the hard-paste variety. The visual difference in fracture is also related to the form of silica present. In hard-paste porcelain, the quartz grains are tiny, tough, single crystals and a smooth fracture takes place through the glass matrix. In soft-paste porcelain, the cristobalite particles have a many-grained "horse's-tooth" structure and fracture occurs between these grains, giving the fracture surface a rough sugary appearance.

CAPILLARITY

Capillary phenomena result from the pressure created by a curved liquid surface. If we pick up a soap film with a wire loop, the film is attached at the edges and the stable configuration is a flat sheet. If we apply gentle pressure by blowing on one side, we can form spherical soap bubbles. If we apply just the right pressure and blow the film out to form a hemisphere, when we stop blowing the extended soap bubble will pop back into position as a flat plate (Figure 12.3). A disturbed surface always moves to become flatter. If we make a smaller loop, we find that we have to blow harder to form bubbles. Glassblowers are familiar with this phenomenon; it takes a lot more effort and pressure to form the bubble than to expand it.

Capillary effects are familiar to most of us from school experiments in which we observed liquid rise in a fine glass capillary tube, as illustrated in Figure 12.4. If we imagine the microstructure of fine clay particles enclosing water films in a plastic body or particles enclosing a viscous silicate liquid during firing, we can visualize this same phenomenon as

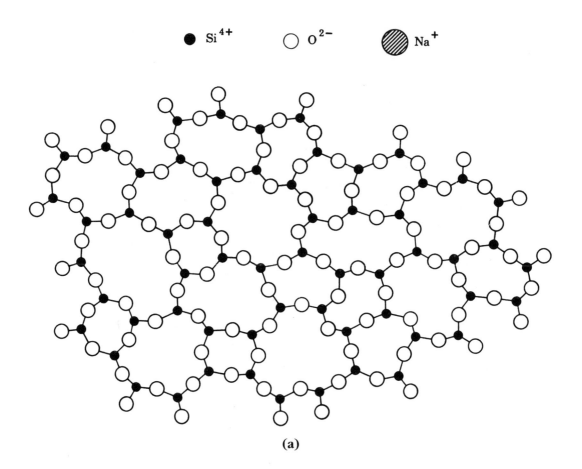

Si^{4+} O^{2-} Na^{+}

(a)

Figure 12.2. (a) The structure of glass is a random silicon–oxygen network. (b) When a flux such as soda increases the oxygen–silica ratio, the melting point is lowered as the network structure is broken down. (c) In a crystal all the constituents are ordered into a regular repeating structure.

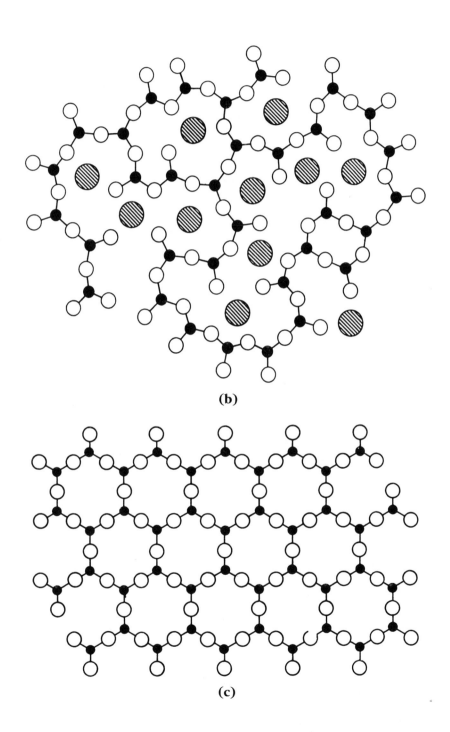

(b)

(c)

shown in Figure 12.4b. The capillary effect occurs at the junction between particles where the tendency of the curved liquid surface is to suck the particles together as in Figure 12.4b. This is precisely the case when the last liquid is drying from a body after forming, and also when the first liquid forms during firing. When just the right amount of liquid is present to fill space between particles, they are held in contact by the capillary effect where they meet at the surface as shown in Figure 12.4c. This is what happens in a drying body in the leather-hard state and in porcelain during high-temperature firing. In a wetter state (Figure 12.4d), the particles are separated by lubricating liquid films and the liquid at the surface has a flatter configuration, thus exerting less pressure; deformation is easier, but so is the danger of slumping.

Capillarity is the principal factor affecting how one shapes a clay body paste, and it is the major force effecting the consolidation and densification of a body at high temperature during firing. One of its main characteristics is that its force becomes stronger as the degree of curvature increases, that is, as the capillary size decreases. This is why fine clays are needed for ceramics. A second important characteristic is that it is quite a weak force. As a result we can shape clays with our fingers, and do not need the

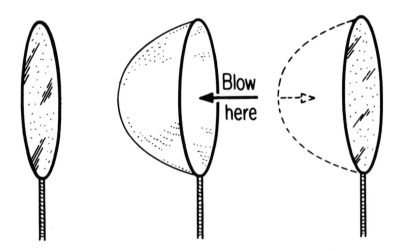

Figure 12.3. (a) A soap film held on a bubble-blowing ring forms a flat sheet of minimum surface area. (b) Steady, gentle blowing extends the film to become a hemisphere. (c) If we stop blowing, the half-bubble springs back toward its concave side. All curved surfaces tend to move in this direction.

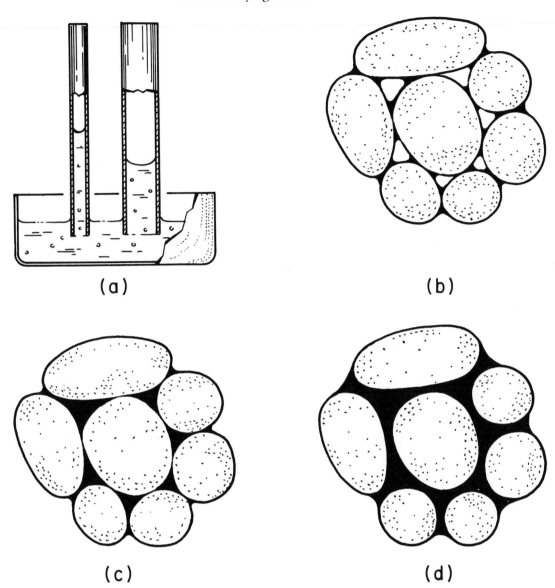

Figure 12.4. (a) One of the classic ways to measure surface tension is to observe the rise in a fine glass capillary tube. (b) The same capillary pressure is exerted by the first liquid to form on heating earthenware and the last liquid to leave a drying solid. (c) When the liquid just fills spaces between particles in contact, we have reached the leather-hard point in drying and a maximum capillary effect sucking particles together during firing. (d) More liquid allows thicker films and easier flow of particles during shaping, but may also allow slumping.

hammer blows used to forge metals. However, because the capillary forces are weak, both the shaping and firing of ceramics are extremely sensitive to our choice of materials and how we treat them. At the leather-hard state, the capillary pressure holding clay particles in contact is about 50 pounds per square inch—about half the pressure that can be exerted by a person pressing hard on the ball of the thumb. The pressure applied by rubbing the surface with a burnishing stone is enough to rearrange the particles and densify a surface layer. With clay with the larger liquid content that produces the workable plastic state necessary for throwing, the pressure needed to raise a cylinder at the potter's wheel is about a third of this, perhaps 10 or 15 pounds per square inch. Because the surface tension of glass is about five times that of water, the forces that suck together the particles of a body during firing are in the range of 50 to 500 pounds per square inch.

The tendency of liquids to wet solids is also a capillary effect. Liquid glazes flow out over the surface much as water does over a clean glass. In contrast to glass, wax has a low surface energy and a drop of water placed on it tends to ball up, as illustrated in Figure 12.5b. This is the physical basis for using waxes and similar materials in preparing resist designs. When the surface of glass has an oily film, as is often the case with a window pane, a liquid drop flowing down it tends to ball up at the lower edge even though the trailing edge is completely wet, as shown in Figure

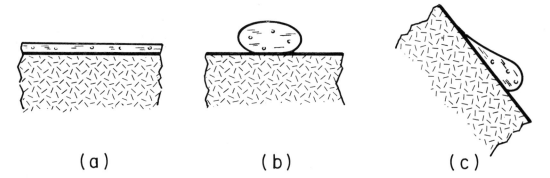

(a)   (b)   (c)

Figure 12.5. (a) Lead glazes spread out and completely wet a surface, also penetrating into the body. (b) A drop of water on a wax surface forms a ball and does not "wet out." (c) On a window pane the advancing edge of a water drop is often seen as not wetting, while the trailing edge wets completely. The same phenomenon occurs with alkaline and lime glazes.

12.5c. This process corresponds to the fault of crawling, in which glazes do not spread out after bubbles or cracks have formed during the application process. We saw an example of this in the Egyptian faience chalice described in Chapter 2. The addition of sodium and calcium to silica tends to increase the surface tension, and alkali-lime glazes are more susceptible to crawling and nonspreading than other compositions. In contrast lead oxide decreases the surface tension of a glaze and lead glazes wet out more effectively and penetrate into the body for better adherence. Lead glazes also form smoother surfaces. The combined advantages of better gloss and better adhesion are powerful reasons to value lead oxide as a glaze constituent.

EFFECTS OF TEMPERATURE

In Chapter 9 we recounted how Count von Tschirnhaus observed that while neither lime nor quartz could be melted alone, a mixture of the two was easily made molten in his solar furnaces by using burning lenses. This was an early observation of the influence of mixing (that is, forming a eutectic mixture) to give lower temperature melting and comes under the rubric of what we now call phase equilibria. An American genius, Professor J. Willard Gibbs of Yale University, laid the foundation for this subject in 1874.

According to phase-equilibrium rules, when we add one constituent to another, the melting point is lowered, as when we spread salt on ice. If we add a third component, the melting point is lowered even more, and with a fourth component, even further; but then it begins to become a bit tricky. A single pure material melts at a single temperature; ice, for example, always melts at the freezing point, 0°C. If we add some salt to ice, a little liquid forms at a very low temperature, about −40°C, but the mixture does not become completely liquid unless the temperature is raised to about −2°C. That is, in mixtures there is a *range* of melting temperature and it is useful to think about the two end points: the *solidus* temperature is the lowest temperature at which any liquid at all is formed, and the *liquidus* temperature is the lowest temperature at which the sample is entirely molten. For our salt–ice example, this melting range would be from −40°C to −2°C. For the Medici porcelain, the melting range was small and it was very difficult to fire that ware without warping or slumping. For triaxial flint-clay-feldspar bodies, which compose fine English stoneware, Chinese porcelain, and European hard porcelain, the melting range is wide and it is relatively easy to fire dense, hard, impermeable ware successfully, as discussed in Chapter 1.

All ceramics of interest to us have several constituents, which mostly affects their behavior at the beginning of the melting process when just a little liquid is formed at the contact points between particles. This is the liquid that glues the particles together to form the sort of structure found in earthenware after firing at 700°C, as illustrated in Figure 12.4b. Aside from helping us understand that a bit of liquid is present at quite low temperatures because of the many constituents that make up the body, and that the amount of this liquid remains small until a temperature is reached at which the major constituents begin to melt, the phase-equilibrium diagrams seen in ceramic texts are not of much use with regard to earthenware pottery; they are mostly limited to two or three constituents. For porcelain and stoneware fired to a higher degree of vitrification, three-component phase diagrams can be quite useful, as discussed in Chapter 1 and in connection with particular objects.

As the temperature of a porcelain or a glaze is raised, an increasing amount of viscous liquid forms; that is, the solids present are dissolved into the solution. Naturally enough, as the temperature is lowered, the reverse occurs. If we cool a liquid silicate rapidly, however, there is not time enough for this to take place, and we end up with a solidified liquid—a glass. If we cool more slowly, a larger amount of solid will form; that is, the *rate* of cooling can be a major factor in the visual appearance of ceramics. In Jun glazes we first form an emulsion during slow cooling, and this results in a blue color; subsequently calcium silicate crystals form to give a cloudy appearance. If a sample is cooled quickly, there will be neither opalescence nor cloudy whiteness; if the sample is cooled even more slowly, too many wollastonite crystals form and the glaze becomes white rather than translucent, as shown in Plate IXb. In contrast celadon glazes have a composition in which precipitation is less likely during cooling; to maintain the concentration necessary for translucency, the kiln master must underfire so that a clear liquid does not result in the first place. Both of these are tricky operations to do perfectly; as a result, there is a wide range in the optical quality of Song Dynasty glazes.

When high temperatures are reached during firing, atomic vibrations are intensified and become stronger as the silicate liquid matrix of a porcelain becomes more and more fluid. At the normal firing temperature, the consistency of the silicate matrix is like very stiff honey, but the fluidity is extremely temperature sensitive; near the firing temperature, it is multiplied some 100 times for each 100°C temperature change. This change, together with the increased liquid content at the higher temperature, explains why only a few compositions are suitable for producing a porcelain in traditional kilns. Most slump when even slightly overfired. The glazes flow over the surface like light to heavy cream, and their response to temperature is less dramatic. The fluidity of a glaze changes by a factor of three when the temperature changes by 100°C. Thus temperature control for satisfactory glost firing is less difficult than for firing porcelain. This explains in part why a sixteenth century practice that was suitable for producing tin-opacified glazes on an earthenware body found porcelain production such a challenge.

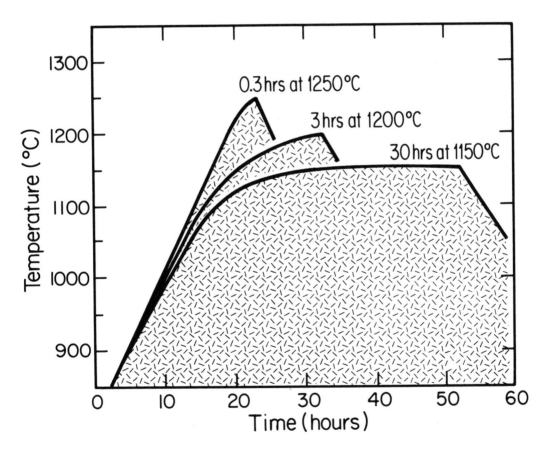

Figure 12.6. Because firing processes take place faster at higher temperatures, the three time–temperature firing procedures will have equivalent results.

For the same reason of increased atomic mobility, the rate of reaction between glaze and body to form a layer of anorthite, the rate at which quartz grains dissolve in a glaze or body, and the rate of formation of wollastonite in a soft-paste body all proceed about ten times more rapidly when the temperature is increased by 100°. The combination of increased speed of reaction and increased silicate fluidity at the higher temperature means that equivalent firing results can be obtained either by holding the sample for a long time at a lower temperature or for a shorter time at a higher temperature. If a fine earthenware or porcelain can be successfully fired in three hours at 1200°C, practically the same result can be obtained in 30 hours at 1150°C—or, if a sufficiently long time were allowed, say 3000 hours, (or four months), at 1100°C. On the other hand, the firing temperature were increased to 1250°C, only 20 minutes would be required, but control of the process would be difficult. Thus a wide range of different time and temperature envelopes can lead to equivalent results, as shown in Figure 12.6.

RECOMMENDED READING

Kingery, W. D., H. K. Bowen, and D. R. Uhlmann, *Introduction to Ceramics*, John Wiley & Sons, New York (1976). Comprehensive, but more advanced than appropriate for all but the most intrepid. Requires college-level chemistry and mathematics.

Lawrence, W. G., and R. R. West, *Ceramic Science for the Potter*, 2nd ed., Chilton Book Co., Philadelphia (1982). Much of this is specifically aimed at potters, but the discussions of science are widely applicable.

Norton, F. H., *Elements of Ceramics*, Addison-Wesley Press, Cambridge, Mass. (1972). Another excellent discussion of materials, methods, and products.

CHAPTER *13*

SHAPING AND FIRING

T he historical development and uses of different body formulations, shaping methods, and firing procedures were discussed in Chapter 1 and applied to individual objects in Part II. The more systematic presentation of this chapter will make clear that superficially different formulations and procedures are based on only a few technological concepts. Visualization of these concepts is the best way for a nonspecialist to understand the technology.

CERAMIC BODIES

At the beginning of ceramic production and most commonly thereafter, local availability of raw materials determined body formulations. As artisans became more sophisticated and special objectives were defined, appropriate materials were actively sought. While there is an infinite variety of ceramic body and glaze formulations that a careful ceramic technologist might wish to differentiate, there are only a few conceptual variations.

Permeable Earthenware

Deposits of clay with sufficient plasticity for forming ceramics are found almost everywhere; they have been shaped and fired since village life first developed in the neolithic period 8,000 to 10,000 years ago. Almost from the beginning, clays have been purified by thoroughly mixing them with water, occasionally adding a bit of potash to obtain a good suspension, and settling out coarse particles, sticks, and stones. Most of these clays are easy to fire into hard, porous products because they contain considerable iron, lime, soda, potassia, and other impurities. These form a small amount of viscous liquid that acts as a glue, holding the particles together at the contact points at temperatures as low as 700°C. The resulting structure is similar to that illustrated in Figure 12.4b.

Body formulations are not very critical, but clay selection is neither arbitrary nor unimportant. Nonplastic minerals present in the clay or intentionally added (sometimes called temper) affect results in three different ways. The first is to decrease the drying shrinkage; sandy clays or clays with a lot of nonplastic added have less drying shrinkage, which makes the joining of separately formed parts easier, as well as the modeling of figures and, indeed, almost all shaping. Second, the workability of clays with a high alkali content is improved by adding limestone or clamshells as temper; for limey clays saltwater additions often do the same. Third, nonplastic additives can alter the contraction on cooling; limey clays and clays with a high quartz content have a higher contraction on cooling so that there is less tendency for glazes to craze or spall. Piccolpasso in his 1557 work *Three Books of the Potter's Art*[1] recounts that limey clays are better for decorated majolica while red-burning clays (which have a lower thermal expansion and contraction) are preferred for ordinary kitchen ware.

Iron oxide is a principal constituent of permeable earthenware clays, and it was found by about 6000 B.C. that color could be controlled by adjusting the furnace atmosphere—plenty of air to maintain the iron oxide in the red oxidized hematite form (Fe_2O_3 has 1.5 oxygen atoms for each iron), or a smokey flame to reduce iron oxide to black magnetite (Fe_3O_4 has only 1.33 oxygen atoms for each iron). Using a fine-particle-size, alkaline-rich iron-containing clay as a slip, ware was often fired in a reducing atmosphere to a temperature at which the painted slip vitrified to a glossy black surface while the body remained gray. Then the kiln was opened to the air and cooled in an oxidizing atmosphere; the permeability of the body allowed oxygen to penetrate its interior and reoxidize the iron to form a pink or buff color while the impermeable black glossy decoration remained black. Close examination of a wide variety of ware made near the eastern Mediterranean during this and much earlier periods shows that the technique was in wide use. As shown in Plate IIIb, areas where the painting is thin show traces of a reddish tint corresponding to partial reoxidation on cooling. Roman terra sigillata used a slip in a similar way but with the firing done entirely in an oxidizing atmosphere to form a glossy red surface.

White Quartz-Paste Bodies

As a principal body ingredient, quartz has two advantages. First, when flint nodules or quartz pebbles are crushed, the resulting powder is pure and white. Second, the contraction of quartz on cooling is large, so that it is compatible with alkaline glazes. Each of these characteristics contributed to the success of Egyptian faience, which was simply powdered quartz bonded and coated with alkaline glass formed by the efflorescence of soluble salts. Later, white Islamic wares were made with a mixture of ground quartz, premelted glass frit, and a highly plastic white clay. These compositions were the historical forebears of Medici porcelain and soft-paste porcelain in which the quartz constituent was a lesser fraction of the whole.

Vitreous Stoneware

By the end of the Shang Dynasty in China (about 1000 B.C.), furnace temperatures had reached 1200°C. At this temperature proto-porcelain stoneware based on an iron oxide-containing clay-mica-feldspar-quartz mineral raw material could be fired to form a strong, high-density, impermeable gray-colored stoneware. This success resulted from the gradual parallel development of lowered iron content and increased kiln temperature over several centuries. A similar product was made in Germany during the fourteenth century using natural deposits of clay containing feldspar, quartz, and other impurities. Toward the end of the seventeenth century, similar ware, but more refined, was made in England. In 1708 Böttger introduced a stoneware based on a mixture of red clay and a limey clay, and the practice of adding gypsum or lime as an auxiliary flux became widespread. Stonewares of various depths of color are based on mixtures of clay, quartz, feldspar, lime, and iron oxide in various ratios. In all of them, fine mullite crystals in an alkaline silicate glass are an essential element of the microstructure.

White Porcelain

When kiln temperatures in China reached about 1300°C during the Han Dynasty (221 B.C.–220 A.D.), it was possible to obtain a dense vitreous body with an iron content of less than 1 percent, and a white porcelain resulted. It was made from china stone, a natural mixture of quartz, mica, feldspar, and kaolin. This general composition later developed into the "triaxial" mixture of quartz, feldspar, and kaolin that became the basis of European hard-paste porcelain and semivitreous whitewares. At Meissen Böttger used a higher firing temperature and found that a clay-gypsum mixture with low iron content would also make a satisfactory white porcelain. Later, in Europe, feldspar was used as a constituent in addition to gypsum or lime. In all of these wares, a mixture of fine mullite crystals in an alkaline glaze, often associated with quartz grains, is the essential microstructure. A quite different white porcelain was the short-lived Medici material, which used a manufactured alkali-silicate "sinter" together with quartz and a white clay. This approach was improved and perfected with the development of soft-paste porcelain, which also employed an alkali-silicate sinter but used it in conjunction with a lower clay content and added lime. The essential microstructure was a mixture of cristobalite grains and fine wollastonite crystals in an alkaline glass matrix.

Modifications of these basic formulas were the subsequent use of a mixture of bone ash (calcium phosphate) and feldspar with clay and quartz called English bone china, and a mixture of melted frit and feldspar with clay and quartz called Beleek porcelain.

Slips and Glazes as Part of the Body

Thus far we have described the development of white quartz-paste bodies and white porcelains as grounds for monochrome glazes or polychrome decoration. Many quartz-paste bodies were made from less pure materials that were yellow or gray in color and covered with a thin, white, surface layer prepared from a pure white quartz. A similar result was obtained by the formation of a white reflective layer under the glaze of buff or gray Chinese stoneware attributable to the reaction between the glaze and the body. Another technological solution was to apply an opaque white glaze to cover a buff or gray earthenware body, as was done for majolica. Piccolpasso describes how a mixture of finely ground quartz and calcined lees of wine was sintered under the furnace to form a hard rocklike mixture of alkali silicate glass, which was milled together with a calcined mixture of lead oxide and tin oxide (pure tin when calcined gives a gray powder). The tin glaze applied to the surface of the earthenware served as the ground for the painting. After painting, the ware was often coated with a lead glaze; the tin-glaze layer was as much a part of the body as of the decoration. A variety of clay slips have been used to alter the surface color of clay bodies or as decoration, with or without subsequent glazing.

Summary

There are an infinite number of specific combinations and formulations of ceramic bodies, but they can be divided into five generic families on the basis of the materials used and microstructures achieved.

1. Permeable earthenware
   Pottery
   Terra-cotta figures, amulets, tokens, etc.
   Brick and tile
2. White quartz paste
   Egyptian faience
   Islamic quartz-clay-frit ware
3. Stoneware
   Quartz-clay-feldspar
   Böttger red ware (clay-gypsum)
4. White wares and porcelain
   Hard-paste porcelain (quartz-clay-feldspar)
   Semivitreous wares (quartz-clay-feldspar)
   Böttger porcelain (clay-gypsum)
   Wedgwood jasperware (clay-barium sulfate-gypsum)
   Medici porcelain (quartz-clay-alkali silicate sinter)
   Bone china (quartz-clay-feldspar-bone ash)
   Beleek porcelain (quartz-clay-feldspar-frit)
5. Engobes and underglaze coatings
   Clay on clay
   Quartz on quartz
   Tin glaze on earthenware

SHAPING AND DRYING

The shaping of ceramic masterpieces depends on the plastic properties of the clay. A body is "plastic" when some minimal force must be applied to change its shape; once this force is exceeded, deformation continues until the pressure is removed. The pressure just sufficient to induce deformation is called the "yield point," which must be sufficiently high that slumping and distortion do not occur under the force of gravity, but not too high for the forming method used. Ware becomes stiffer (a higher yield point) with less water and softer as more water is added, as shown in Figure 13.1. "Fat" clays allow extensive deformation over a wide range of water content. "Lean" clays have a smaller range of extension. "Short" clays have a smaller range of water content over which they can be shaped. It might seem desirable always to use clays of the best plasticity, but we shall see later that these clays are too slippery and have such a large drying shrinkage that they are impractical.

The clay minerals are very widespread special materials composed of platey particles of hydrated aluminum silicates that have a fine particle size—individual particles are in the range of 0.1–10 μm (0.001–0.01 mm), as illustrated in Figure 1.8. When mixed with water, a lubricating film develops between particles that allows them to slide over one another. These films are thin, typically about 0.05 μm, but still appreciable in terms of the particle size of the clay. The thickness of the water films and their lubricating effectiveness depend on a complex way on the type of impurities, organic soil acids, and amounts of salts or lime present in the clay.

As would be expected for natural minerals formed from different starting materials, and often transported long distances before being deposited, the microstructure of clays is quite variable, as shown in Figure 13.2. Micaceous sericite clay such as used in classical Chinese bodies at Ching-te-Chen are platelets several micrometers in dimension, similar to kaolin; limey clays from Greece and Italy that are mostly illite (another clay mineral) are of finer particle size but still very plately; while montmorillonite (another clay mineral) from the Near East is even finer, but somewhat less platey. The finest-particle-size clays such as bentonites are more plastic than the larger-particle-size kaolinites. Limey clays tend to be more workable than salty ones, but there can be problems. It is generally found that the yield point is increased if calcium ions are present. When there is too much sodium or potassium in the form of soluble carbonates or silicates, the water films become thicker and a substantial decrease in the yield point makes it impossible even to shape the clay. Some clays with an excessive lime content are improved by the addition of saltwater. Finding a proper balance depends very much on the particular clay and its impurities. The fine-particle-size clays such as bentonites, which have a higher plasticity than larger-particle-size clays, are also more susceptible to the influence of impurities.

The lubricating water films between particles that are necessary for plasticity are bad actors when it comes to drying shrinkage. A clay with

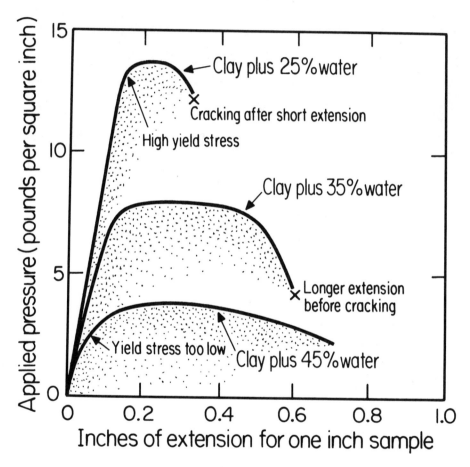

Figure 13.1. A higher force is necessary to deform a stiff clay with lower water content. As the water content increases, so does the total extension before cracking. In addition to water content, the shape of these curves is affected by particle size, particle shape, amount and type of nonplastic additions, salt and lime content, and rate of deformation.

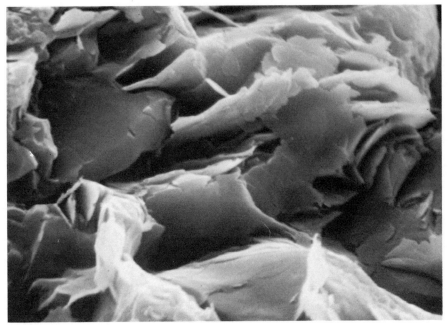

a

Figure 13.2. (a) Unwashed china stone (petuntse) from Ching-te-Chen, China, consists of micaceous sericite clay platelets less than a micrometer thick but several micrometers across. (b) A calcerous illite clay from Corinth consists of much finer platey particles and has a much higher impurity content (potassia, calcia, iron, titania). (c) A limey montmorillonite earthenware clay from Hajji Firuz, Iran, is even more impure and has a finer particle size but a less well-developed platey nature. (All at 1000X.)

b

c

a particlel size of 1 μm (0.001 mm) has about 100,000 particles, and thus also 100,000 water films, along a 10-cm length. If these are each 0.05 μm thick, the linear shrinkage required to eliminate them during drying is about 5 percent. As the water content decreases during drying, capillary pressure of the water at the surface sucks the particles together, as discussed in Chapter 12, until they come almost into contact at the leather-hard state (Figure 12.4). When the surface becomes light in color as the surface water film departs with a bit more drying, the particles are in contact and there is no further shrinkage or plasticity even though further drying is necessary to get rid of the remaining water. The relationship between shrinkage and water content is shown in Figure 13.3.

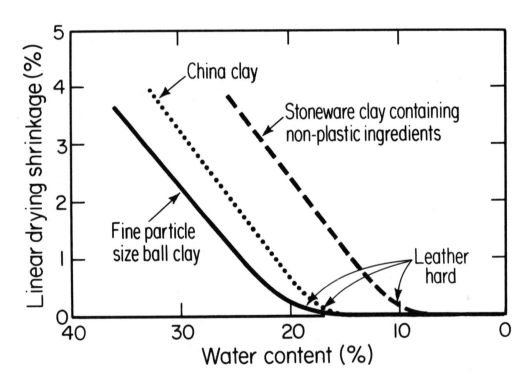

Figure 13.3. As the water content of a plastic clay decreases during drying, there is a shrinkage corresponding to the lost water that continues slightly beyond the leather-hard condition.

Preparing the Body

Natural clays are formed under a variety of geological circumstances. More often than not, there are other constituents present in the mined clay so that washing the clay to settle out twigs and larger particles is necessary to form a workable batch. Many clays are formed under strong geological compaction and can be broken up only slowly into their ultimate particle size to develop their latent plasticity. If these clays are exposed to the weather (wetted, dried, perhaps even frozen and thawed), this decomposition occurs more readily. When organic materials are present or the clays are stored in a wooden cask, fermentation results in a "sour batch," which also tends to separate the clay particles.

Although pure clay may have good plasticity, its high shrinkage during drying can cause warping, and even cracking, such as seen on the surface of a dried mud flat. A corrective for this is to add larger-grain-size non-plastics, or "temper," which have fewer water films and therefore less drying shrinkage. As temper is added, the workability is decreased somewhat, but about half the clay can easily be replaced with nonplastic, thus cutting the drying shrinkage by about half. The nonplastics also reduce the firing shrinkage; in addition, they influence the contraction on cooling. Quartz and lime in particular increase the cooling compaction and eliminate some of the cracking and spalling that otherwise would occur with alkaline glazes. It takes skill and experience to get the mixture right. If the nonplastic particles are too large, the shrinkage of the clay during drying may open up fissures adjacent to the temper particles and cause weakness in the ware after it is dried and fired. For thick-walled crudely formed ware, we can accept higher amounts and larger sizes of nonplastics than for finely finished ware. High lime concentrations lead to stiffness and shortness in some clays, while sodium salts provide greater extensibility. If there is a choice, additions of lime or gypsum are generally preferred to an excess of alkali; this is probably one of the reasons why crushed shell has been a popular temper, even though its firing characteristics are quite bad. (Another reason is the ease of crushing heated shell.)

For contrived bodies such as French soft-paste porcelain and Islamic quartz paste, as little as 10 percent of a highly plastic clay is sufficient for workability by skilled artisans; this is also true of Chinese bodies, which contain no highly plastic ball clay. However, these bodies are "short" (i.e., workable only over a limited water content), so they have to be formed rapidly, and correctly the first time. They do not have the forgiving user-friendly characteristics of bodies used by most modern potters. For fine wares each of the body constituents is reduced to an appropriate particle size by grinding. Assurance that the particle size is satisfactory is usually controlled by screening a slurry through a piece of cloth to eliminate oversize particles. The most typical compositions consist of about 50 percent clay and 50 percent nonplastic, which gives suitable plasticity along with satisfactory drying behavior. Hard porcelain is often made with about 25 percent ball clay (fine particle size, high plasticity), 25 percent china clay (larger particle size, less plasticity), with 25 percent feldspar and 25 percent flint added as nonplastics. However, soft-paste porcelain, which uses a very-fine-particle-size, highly plastic, limey clay, is made with as little as 10–15 percent clay. This is also true for Islamic quartz-frit-clay bodies, to take advantage of the excellent plasticity of fine-particle-size montmorillonite clays.

For any body a uniform water content, wetting of all of the fine particles, and elimination of air bubbles are necessary. This is accomplished by a "wedging" process, which consists of repeatedly shearing the clay. A variety of methods have been used, including standing on the clay and repeatedly shearing it (foot wedging), cutting lumps of plastic clay with a wire and slamming the parts together, beating with wooden mallets, and various hand-kneading procedures. Modern manufacturers use a de-airing method that applies a vacuum to the clay while shredding it and subjecting it to high shearing stresses; then a column is extruded through a die for subsequent forming.

Modeling (Pinch Forming)

The earliest toys, cult figures, and tokens, modern sculpture, Egyptian faience, Song Dynasty dragons, and appliques of all kinds have been hand modeled from plastic clay. For fine detail work, the most important factor is good plasticity. This requires a substantial amount of a well-dispersed clay, often one that has considerable organic material naturally present or formed during aging. Larger sculptures use terra-cotta bodies to which a larger amount of nonplastic is added to minimize drying shrinkage and prevent cracking. Between modeling sessions the work is covered with a wet cloth or stored in a wet cabinet to prevent drying. For shorter periods an area to be worked may be left overly thick and the outer clay later removed prior to shaping the inner wetter material.

There is almost no limit to the fineness or coarseness, crudity or precision, of modeled forms. Undercuts and complicated shapes, rolled strands of clay, paper-thin petals, solid or hollow balls, and all sorts of other shapes can be formed. The use of modeling tools on plastic clay gives an artist great freedom to decorate surfaces and refine shapes. As each work is slightly different, this is not a method for mass production. Modeling tools come in a variety of sizes and shapes that are designed either to push the clay about or to trim it, as required.

Slab and Coil Building

If clay is spread between the hands or rolled out on flat surface to form a slab, such slabs can be assembled into a vessel by pressing or kneading them together. This practice was widespread during the early stages of Near Eastern production, but circular vessels were more often fashioned by laying out a slab of clay as the vessel bottom, turning up an edge all around, and then coiling a long rod of clay (produced by rolling it between the hands) around and around the circumference to build up the wall. In this method, to form a good overlapping joint where the coils or slabs come together, a kneading motion between thumb and fingers is used that requires strength and dexterity. A skilled artisan can build up such a wall very quickly. Less skilled individuals require a softer, more plastic clay and have to build up the wall section by section, allowing it to dry partly between additions, a more difficult process.

For easy rotation the vessel may be built on basket work that can be rotated, on a layer of cloth or piece of pottery or plastic, or on a wheel, which can be quite crude. A thick piece of wood in which a hole has been drilled so that it can be slipped over a post driven into the ground is quite satisfactory; this is sometimes called a "slow wheel," a "tournette," or a "turntable," in contrast to throwing on a fast wheel in which the wall is raised, thus utilizing the centrifugal force of the wheel. If the potter sits on the ground, the tournette can be rotated with one toe as the wall is built up.

Skill resulting from years of practice can lead to quite remarkable effectiveness, as to both speed and precision of form. To increase production speed and obtain better uniformity, potters have invented a number of special ways in which to hold the fingers, brace the body, and use simple tools. With a crude, thick, wooden disk on a post, fairly rapid rotation permits simultaneous coil addition and kneading, which thins the original coil diameter and raises the wall. Ware can be made at a rate not much slower than that of throwing. Guides such as a bamboo ring inserted around the mouth can lead to quite good circular cross sections. Often calipers or other measuring devices are used. In some cases an external template or "quarter mold" of circular section has been used against which the coils are shaped and formed.

The main modern application of coil building has been for large shapes of too heavy a cross section to be thrown on a wheel. Good joining of the added coils is required. Lower sections must be allowed to dry somewhat to develop the yield strength necessary to avoid wall buckling during subsequent forming. If the ware dries too much, differential shrinkage will result and form cracks, so there must be a balance between the rate of clay application and the rate of drying, which can only be controlled through skill and experience.

Shaping with Paddle and Anvil

Local variations in water content lead to variations in drying shrinkage that can easily lead, in turn, to local stresses and cracking. Radiographs of ware formed at low hand pressure always show regions of internal porosity and poor consolidation. Even if visible cracks do not appear during the drying process, the lower density can lead to defects after firing, a difficulty that remains a major problem in modern ceramic production. Particularly during coil construction, when two coils of clay are brought together, there tend to be water layers, contaminants, and oriented clay particles on the surface of each, and so extensive kneading of the join is necessary to achieve good adhesion. To consolidate the body and break up such boundary layers, the application of higher pressures on a stiffer paste than can be manually worked is helpful. To accomplish this, one popular process involves the use of a round stone as an anvil; the clay is beaten toward it with a wooden paddle, often with a rough surface texture to help develop compressive stresses rather than merely thin the point of contact. If this is done with an upward rocking and beating motion, the wall simultaneously is raised and uniformly thinned at the same time that the body is made denser and more uniform. The higher pressure is necessary to deform the stiff paste with its lower water content (see Figure 13.1).

Much the same result is achieved in wheel-thrown ware by ribbing—that is, compressing and extending the wall by simultaneously pressing inward with the hand, or tools, as they are drawn in an arclike motion across the wall.

Molding and Mold Making

For thousands of years, in order to form complex shapes and many pieces of the same size repetitively, clays have been pressed into or over molds carefully constructed of fired earthenware. Used widely in the Mayan and Inca cultures, plaster of Paris (gypsum plaster) replaced earthenware in Europe as the principal mold material during medieval times. Indeed the preparation of plaster-of-Paris molds is a major topic of Piccolpasso's sixteenth century work, *Three Books of the Potter's Art.*[1] By molding separate parts and sticking them together with a slurry of the body material, complicated shapes can be formed. Those who are used to thinking of ceramics in terms of the potter at a wheel almost always underestimate the extent to which historically important luxury wares have been formed by molding. Except for the Song Dynasty pieces, molds were used in producing every one of the ceramic masterpieces we illustrate in Part II.

Crude shapes such as brick and tile are often formed in wooden box molds, many of which have the mold sides fitted over a raised platform attached to a separate bottom plate. A lump of clay of about the right size is thrown into the box mold, the top is cut smooth with a wire, and the sides are slipped off so that the brick or tile can be removed for drying. To avoid sticking, molds are sometimes wetted or coated with dry clay or sand.

In China and the Near East, molds were made from a plastic clay that was shaped by throwing, modeling, molding, incising, and carving. Master models of wood or clay were often constructed as the first step. After careful finishing, often with a design carved on the surface, the mold was fired to the low temperature necessary for stability but with much remaining porosity. It was then touched up and ready for use. Gypsum rock calcined at baking oven temperatures dehydrates to form plaster of Paris, and this was the preferred material in medieval and later European practice. On mixing with water, a slurry is formed that sets into a hard, porous mold. Molded decorations such as appliques or "sprigged" designs have been formed in wood, plastic, plaster, metal, and earthenware molds. Often the originals are modeled oversize and then a sequence of drying and bisquit firings with their associated shrinkage is used to reduce the size.

Since the piece must be removed from the mold after it dries and shrinks a bit, there cannot be any undercuts in the molded shape (but undercuts can be carved in after the ware is partly dried). For molding over a convex mold, a stiff clay must be used that can be removed before drying shrinkage leads to cracking. For complicated shapes the mold maker's art is difficult and critical; a sculpture may be assembled from several separately molded parts. On the other hand, a plate or the molded interior of a bowl usually will be made on a single simple mold. Parts of figures, tea spouts, narrow-necked jars, square bottles, and many other shapes have been produced by rolling or pressing out slabs of clay, carefully pressing them into separate molds for each portion of the piece, trimming the edges carefully, roughening them slightly, dampening them with a touch of slip, and carefully pressing the mold halves together. This technique was used by pre-Columbian potters in the Americas as well as porcelain manufacturers in the European tradition. After enough drying to allow removal from the mold, the join was scraped and trimmed and usually smoothed over with a dampened wooden or metal finishing tool. Obviously molding requires time and skill.

Throwing on a Wheel

When specialized craft production began about 3500 B.C. in the Near East, potters increased the weight of the wheel and its rate of rotation so that the wheel's momentum would provide the energy necessary to allow the potter to pull up the wall and shape the piece. Wheels have been developed in a variety of forms in several different cultures, but all of them achieve this basic purpose. Some are rotated by the potter with a foot or a stick, and some are turned by an assistant by hand, foot, stick, or pulley. Modern wheels often have electric motors. For throwing on a wheel, the ware is first centered, then shaped into the form desired. For production of small objects, it is common to throw "off a hump"—that is, a large mass of clay is kept on the wheel with small cups or bowls thrown from the top and cut off in such a way that many are made sequentially. After its invention, throwing on a wheel became the principal technique for pottery manufacture. It requires a body with good plasticity, and one that is well prepared. When these conditions are met, a variety of shapes and forms can be produced and a rate of production maintained that is much higher than that achieved by modeling or molding.

Both modern art potters and village artisans making utilitarian ware typically work with a body that has good plasticity and allows direct artistic expression as well as the rapid production of many pieces. Luxury wares in porcelain bodies are typically "short" and require rapid forming to the approximate shape and wall thickness desired. An increased water content developed by remaining too long on the wheel would be disastrous. Often these wares were shaped to final size after partial drying by pressing them over or into a rotating mold. Extensive trimming in the leather-hard state might be used to obtain the proper wall thickness. In many instances ware was thrown in two sections and then joined after partial drying. Pressing plastic clay into a rotating mold and finishing the surface and foot by turning with chisels or profiled tools is an ancient version of the modern mechanized process, or "jiggering," which does the same thing on a motor-driven rotating mold.

Assembly and Joining

The extent to which the assembly and joining of parts are necessary in the production of ceramics is hardly realized; actually they are the rule rather than the exception. A principal reason for joining is that it permits maximum extension in forming the wall of a vessel. This is particularly important for "short" compositions such as porcelain. The height of a wall 3–4 mm thick is typically limited to about 20 cm; the maximum height to which a thicker wall can be raised is typically 50 cm or so. To make a larger vessel or one with a narrow neck, it is common to form it in two pieces and then join them together after they are nearly dry.

Handles are separately modeled or molded and then joined to the cup or pitcher or jar. Spouts are separately made and added to teapots or pitchers. Decorative appliques are molded and then added to surfaces. In every case the principal steps in the joining processes are to roughen the surface (to eliminate orientation of the platey particles), to dampen with a slip, and then to press together at the same moisture content so that differential shrinkage does not lead to stresses and cracking at the join. After joining, the surface of the join must be roughened and then smoothed to avoid particle orientation that will lift the join during the firing process. Close examination of joins very often shows at least some cracks or separations.

Slip Casting

Most ceramic ware formed in molds is now made by a slip-casting process in which a fluidized slip is poured into a plaster mold that acts as a sponge, sucking water out of the slip, and building up a clay wall following the contours of the mold. The clay layer at the wall gradually stiffens as it dries; then the mold is inverted and the remaining liquid slip poured out, leaving a hollow form. Slip casting is used for complex figures and also for narrow-necked vessels and vases. However, this process did not become widespread until the middle of the nineteenth century.

Drying

As shown in Figure 13.3, water evaporation during the early stages of drying is accompanied by a shrinkage that continues until the particles come into contact at the leather-hard stage. At that point the surface film of water disappears, the surface color changes from a brownish to a whitish tone, and the danger of cracking and warping has passed. If drying during the initial shrinkage stages is not uniform so that one part or one side of the ware dries more rapidly than another, and thus shrinks more, drying cracks and warpage can result. For joining parts together, it is best to have them dried almost to the leather-hard state where the residual shrinkage and the differential shrinkage between parts are not so important. But what is necessary is that the moisture contents of both pieces be the same.

During drying there is continual evaporation of water from the surface. Any salt dissolved in the water will migrate with the water to the surface, from which evaporation takes place, and become concentrated on that surface. Once the leather-hard state has been reached, there will be internal evaporation; from that point on, salts are concentrated at the contact points between particles where the last traces of liquid are present as lens-shaped droplets resulting from capillarity, as illustrated in Figure 12.5. This drying process was the basis for the manufacture of Egyptian faience (Chapter 2); any soluble salts present in clay bodies are also concentrated near the surface and at the contact points between particles. The increased salt concentration where particles touch makes these points fuse together during firing. When chlorides are present, as when seawater is used, there tends to be a reaction with the iron and titanium oxides in the body such that ware may have a "bleached" surface layer that sometimes is mistaken for slip. When soluble chlorides deposit at iron oxide ocher decorations, they can cause evaporation of the iron from one piece and its deposition on a neighboring piece, resulting in "ghost" decorations in stacked ware. Bricks containing calcium sulfate tend to exhibit efflorescence after firing; calcium sulfate is not completely decomposed during firing, and when water soaks into the porous brick, a portion dissolves and is deposited at the surface, forming the white scummy film that is a fairly common brick defect.

FINISHING

One of the differences between ceramic masterpieces and ordinary pottery is the amount of effort and skill invested in the finishing operation. Throwing a pleasing shape on the wheel is only a small part of producing outstanding ceramics. For much ware a surface coating is then applied that can be considered part of the body. Quartz-paste bodies that are not pure white might be dipped into or covered with a slurry of the same body type but of purer ingredients to impart a good white color. Red or buff clay bodies are often coated with a clay that is whiter or redder than the body itself. For burnished ware a slip layer of a fine-particle-size levigated clay, perhaps with a bit of ash and even some added ocher, will give a glossy surface. A special case is the underglaze tin-opacified ground with which the majolica body was coated before painting; this is usually considered part of the glaze, but it served a "body" function as the underglaze ground.

When the ware has been dried to the leather-hard state, most of the interparticle water films have been removed, the yield point substantially increases, extensibility of the ware is much decreased, and there is little further drying shrinkage. It is in this condition, as a stiff plastic, that the ware best can be incised, carved, or trimmed. Final trimming to shape and forming of the foot is usually accomplished by chucking the piece on a wheel or a horizontal lathe and turning. To obtain a uniform, thin wall of the proper shape, ware may be thrown a bit thick and then turned down to the desired form and wall thickness, checking it with template and calipers. Superthin walls such as found on Chinese "eggshell" wares may be shaped by turning the internal surface and then building up the wall thickness by glazing the inside. After the glaze dries, the outside is turned to its final thinness and glazed. In this way sufficient strength of the thin wall is maintained during the critical finishing process.

Hand carving of inset panels, undercuts, and final touching up of sculptures and bas relief decorations require great skill. To increase the translucency of thin ware, Persian potters cut small holes as windows through the wall, which they filled in with glaze (similar Chinese wares are called "rice grain" porcelain). Depending on the depth of carving, incised designs on the surface can appear as almost invisible shadows or as bold compositions when glazed. Geometrical or free-flowing organic patterns may be scratched in with a pointed or comblike tool. Designs may be carved through an overlain slip layer to reveal the underbody (sgraffito), or whole sections of the slip may be cut back to form the design. Hand-carved and incised wares offer many opportunities for artistic expression but require much skill for its effective realization.

While clay ware is best joined together and finished in the stiff plastic condition generally described as leather hard, frit porcelain bodies, which have a higher content of nonplastics, do not have the green strength necessary for easy carving. For these materials animal glue or gum or some other strengthening agent was often added to increase the dry strength so that finishing operations could be carried out in the bone-dry state. For the soft-paste porcelains made at Sèvres, a mixture of black soap and parchment glue was added to provide sufficient dry strength. In present-day Iran, vegetable gums are employed for the same purpose. Although documentary or archaeological evidence is not available, it is quite certain that such additions were also utilized for paper-thin or carved Islamic quartz paste and for Egyptian faience.

From very early times, it has been known that burnishing a clay surface by rubbing produces a surface sheen after firing. This effect results from the aligning of the clay platelets in the plane of the surface, and from densifying the surface layer by applying high pressure. It can be carried out dry or wet, but is most effective at the leather-hard stage. Burnishing may be accomplished with a pebble, a piece of hard wood, or any smooth, hard material. Techniques derived from the jewelry trade that involved leather polishing wheels were practiced by Meissen and Wedgwood in the eighteenth century. Burnishing works best with fine-sized platey particles, and a slip coating of levigated illitic or kaolinitic clay is particularly effective—and even more so if a little potash is added during sedimentation to provide alkali to the surface layer. Clays suitable for burnishing already have a sheen before firing.

FIRING

There are two quite different aspects to the technology of firing. One is related to the effects of temperature, time, and kiln atmosphere on the ware produced. Another is the matter of kiln design—how to achieve these conditions.

Changes in the Body During Firing

In the drying process, the water that serves as a lubricant between the clay particles evaporates and leaves behind some 30–50 volume percent of empty space. As a result unfired ware is weak and permeable. During firing the final bit of moisture evaporates, and then, at low red heat, clays decompose, evolving more water vapor. At the same time, some of the organic materials present in the body vaporize and, if time and conditions allow, hydrocarbons and residual carbon burn and disappear. For these processes to be completed, this stage of firing must be carried out slowly and with plenty of air.

Earthenware clays contain not only quartz and feldspar particles, but also soluble alkalies and alkaline earths, iron carbonate and oxides, sulfates, and other impurities in small amounts. During drying the soluble impurities tend to concentrate at the contact points between particles. This results, during firing, in the formation of a small amount of liquid when the temperature reaches 600–800°C. The liquid forms as tiny concave lenses due to capillary pressure that glues the particles together, resulting in a structure such as shown in Figures 12.5b and 13.4a. These lenses join or "sinter" the particles together, strengthening the body without much shrinkage. Earthenware bodies may exhibit as much as 15–30 volume percent porosity after firing, which makes them permeable and weak. As firing continues and the temperature increases, the sintering process continues, but there is a broad range of temperature where not much more liquid forms and more or less equivalent results are obtained. The firing temperature is not very critical so long as it is not too high. In this regime unglazed earthenware can be stacked without the pieces sticking to each other.

a

Figure 13.4. Changes in the microstructure of an iron-containing earthenware shard from Karanova, Yugoslavia. (a) At 700°C there is little change from its appearance before firing, but liquid has formed, attaching the particles together to provide a useful permeable product. (b) At 800°C reaction produces a mixture of crystalline particles in a glassy matrix, forming a harder, less permeable ware. (c) At 900°C the ware consists entirely of a viscous liquid that will barely hold its shape. Higher firing temperatures would cause slumping or bloating.

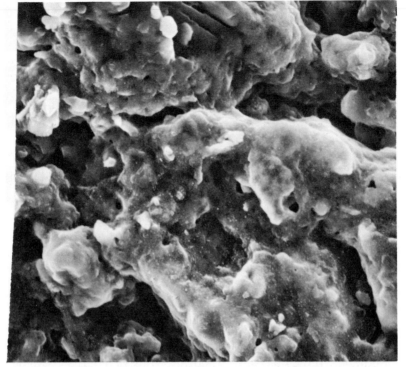

b

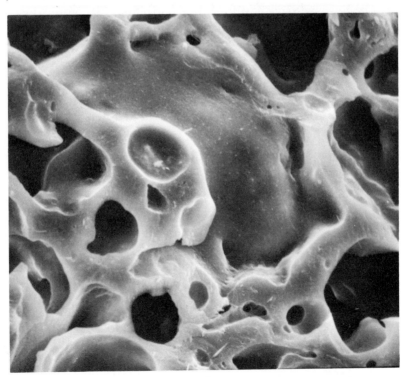

c

Depending on the composition, as the temperature reaches the range of 800–900°C, the clay and fluxes react to form a mixture of viscous silicate liquid and crystalline material, and at this point the composition becomes critical to what happens. Some compositions melt completely to form a viscous liquid at temperatures just above 900°C, but complete melting in the range near 1100°C is more common. If limestone ($CaCO_3$) is present, it decomposes to form quicklime (CaO) at about 800°C, and a higher temperature is necessary for it to react with the surrounding body. As a result there is a critical firing temperature range that must be avoided to prevent "spit out" caused by residual quicklime (when the quicklime reacts with the atmosphere, it expands and pops out bits of clay). But by far the greatest difficulty with earthenware is that it tends to become entirely liquid rapidly once the temperature is raised above about 1000°C. When that happens the ware is overfired and bloats or slumps. That is, while a wide range of temperatures will result in satisfactory firing of porous permeable earthenware, the temperature range at which dense impermeable products are formed without slumping or bloating is quite limited.

The iron oxide in most earthenware clays transforms into particles of red hematite (Fe_2O_3) at red heat if there is enough air to provide oxidizing conditions. If the fuel is damp and air is constricted, there will be a reducing atmosphere and black magnetite (Fe_3O_4) will form. The reaction, which can be reversed back and forth by controlling the combustion process, is:

$$\text{Black magnetite + Oxygen} \underset{\text{Reduction}}{\overset{\text{Oxidation}}{\rightleftharpoons}} \text{Red hematite}$$

If earthenware has much iron oxide and is heated above 800–900°C in reduction, magnetite acts as a flux to form more silicate liquid and a harder, denser product results (which is also more likely to slump) than if oxidizing conditions were used.

In modern production high forming pressures pack the particles tightly together, resulting in a higher green density, and thus less porosity after firing. By burnishing the surface with a fine, smooth pebble, locally high pressures are achieved that orient the clay particles and compact them so that the initial porosity is much less in a thin surface layer as compared with the underlying material. This combination of compaction and orientation in the burnished layer accelerates the sintering process and consolidation of the layer during firing. A denser, lower porosity material with a glossy surface results. This is enhanced when the burnished layer contains extra alkali that forms a more liquid phase to aid consolidation during firing (as in Greek black-on-red ware and Roman terra sigillata).

To achieve hardness, impermeability, and whiteness, special compositions are required that allow densification without excess slumping. As shown schematically in Figure 13.5 and in the microstructures of both hard-paste and soft-paste porcelain (Figures 1.3 and 1.4), this is accomplished by having large, relatively inert particles embedded in a mixture of fine particles and a viscous silicate liquid. In the case of widely used quartz-feldspar-clay compositions, the clay decomposes to form mullite crystals in a silica-rich liquid, while the feldspar contributes alkali to the silicate liquid in which the quartz slowly dissolves. In the resulting microstructure, the mullite needles stiffen the glass during firing and afford

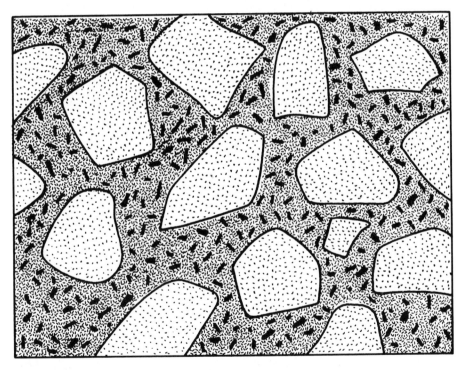

Figure 13.5. Schematic illustrations of bodies formulated for successful firing over a wide range of time and temperatures. These bodies have refractory grains dispersed in a viscous silicate liquid containing an extensive network of fine crystallites that stiffen the liquid and prevent excessive slumping.

good physical properties after cooling. Even more important, these compositions are self-correcting; as the temperature and firing time increase, more liquid forms, but more quartz also dissolves, making the larger amount of silicate liquid even stiffer. This is illustrated in Figure 12.6, which shows that longer times at lower temperatures give the same results as shorter times at higher temperatures. It is really a wonderful system.

Kilns

The final test of ceramic artisanship comes at the moment the kiln is opened. Successful firing is so essential to producing a ceramic masterpiece that it seems appropriate to devote a separate discussion to kilns. In theory it is simple enough. Transforming a soft porous clay shape into a stonelike product requires exposure to high temperatures in a kiln that consists of:

1. A source of heat.
2. Setting space for the ware.
3. A means of heat transfer from the fire to the ware.
4. A container that surrounds the ware and keeps it hot.

Almost every possible arrangement for combining and utilizing these elements has been used. Key factors in determining the degree of sophistication required are the temperature level, temperature control, type of atmosphere, atmosphere control, care in setting, and protection of the ware during the firing process.

For crude earthenware we have seen that temperatures in the range 700–1000°C are sufficient. This temperature level can be reached with gross inefficiencies in each of the kiln requirements, although better arrangements provide improved fuel efficiency and temperature control uniformity. In contrast, for firing porcelain at a temperature of 1300°C or more, the increased shrinkage during firing requires care in setting the ware within the kiln. The glaze must be protected from direct contact with the flame, and to reach this level of temperature with some degree of temperature uniformity necessitates efficiency of heat generation, heat transfer to the ware, and heat containment. The technical solutions for obtaining these results were found early in China, but not until the eighteenth century in Europe. The traditional story that the European development of hard porcelain was mostly a search for suitable materials is a wonderful half-truth—a much more important search was for an efficient firebox!

The simplest arrangement—one used from the earliest times and by many primitive people, and which is quite satisfactory for firing permeable earthenware with a minimum of bother—is to have the fuel and ware stacked together, surrounded by a temporary (or fairly permanent) enclosure to confine the heat. One way of doing this is to heat the ware over the fuel at the center of a fire, and lean pieces of wood around the outside, so that while much of the heat resulting from combustion is lost to the surroundings, the central region temperature rises to between 800 and 900°C (Figure 13.6a). In a more sophisticated version, such as used by southwestern native Americans in this century, the ware is stacked on rocks or a simple grill with fuel underneath and surrounded by a pile of added fuel such as dung cakes, which burn to form an insulating layer that holds the heat in the interior. If the ware might be harmed by contact with the dung, a layer of shards can be interposed between it and the ware, or a layer of ashes or pieces of sheet iron used instead of dung. A portion of the enclosure might be permanent, as in pit firing. A commercial technique used well into the twentieth century for firing brick has been to stack fuel and bricks together within the enclosing walls, and then to drop coal in among the bricks being fired (a skove kiln). Where careful stacking of the ware is unnecessary (unglazed ware, low firing shrinkage) and a temperature level above 1000°C is not required, this is an inexpensive, satisfactory arrangement.

A more sophisticated firing practice involved the separation of the heat source from the stacked ware. Our earliest evidence of this technique is found at the Chinese neolithic site of Pan-Po, where an underground tunnel conducted the flame from a fire through channels to a setting area enclosed by what was probably a temporary heat-containing enclosure (Figure 13.6b). This arrangement is not much different in concept from Romano-British kilns, which have been excavated, rebuilt, and tested to show that they achieved a firing temperature above 1000°C. Similar Greek kilns are illustrated on black-and-red painted ware. Egyptian tomb paintings suggest that early kilns there had a shaft construction, with a fire directly under a perforated floor supporting the ware, similar to a Renaissance design described by Piccolpasso. Frequently in medieval and Renaissance kilns, setting space for sintering glazes or bisque firings was reserved at the rear of the firebox (Figure 13.6c). In these and many Near Eastern kilns, a fairly large firebox allowed the use of brush and other bulky fuels.

In modern kilns we have optical and electrical pyrometers that measure

1 meter

a

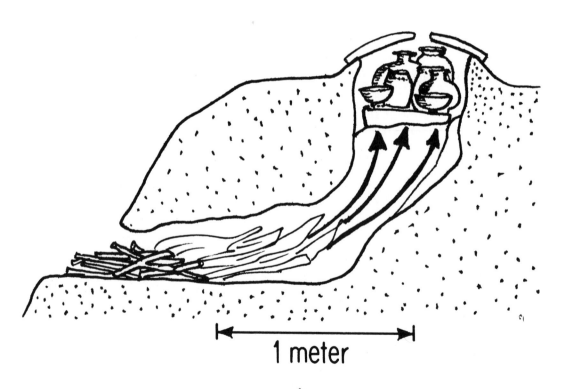

1 meter

b

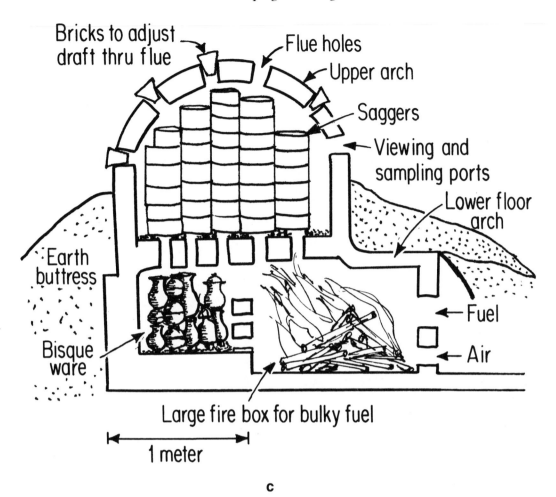

Figure 13.6. (a) The simplest kiln consists of war stacked together so that the fuel itself forms the enclosure. (b) At Pan-po in neolithic China, the firebox was connected by a tunnel to a separate setting area. (c) Medieval and Renaissance kilns frequently had a large firebox suitable for bulky fuels and a separate setting space at the back of the firebox for fritting glazes and firing bisque ware.

temperatures, as well as cones of carefully prepared material that bend after a given amount of firing—indicators invented in antiquity and used by Böttger at Meissen. In depending on these aids, we have lost much of our ability, which comes from experience, to identify the kiln temperature by the radiated color. The color scale of temperature is approximately:

Barely visible red	525°C
Dark red	700°C
Cherry red just beginning to appear	800°C
Clear red	900°C
Bright red, beginning orange	1000°C
Orange	1100°C
Orange-white	1200°C
Dull white	1300°C
Bright white	1400°C

In his work on Renaissance pottery, Piccolpasso describes quite clearly how the fireman is attuned to this color variation to judge variations in temperature and how the temperature can then be stabilized by adjusting the firing or opening flues to allow more hot gases at a higher velocity to reach the cooler part of the furnace.

Another ancient method of judging the firing process was to withdraw a small sample from the kiln for examination. This practice led to the temperature indicator invented by Wedgwood in the mid-eighteenth century, which consisted of a carefully prepared cylinder of a selected clay. During firing the clay cylinder was withdrawn from the furnace and its diameter measured by pressing it into a wedge-shaped opening in a brass plate with an engraved scale.

To understand the operation and problems associated with attaining the temperatures necessary for porcelain, we must digress into questions of heat generation, heat transfer, and temperature measurement. When the firing and setting chambers are separate, heat enters the setting area as a flow of hot gas. Some part of this gas heats the ware and inner kiln wall with an efficiency that depends on the difference in temperature between the gas and the ware (the gas must be hotter than the ware) and also on the velocity of the gas (when the gas moves over the solid more rapidly, there is greater turbulence and heat transfer is more effective). Much of the heat content of the gas leaves the furnace with the hot exiting gases, some heat is conducted out through the furnace wall and lost, and the rest heats the ware. At the highest temperature reached by the kiln, the amount of heat entering is just equal to the heat emitted through the walls of the kiln plus that lost with the exiting gas. Thus one might achieve a higher temperature by having better insulated walls so that less heat is lost through them, by more and hotter gases entering the kiln, or by a higher gas velocity.

As illustrated by the neolithic kiln at Pan-Po (Figure 13.6b), the Chinese had developed early cave-type kilns in which the surrounding soil provided excellent insulation, and these are still used in China today. By the Warring States period (481–221 B.C.), they had also developed multiple chimneys at the rear of a cross-flow cave-type kiln that provided a good draft and efficient combustion. These basic ideas developed into the Song Dynasty northern Henan kilns used for jun stonewares (Chapter 4, Figure 4.2) and the Ching-te-Chen cross-flow kilns beginning in the T'ang Dynasty (Chapter 8, Figure 8.2). If good insulation is employed, the outer kiln wall temperature is kept low—when it is at 100°C, only one-twentieth as much heat is lost as at 400°C. Firing the flame-belching kilns of Europe was an exciting experience, but porcelain temperatures could not be expected. (Nor were they required; for rapid firing of ware to 900–1050°C, Renaissance majolica kilns were satisfactory.)

Chinese kilns and most European kilns relied on wood as a fuel. The combustion of wood (and coal) is mostly preceded by gasification of the combustible elements, which actually absorbs energy. The flame temperature achieved depends on having the correct ratio of fuel to air, and can be greatly increased if the air and vaporized fuel are preheated prior to actual combustion. This is achieved by careful design of the firebox so that primary air passes over the fuel, causing vaporization; secondary air passes over the hot ashes and is preheated before the vaporized fuel and air mix and combustion occurs in a long flame. As discussed in Chapter 9, Böttger's success in firing his new porcelain composition in Europe was attributable as much to his firebox design as to any other factor. In all porcelain kilns, close packing of the saggars and adjustment of the flues to control the velocity and flow of the hot gases are essential.

Kiln temperatures can also be increased by the shear volume of combustion gases introduced. In the northern Chinese kiln described in Chapter 4, two fireboxes were employed, thus putting twice as much heat into the kiln. Some eighteenth century porcelain kilns had as many as seven separate fireboxes spaced around the circumference of a cylindrical kiln.

The third type of design, developed in southern China and used for manufacturing the Longquan celadon described in Chapter 3 (Figure 3.5), is even more efficient. This is the hill-climbing dragon kiln, which consisted of a long tunnel rising at an angle of about 15 degrees, with a thick insulating arch over the top. Entry ports along the side allowed the insertion of fuel and generation of a fire that moved up along the tunnel during the firing process. Air for combustion was preheated by the cooling ware below the fire to get a long, hot flame. The exhaust gases passed over and preheated the ware above the flame, and thus efficiently extracted the heat content of the cooling gas. (This principle is equivalent to that of the most modern tunnel kilns, in which the flame is held constant in position and the ware is pushed along a tunnel past the fire. After first being preheated in the combustion gases, the cooling ware serves to heat the combustion air to allow efficient high-temperature burning.) The dragon kiln was later divided into separate chambers in which the ware was loaded and stacked more easily (rather than the worker having to crawl in and out along the tunnel); these were called step kilns. Similar kilns, often with the chambers arranged in a continuous circle, are used today for brick production.

Whereas earthenware without glaze has a low firing shrinkage and can be stacked in an open setting, as can porcelain when it is bisque fired at low temperature, soft-paste porcelain and English bone china have a firing shrinkage of about 10 percent and contain sufficient liquid silicate at the firing temperature that the ware is easily deformed. Ware directly exposed to the fire and developing local hot spots would be ruined. Setting ware in such a way that deformation does not occur and temperature is equalized requires experience—often each piece has to be set on its own bed of sand and enclosed in a clay saggar that protects it from contact with flames, and also provides a high thermal mass that evens out local variations in temperature. The saggars are stacked into high columns and are anchored by wads of clay in an arrangement that has been found to give satisfactory gas velocities for temperature uniformity and control. For porcelain made in the one-fire process with the glaze already applied, care must be taken not to mar the glaze during firing. Flatware can be set on an unglazed foot. Sometimes bowls were gilded at the rim, in which case the glaze on the rim could be wiped off and the ware set upside down. Many special tricks based on ingenuity, skill, and experience were developed.

Defects that may have been introduced in the ware during forming tend to be exaggerated and to show up after firing. Other defects can result from inadequate control of the temperature, temperature distribution, setting procedures, and atmosphere during the firing process. As a result kiln firing has usually been a specialized operation, one that has to be done well to produce ceramic masterpieces successfully.

RECOMMENDED READING

Bourry, E., *A Treatise on Ceramic Industries*, A. B. Searle translation, 4th ed., 1926 (1st ed. 1901), Aberdeen University Press, Aberdeen (1926). An understandable discussion of materials, methods, and firing procedures in use at the end of the nineteenth century.

Cardew, Michael, *Pioneer Pottery*, St. Martins Press, New York (1969). An excellent discussion of material selection, forming methods, and furnace construction effectively carried out with primitive tools.

REFERENCE

Piccolpasso, Cipriano, *The Three Books of the Potter's Art* (1557), R. Lightbown and A. Caiger-Smith translation, Scolar Press, London (1980). Compositions, forming methods, furnace construction, and decorating techniques of the Renaissance are discussed.

14

GLAZES AND DECORATION

The innumerable possible variations of shape, form, and design are important in making ceramics a wonderful medium for expression. Archaeologists rely on these elements in defining pottery typologies that determine relative chronologies and archaeological periods. In addition there are enormous possibilities for variations in surface texture, color, reflectance, translucence, and luster that can be combined in various ways to accomplish a particular purpose of the artisan or artist. Understanding how these effects are achieved can make us more aware of both the opportunities available to the artist and the limitations imposed, thus adding to our knowledge and appreciation of form and design.

GLAZES

A glaze is simply a continuous layer of glass coating the surface of a ceramic. Glazes have compositions similar to those of other glasses except that more alumina is added to render them less fluid at high temperatures so that they do not flow down the vessel wall into a pool at the foot. Within the glass coating are usually bubbles and crystalline particles. The glaze provides a hard, nonabsorbent, impermeable, easily cleaned surface and allows for a variety of colors and surface textures. It also adds strength to the ware and helps prevent chipping. Glazes are usually applied by painting, pouring, dipping, or spraying a water suspension of the ingredients.

The glaze may be applied to and fired on a raw body or applied to a once-fired body in a second glost firing. Glazes may be clear, colored, or opaque; contain tiny or visible crystals; and have glossy or velvety matte surfaces. We refer to a colored decorative glaze layer applied on top of a base glaze as an overglaze enamel. Potters and engineers concerned with glazes usually divide compositions into "raw" glazes, which contain naturally insoluble raw materials, and "fritted" glazes, in which soluble (or poisonous) ingredients are reacted or melted to be made insoluble before mixing with other ingredients. If a soluble constituent were included in the batch, it would effloresce on the surface during drying, resulting in a nonuniform composition and poor surface properties.

In the chemical analysis of a glaze, the data are given in weight percent of the various oxides included. We know that to form a glass we should usually have 60–70 percent silica (but perhaps as little as 30 percent for a high-lead glaze or one in which boron oxide replaces some of the silica). There should be a few percent of alumina for adequate viscosity, and the rest should consist of alkalies and alkaline earth materials that act as "fluxes" to lower the melting point, as discussed in Chapter 12. For a more detailed analysis, which goes beyond our needs, a German ceramist, Hermann Seger, suggested using formulas based on molecular weights. One molecule of K_2O is heavier than one molecule of Na_2O, but they have about the same effect, molecule for molecule. In the formula based on molecular weight, Seger suggested that we divide the constituents according to their purpose: alkalies and alkaline earth elements as modifiers or fluxes (K_2O, Na_2O, CaO, MgO, PbO—in general, R_2O and RO where "R" is any metal); intermediates (R_2O_3 such as Al_2O_3, Fe_2O_3); and glass formers (SiO_2, B_2O_3, RO_2). For ease of comparison, we take the R_2O plus RO as totaling one molecular unit to arrive at the Seger formulas:

A raw lead glaze fired at 900°C:

Modifiers	Intermediate	Glass Former
0.1 K_2O		
0.2 CaO	0.2 Al_2O_3	2.0 SiO_2
0.7 PbO		

A porcelain glaze fired at 1300°C:

Modifiers	Intermediate	Glass Former
0.3 K_2O		
0.7 CaO	0.6 Al_2O_3	3.8 SiO_2

Neither of these descriptions is of direct use to the potter, who needs to know what ingredients to mix together. The weight percent oxides or Seger formulas must be recalculated in terms of convenient ingredients available for making up a batch; various raw materials may be used, within limits. Feldspars are the only convenient insoluble source of alkali, but their use poses a limitation since they also contain alumina (i.e., the formula for potassium feldspar is $K_2O \cdot Al_2O_3 \cdot 6SiO_2$). If alkali is derived from soluble soda ash (Na_2CO_3) or potash (K_2CO_3), or if soluble borax ($Na_2B_4O_7 \cdot 10H_2O$) is used, a portion of the glaze is usually premelted to form an insoluble frit, to avoid problems with efflorescence of the soluble salts. There are rules potters follow to obtain an easy-melting and insoluble frit. Lead could come from red lead (Pb_3O_4), litharge (PbO), or white lead ($2PbCO_3 \cdot PbCOH_2$)—white lead is specified in Chinese formulas and continues to be preferred because it stays in suspension better. Clay can be used as a source of alumina and will improve the suspension—but too much can cause excessive shrinkage on drying, leading to cracks. What are now rules for ceramic engineers have traditionally been learned empirically. Potters have usually tried many different procedures and formulations before settling on one that worked.

Raw Glazes

Among the most common glazes made from naturally insoluble ingredients are porcelain and stoneware glazes that contain limestone and feldspar as the principal source of fluxes. Pegmatites, china stone, and similar mineral mixtures of quartz, clay, mica, and feldspar can be used as natural glazes. The earlier Chinese Yue glazes and Böttger's earliest European hard porcelain had a relatively high lime content; in both cases a portion of the lime was later replaced by feldspar.

The other principal raw glaze category covers the lead glazes, in which a principal constituent is red lead (Pb_3O_4), litharge (PbO), or white lead ($2PbCO_3 \cdot Pb(OH)_2$). Litharge is the oxidation product formed on molten lead. If litharge is heated at 300°C or so, it gradually transforms into red lead. Litharge can be reacted with vinegar to form the acetate, which then decomposes to form white lead. Both forms have been known and used since antiquity, with white lead as a paint pigment as well as a glaze constituent. The lead-oxide content can be as much as 60 percent for low-melting enamels, but a whole series of lead-alkali mixtures work well, firing at increasingly higher temperatures as the lead content is lowered.

Other constituents that act as strong fluxes somewhat similar to lead are barium oxide (BaO), zinc oxide (ZnO), and bismuth oxide (Bi_2O_3), which is more expensive but is used in some low-melting enamels, particularly as a flux for gold decoration. Barium carbonate is used as a flux in stoneware glazes; raw glazes containing a lot of zinc oxide are called *Bristol* glazes.

Fritted Glazes

If the available alkali is soluble—such as natron collected in the desert, calcined plant ash (sodium and potassium carbonates), or sea salt—it must be rendered insoluble by premelting it with silica for use as glazes that are to be mixed and milled. This is also true of borax and boron oxide. Fritting is now required to make heavy-metal poisonous constituents such as lead and barium nontoxic. To be insoluble the amount of alkalies such as soda and potassia should not be much more than half the total basic oxide content. The silica plus boron oxide should be one to three times the basic oxide content, so as to form a glass on cooling. Current practice, and that traditional in the Near East, is completely to melt the frit, and, when possible, pour it into water, which breaks it up into small particles suitable for milling. Early glass practice, beginning about 1500 B.C., was to sinter the reactants together and react them in a partially molten state. This process continued in use for European majolica glazes and French soft-paste porcelain. The two different processes have both been called fritting, and this has led to some difficulty in terminology—the French word *fritte* is best translated as "sinter."

The fritted portion of the glaze is ground to a fine particle size together with insoluble "mill additions" such as additional quartz to raise the glaze fusion temperature, clay to aid suspension, white lead (which also has good suspension properties), a tin-lead calcine to give opacity, coloring additives, and pigments. After milling the glaze is usually screened through a fine cloth to eliminate coarse particles.

Application

Success in applying the glaze depends mainly on how well the slurry was prepared. There should be a high concentration of solids, but the particle size controlled so that the suspension remains fluid. A clay addition helps prevent settling, but too much clay results in excessive drying shrinkage and may cause the glaze to crack as it dries. Both the raw materials used and the time of milling must be carefully controlled. Adding water-soluble gums to increase the dry strength is often helpful.

In addition to brushing, glazes are most often applied by dipping the piece into the glaze suspension or by pouring the glaze slurry over the ware, and a variety of clever devices have been utilized to speed up these operations. Spraying is used for large pieces, for delicate pieces where too much water absorption would be harmful, for ware that needs a thinner layer than can be achieved by slipping, and for ware in which a thick layer has to be built up gradually. The early Chinese technique was to tie a silk cloth over the end of a bamboo tube and then blow the glaze slurry from the tube through the cloth. Piccolpasso[1] suggests applying the cover glaze over unfired decorated tin-glaze majolica by loading a brush with glaze and then flicking droplets on the surface or by applying a single, rapid, light stroke. Asperator sprayers are often used, and today compressed-air paint sprayers are the norm. In any of these processes, successive droplets build up on the surface and the rate of application must be adjusted so that there is neither running nor dripping nor a lack of coalescence.

Firing

After thorough drying glazed ware is carefully set in saggars (clay boxes) for protection from flame and ash during the firing process. For most stoneware and hard porcelain, the glaze is applied to the unfired ware (as with most vitreous sanitary ware, electrical insulators, and wall tile), but sometimes a low-temperature bisquit firing precedes the glaze application. In both cases the glaze and the ware are matured together in the highest temperature firing. Careful setting is required to allow the ware to shrink and settle in such a way that glazed areas do not touch adjacent pieces or the saggar wall. The ware is often set on a bed of sand or burned lime, which sometimes has to be ground off the foot with an abrasive wheel after firing. High firing of glaze and body together causes some of the molten glaze to penetrate into the body and produces a reaction layer that greatly improves adhesion. Some body dissolves in the glaze; there is usually an enrichment of alumina and the formation of anorthite ($CaO \cdot Al_2O_3 \cdot 2SiO_2$) or mullite ($3Al_2O_3 \cdot 2SiO_2$) crystals at the interface.

Most semivitreous ware, soft-paste porcelain, and bone china undergo two firings. The glaze is applied to prefired bisquit. Ancient quartz-paste ware was predominantly made in a one-fire process. In the glazes for these wares, lead was a principal constituent; it provided a low-melting-temperature glaze that "wets out" well and penetrates into the body for good adhesion. Since the eighteenth century, lead frequently has been augmented by boron to obtain a harder glaze for the same firing temperature. The most common glaze compositions are lead-alkali-silicate, lead-silicate, and lead-borosilicate.

As applied, the glazes are characterized by 40–50 percent porosity, and during firing the first changes consist of burning out any organic material, decomposing the clays and carbonates, and sintering the glaze particles together to reduce the pore volume. Next there is formation of a continuous glassy phase that has entrapped within it the bubbles left from the pores and formed by decomposition of carbonates, clays, mica, and feldspar. These bubbles work to the surface and break, forming pits, which then smooth out under the influence of surface tension. Gradually the remainder of the ingredients dissolve and there often is a reaction between the glaze and the body. Glazes that look smooth often have a number of shallow pits in the surface, which are most easily seen by examining the glaze under oblique illumination. A long firing time and a nonporous body that does not continue to release bubbles are needed to obtain a particularly good surface.

In enamels applied over glazes, melting occurs at such a low temperature that the refractory pigment particles are not dissolved. The firing must be fast enough that there is no reaction between glaze and enamel and that the enamel does not spread over the glaze surface. As a consequence the enamel is raised from the glaze surface, giving a specular reflection at a wide variety of angles. Often individual brush strokes may be discerned. From the overlap of colors, the order of color application can be reconstructed in much the same way as with an oil painting. The quality of color can be controlled by the thickness of application as well as by the concentration and particle size of the pigments.

Glaze Surfaces

Most glazes are designed to have a bright, smooth reflective surface, which is rarely perfect. Even if there is a mirrorlike surface at the firing temperature, bubbles in the glaze shrink on cooling, forming little dimples that mar the perfect flatness. Overglaze enamels are rarely fired long enough to form a perfectly flat surface. Particularly if cooling is slow, cristobalite or tridymite crystals may form at the glaze surface, resulting in a rough velvety surface and reduced transparency. Matte glazes are compounded with a high alumina content, which, together with calcia or baria, forms crystals at the surface to give diffuse reflectivity and a velvety sheen. The most common crystals are the calcium or barium feldspars ($CaO \cdot Al_2O_3 \cdot 2SiO_2$, $BaO \cdot Al_2O_3 \cdot 2SiO_2$) and wollastonite ($CaSiO_3$), but sometimes mullite ($3Al_2O_3 \cdot 2SiO_2$) appears.

Glaze Fit and Adherence

An important requirement of the glaze composition is that it should "fit" the body—that is, its thermal contraction on cooling should match or be slightly less than that of the body. Since the glaze is usually thin compared with the ware, its actual contraction during cooling is determined by the contraction of the more massive body to which it adheres. If the independent contraction of free glaze would have been greater than the body contraction, then it has to be stretched out to match the body. Tensile stresses in the stretched-out glaze result in cracks. This is a common glaze defect called "crazing." If the adhesion of the glaze is poor or the fit is too bad, the glaze will flake off. If the independent glaze contraction during cooling is less than the contraction of the body, it is forced into further contraction, giving rise to compressive stresses in the glaze. Since the glaze is stronger in compression than in tension, a modest level of compressive stress in the glaze is desirable—it increases the overall strength of the ware. However, if the compressive stresses become too great, the glaze tends to raise off the body at "shivering" cracks and peeling may result. Glaze cracks may also result if the kiln is opened while the ware is hot. Surface cooling contracts the glaze faster than the body, but its adhesion to the body prevents it from shrinking freely, and the resulting tension may cause cracking or fracture (dunting). Sometimes the "defect" of superficial crazing is intentionally induced as a design element. Then the cracks usually are darkened by rubbing in a stain or soaking in a dye.

The high lime and alumina content of porcelain and stoneware glazes and the high lead content of lead glazes give rise to lower values of the expansion coefficient and of contraction during cooling for these formulations as compared with high-alkali glazes. In addition the high-temperature glaze–body reaction of the porcelain and stoneware glazes and the good wetting behavior of lead glazes allow penetration of the glaze into the body and good adhesion. As a result lead and porcelain glazes are less likely to exhibit crazing than high-alkali glazes. This is also influenced by the body composition, however. The siliceous Egyptian faience bodies and Islamic quartz-paste ware, for example, contract more than do clay bodies, and thus can utilize highly alkaline glazes without crazing resulting. (In the early development of glazes used on low-fired, porous earthenware, the fluidity of lead-containing glazes and their penetration into the surface of the body to form a good reaction bond and thus avoid peeling were probably even more important than their thermal contraction behavior.)

On long or repeated exposure, porous earthenware bodies and frit-bonded quartz bodies react with moisture in the atmosphere or soil to form hydration products, thus expanding the size of the original body. (The extent of a similar hydration with time has been used for determining the age of natural obsidian artifacts, and results in the iridescent surface layers of glazed and glass objects that have been buried for a long time.) Because of this swelling of the body, there is a stretching of the glaze. Delayed crazing may occur after a period of time, which can vary from several weeks to years. Many ancient objects on display in museums show crazing that was not present during their useful life.

Glaze Defects

The most commonly seen defects, which may not be defects at all, are crazing and a matte translucent surface. For emphasis we mention again that much of the crazing in older objects is *delayed crazing* that was not present at the time of manufacture or during an object's early life. In extreme cases moisture expansion of the body leads to the glaze flaking off the ware. We have mentioned that there are usually dimples over air bubbles in the glaze. If firing is stopped when bubbles are bursting, deep depressions called *pinholes* result. Another defect often seen is *crawling*, which results from a cracking of the glaze layer during drying that exposes some unglazed body. On firing, the glaze draws back from the crack to leave an area of unglazed bisquit. The fault results from too high a drying shrinkage, low glaze strength, and poor glaze adhesion to the body. Sometimes an *orange peel* surface texture is seen where particles are not consolidated into an even layer during application, and this roughness persists in the fired glaze. *Color spots* or *dirt spots* result from specks of foreign matter and *color variations* are often seen as a result of imperfect mixing or application of the glaze constituents.

COLORANTS, PIGMENTS, AND OPACIFIERS

Colored glazes and enamels can be formed by dissolving a small amount, usually between 0.5 and 4 percent, of the coloring oxide in the glaze. Copper oxide, for example, when dissolved in the alkaline glaze on the Egyptian faience of Chapter 2, is a beautiful blue. However, copper oxide dissolved in a lead-silicate enamel, such as for the K'ang Hsi plate described in Chapter 8, is a clear green, whereas it imparts a turquoise color to the lead-alkali-silicate glaze used on the Iznik tile of Chapter 6. Other common solution colors are iron, which in an alkaline glaze gives a light greenish blue but in a lead glaze is yellow or brown; manganese, which gives a purple color; cobalt, which in alkaline or lead glazes gives a clear blue color (but is green in high-potassium glazes); nickel, which gives rise to a gray tone; and chromium, which varies from colorless to green. In high-lime glasses containing appreciable alumina, copper oxide is green. The sensitivity of the surroundings to the color produced means that minor constituents such as sulfur, fluorine, and carbon can also have a great effect.

Colors also vary with the state of oxidation or reduction of the glost firing. Copper is a bright blue in an oxidized alkaline glaze, but it becomes more greenish, and may even turn clear, as the firing is reduced slightly. Manganese is purple in oxidation but brown in reduction; iron in low concentration is green in celadons or blue in jun ware. As the iron concentration increases, the color darkens to brown and then toward black, the degree of blackness depending on the glaze thickness. Colors of transparent or translucent glazes also depend on the color of the underlying body; celadons that are green on a white body become olive or gray-green on a darker underlying body. W. A. Weyl's entire book on *Colored Glasses*[2] is devoted to the range and nature of these solution colors.

A quite different type of color results from the precipitation of tiny colloidal particles of gold, copper, or silver in a reducing atmosphere. Tiny here means very small indeed, about 100 nanometers, or a millionth of a centimeter. When present in sufficiently fine particle size, copper and gold result in a red color, where silver more often has a yellow tint. As the size of the particles increases, the colors become more purplish, then a livery brown. The most sensitive colorant is gold, of which only 0.01 weight percent is required; cooling and reheating give the best gold-ruby color. Copper colloids are similar to gold, but a larger concentration is needed, 0.1 to 0.5 percent. If the copper is present in small amounts, it forms copper metal particles and the transparent bright red color of Chinese *sang-de-boeuf* glaze results; higher concentrations tend to form copper oxide crystals, Cu_2O, which give a darker brick red.

Many of the colorants used for glazes and enamels do not dissolve but rather function as pigment particles in the same way that pigments are used in paint. As most pigment materials dissolve at high temperatures, only a few can be used as underglaze colors in hard porcelain, whereas the range of colors available for low-firing enamels is much greater. One of the earliest pigments was "Egyptian blue" crystals of copper calcium silicate manufactured in antiquity by grinding together quartz, malachite, and lime, along with a bit of alkali "flux" to speed up the reaction. The same type of process is used today to form a wide range of colors. Pigment ingredients are intimately mixed with a flux, often borax, which forms a liquid on heating to accelerate the reaction process. After the crystalline pigment is formed, the borate flux is removed by dissolving it in acid; the pigments then are milled to obtain the fine particle size necessary for effective light scattering. Widely used ceramic pigments have been lead antimonate (Naples yellow), chromium oxide (green), iron oxide (Fe_2O_3, red-brown), manganese oxide (black), iron oxide manganese oxide mixtures (burnt umber, burnt sienna), black iron scale (Fe_3O_4, black), and chromite-ferrite spinels ($[MgFeAlCrTi]_3O_4$, black). White pigments such as tin oxide (SnO_2), arsenic oxide (As_2O_3), and calcium antimonate are discussed in Chapter 12 in their role as opacifiers.

Beginning with the chemical (and ceramic) revolution in Europe at the opening of the eighteenth century, there was an explosion in color development and decorative techniques. It was found that a mixture of alkalies provided a more effective flux than any alkali alone. In addition to lead oxide as a flux, bismuth oxide, barium oxide, fluorspar (CaF_2), and especially borax and boric oxide, were widely employed. Uranium was used for yellows and oranges. Most important, constituents were reacted to form a wide range of compounds and tints not found in nature. Cobalt oxide when reacted with a mixture of magnesia, lime, and alumina produced sky blue; when reacted with pegmatite, clay, and nickel oxide, it produced Delft blue; when reacted with pegmatite alone, it gave Sèvres blue; when reacted with pegmatite, rouge, and manganese oxide, it resulted in Sèvres blue-black; and when reacted with zinc oxide and alumina, it gave deep sea blue. One of the most popular stains was the purple of Cassius resulting from precipitation of gold with tin chloride; a similar color based on gold-ruby glass is prominent in the *famille rose* palette of Chinese ware, which began to be made toward the end of the K'ang Hsi reign.

The sensitivity of pigment colors to processing variations is illustrated in Plate XXI, which shows a set of test samples with identical concentration of iron oxide pigment. The difference in the colors is that the pigments were calcined at different temperatures. As the calcination temperature increases, the particle size of the pigment increases so that the resulting color changes from a clear coral red to a brownish gray. This range of iron-red colors can also be seen in the K'ang Hsi *famille verte* plate described in Chapter 8. Minor impurities and the flux used are also found to be critically important to obtaining good oranges and bright reds. Also shown is a range of Cassius pinks and purples that were precipitated from exactly the same solutions, but with the mixing speeds varied. Rapid mixing gives a light pink, while slow mixing results in a darker purple color.

We have discussed the role of white pigments as opacifiers, but they also play a strong role in brightening colorants in solution by providing diffuse reflection of light back to the surface, as illustrated in Figures 5.5 and 12.1. Tin oxide has been by far the most widely used white pigment, as it is easy to prepare in fine particle size by oxidation of a lead–tin mixture, is insoluble, and has a high refractive index. Tin oxide dissolves in higher temperature glazes, as do other effective opacifiers, so that dense, white, opaque porcelain glazes are not possible. In high-lime glazes, opacity results from calcium silicate ($CaSiO_3$) precipitation if cooling is slow.

White bodies may be opacified or colored with stains by adding up to 10 percent of pigment and thoroughly milling to achieve uniformity and avoid mottling. The jasperware bodies of Wedgwood, which consist of barium sulfate grains immersed in a barium-aluminum-silicate matrix, were thought to be particularly good for stains. Red stonewares, and also red brick, depend on the presence of red iron oxide, Fe_2O_3, as the colorant. As the temperature is increased above about 1100°C, a partial reduction begins to give a darker color—becoming a chocolate brown and then transforming to black magnetite, Fe_3O_4, at 1400°C in air. In more reducing atmospheres, this transformation occurs at lower temperatures, so that ware fired with a smokey flame is gray and then black at temperatures as low as 500–600°C (dull red heat). Brick and terra-cotta colors are much affected by other constituents as well, with calcium oxide in the clay giving a buff color, and manganese impurities resulting in brown.

Thus we see that several variables affect the final color achieved. These include (1) the number and concentration of colorants, (2) the amount and type of opacifier or pigment particles, (3) the size of the pigment particles, (4) the composition of the glaze, (5) the state of oxidation or reduction of the colorant, and (6) the presence of small amounts of constituents such as carbon and sulfur that react with the primary colorant to form compound "chromophores." Even though there are only a few basic colorants, the opportunities for subtle and not-so-subtle variations are staggering.

SLIPS AND UNDERGLAZE DECORATION

Surface coatings that have a composition similar to that of the body are called slip coatings or engobes. (These terms are essentialy similar, with slip suggesting a natural clay-based composition and engobe a more opaque white or contrived composition.) The objective is to provide a smooth surface with a color different from that of the underlying body. The coatings are achieved by applying a liquid suspension of a special clay or formulated mixture to the unfired ware by dipping, pouring the slurry over the piece, or painting. Often the slip composition is a whiter clay (in more recent times with the opacity enhanced by tin oxide or some other whitener) or a clay with higher iron content to afford blacker or redder color, depending on the firing atmosphere. The slip can be painted to furnish a design as in neolithic ware that used clays containing high concentrations of iron (red), manganese (black), or chromite spinel (black). Resist decoration can be accomplished by painting the ware with a wax before applying the slip. Designs can be added by combing or rubbing with a finger while the slip is wet or by using sgraffito techniques after it is dry—that is, incising or scratching through the slip layer it is to reveal the underlying body. Background areas or sizable design elements may be scraped away.

A different application of slips and engobes is to cover an underlying buff, red, or gray body with a white coating as a ground for subsequent decoration. The Iznik tile described in Chapter 6 was molded in an impure yellowish-gray body and then coated with a layer of purer white quartz paste before bisque firing. This provided a good white ground for painting; after painting the tiles were coated with a lead-alkaline glaze and fired. Some earthenware clay bodies have been coated with a white clay and then bisque-fired before painting. Sometimes a three-step process was used—form and first fire, coat and second fire, paint and glaze for the third fire. The most widely used method of majolica manufacture was to apply a tin-opacified underglaze coating on bisque-fired earthenware. The design was painted onto this white underglaze layer and often covered with a sprayed-on lead overglaze. Then the white underglaze ground, underglaze painting, and surface glaze were fired together.

Technically it is required that the engobe fit the body—that is, have the same or less contraction on cooling. Thus we have quartz frit on quartz frit or clay on clay. For majolica bodies coated with tin-opacified lead alkaline underglaze ground, relatively high lime bodies that contract substantially upon cooling were used to get a better glaze fit. (The same potters used a red firing clay for utilitarian ware.)

For painting underglaze designs, the ground is generally a prefired white bisquit ware, but this is not always the case. Most Chinese underglaze painting was done on unfired ware. European majolica was painted on bisque-fired ware that was dipped into or painted with an underglaze layer of tin-opacified white ground. White clay engobe layers on clay ware and white quartz-paste layers on quartz-paste ware were sometimes bisque fired, but usually not.

Ceramic colors require careful preparation for successful results. The coloring ingredient, plus any added white pigment extender such as quartz or fired white clay or tin oxide, often mixed with a 20–30 percent frit or flux addition, were frequently baked or calcined together, and then remilled to form a more uniform mixture. Without such preparation the colors would appear blotchy and the intensity of color and flow of the color during application would be hard to control. Water-based paints with gums or glue added to furnish proper adhesion have been the traditional method. Oil media have also been used. In this case it is necessary to preheat the underglaze decoration to a red heat to eliminate the organic material before firing; otherwise bubbling of the color will result.

The principal underglaze colors used for Chinese hard porcelain were cobalt blue and copper red. The cobalt ore was described by Père d'Entrecolles as being first washed, then roasted for 24 hours, then re-washed two or more times in boiling water, then ground for a long time before it was ready to use. Analyses indicate that one part of this was mixed with one part glaze stone (pegmatite-like quartz, mica, feldspar mixture) and one part lime, then mixed with water and animal glue to prepare the paint. Pure cobalt oxide is an intense colorant and was often melted with a potash-quartz mixture to make a blue glass, smalt, used as the pigment. Underglaze red was a mixture of 15 percent copper oxide, 21 percent red clay, and 65 percent limestone, also prepared as a finely ground mixture in water with an animal glue binder. The red required heavy reduction and often became grayish. The underglaze painting was coated with glaze by dipping, painting, or spraying, and then fired at the high temperature (1250–1300°C) necessary for hard porcelain, which greatly restricts the spectrum of colors available. In fact blue and red were practically the only underglaze colors used in China until toward the end of the eighteenth century.

For majolica, quartz-paste, soft-paste-porcelain, and bone-china ware using a lower temperature lead or lead-alkali glaze, the palette of available colors is much extended. Iron oxide red, spinel blacks, and chrome greens were traditional colors based on insoluble pigments. Delft blue was made from a mixture of cobalt oxide, nickel oxide, white kaolin, and pegmatite, which could be used after milling without fritting. Until the end of the eighteenth century, chemical analyses were not available and so each mixture, because the raw materials involved were identified by their place of origin rather than their mineral species or chemical compositions, had to be empirically tested. During the eighteenth century chemical revolution, a host of new pigments, and new methods of preparing them, developed.

OVERGLAZE ENAMELS, GILDING, AND LUSTER

Beginning with the Song Dynasty in China and the twelfth century Minai ware of Persia, pigments were added to low-temperature fluxes for painting on the surface of glazed ceramics, which were then refired to fuse the applied decoration. The overglaze enamel became an integral part of the glaze surface. The method was widely used in both China and the Near East during the fifteenth century. During the K'ang Hsi reign in China (1662–1722), a sophisticated family of overglaze enamels was developed as discussed in Chapter 8. The porcelain body increasingly became a white ground with more and more focus on the overglaze painting. At this time in Europe there was also a change from majolica painting techniques (which required great skill since erasures and corrections were not possible) to overglaze enamels. Lusters as an overglaze painting medium had been in use since the tenth century in the Near East, as discussed in Chapter 5.

The simplest low-melting enamel flux consisted of a finely milled mixture of 25 percent quartz sand and 75 percent white lead. Colorants such as cobalt oxide or copper oxide, which enter into solution in the enamel, were added and the enamel ground wet with mortar and pestle. In Chinese practice the raw ingredients were ground in a water suspension using animal glue as the binder. Particularly for copper colors, to achieve a range of green tones, saltpeter (potassium nitrate) was used, which required fritting the enamel to avoid effluorescence. When iron oxide was used as a pigment, the alumina content was increased to give a brighter red. European practice, beginning in the early eighteenth century, almost always included some boric oxide or borax as an ingredient to make a low-melting lead borosilicate. A typical formula consisted of 67 percent white lead, 22 percent quartz sand, and 11 percent fused borax. At Sèvres a simple lead borate, 67 percent white lead and 33 percent boric acid, was often used as the low-melting flux. Fluxes were melted with copper or cobalt to form greens and blues, but increasingly, as applied chemistry developed new stains, insoluble pigment particles were added to the flux in amounts ranging from 10 to 20 percent, and milled to form a fine, uniform composition. Following the practice of painters, European enamelists mostly used an oil-turpentine medium. During the eighteenth century, the range of colors available increased enormously.

For complex designs and elaborate symmetrical decoration, the designs, before being painted, would be outlined with a dye or with powdered charcoal sifted through a perforated paper. Painting was a separate skill from the potting and often ware was sent to separate shops for decoration (as it still is at Ching-te-Chen). The lead silicate or lead borosilicate enamels vitrify and react with the glaze at a temperature of 650–700°C, which is easily achieved with muffle kilns in which the setting space is separated from the combustion flames.

For gilding, the cheapest method is to incorporate soluble gold salts in a varnish; firing in a reducing atmosphere at about 700°C forms a thin layer of metallic gold, but the adherence is not particularly good. Thicker, richer gilding is done by mixing powdered gold metal with a low-temperature flux, frequently bismuth oxide, and firing at about 700°C to form a brownish color. Burnishing causes the soft metal to flow into a continuous polished layer.

EFFLORESCENCE, ASHES, GALENA, AND VAPOR GLAZING

While glazes and slips have usually been applied by painting, pouring, dipping, or spraying, there are some special compositions for which more direct methods are employed. In the manufacture of Egyptian faience, a paste was made of crushed and milled quartz together with soluble alkali, lime, and copper salts found in the Egyptian desert. After the object was molded into shape, the soluble salts migrated to the surface with the water; during evaporation at the surface, an efflorescent layer of salts was deposited. When this layer was fired at a temperature of 900–1000°C, the salts reacted with the quartz to form a silicate glass. Low-lime formulations have a beautiful blue color; as the lime is increased, the glaze becomes more corrosion resistant, but the color fades to a greenish blue. As discussed in connection with sliplike layers, addition of seawater to the batch gives a chloride layer at the surface, which has a bleaching effect—and saltwater may be used with limey clays to improve plasticity and prevent quicklime formation. We think it likely that the effectiveness of burnishing often depends on small salt concentrations effloresced at the surface.

When ware is placed directly in contact with the flames, the hot ash reacts with the surface of the ware to form a glossy glaze. This can easily be seen on the surfaces of saggars near the firebox and on the brick of long-used kilns. Some potters intentionally placed stoneware pots in the path of the flames to produce an uncontrolled but attractive range of glazing effects. The earliest glazed ware in China and Japan seems to have been made by sifting, or perhaps painting, a layer of ashes on the surface, which reacted with the body to form a glaze during firing; some modern stoneware is ash glazed. In addition to compositional variations, the principal difficulty with ashes as a constituent of mixed and milled glazes meant to be dipped or painted is that the alkali in the ashes is partially soluble and would effloresce on the surface. Ashes used as a source of alkali in Islamic lusterware, Medici porcelain, Iznik tile, and soft-paste porcelain were rendered insoluble by sintering or melting with silica to form a frit.

In another method of direct reaction glazing, which was widely used to form lead silicate glazes, lead ore, or galena (lead sulfide), was milled to a fine powder and then dusted on the surface of dampened ware in a uniform layer. During firing the lead sulfide oxidized to form the oxide, which then reacted with the siliceous clay body to form a lead silicate glaze. The process was easy to use and effective, but generated large volumes of sulfurous fumes, requiring a good flow of hot gases through the furnace during firing. It was not efficient in the use of fuel and must have been detrimental to the environment.

Vapor glazing processes utilize the chemical reaction of a gaseous constituent with the body to create a glassy surface coating. Good alkali silicate glazes result when common salt is introduced into the kiln when the ware is at a temperature of 1150–1300°C. The lower temperature range works for iron-containing red-firing clays whereas a higher temperature is needed for more refractory stonewares. A mixture of vaporized salt and water vapor from the combustion process reacts with the siliceous surface of the ware to form a silicate glass layer. For a salt glaze to form, the body must have sufficient silica. Some earthenware clays with a high alumina content will not form a salt glaze successfully. Salt glazing was extensively used for German stoneware in the sixteenth and seventeenth centuries and in Staffordshire at the end of the seventeenth century. The high temperatures required for German stoneware were in part responsible for the kilns that enabled the successful production of the first European hard porcelain made by Böttger at Meissen in 1708. A special variation of vapor glazing was sometimes used to fire Egyptian faience, and is still employed for the manufacture of Qom donkey beads in Iran. In this process a quartz-paste body is embedded in a powder mixture of calcined lime, sodium carbonate, silica, and charcoal, with some copper added as a colorant. On heating to a temperature near 1000°C, the sodium carbonate diffuses to the quartz-paste body, where it reacts, releasing carbon dioxide and forming an alkali silicate. The carbon in the adjacent glazing powder reduces the amount of CO_2 formed so that the process can continue to build up a glaze layer. As the first liquid is formed, it penetrates into the quartz powder so that the bead shrinks away from the surrounding powder to allow room for the shiny coating to be formed.

Another rather special case has been the use of "smear" glazes in which a thin, sometimes greasy, glaze is developed on bisquit ware by painting the glaze on the inside of a closed saggar. The alkaline glaze constituents vaporize and react with the silica-rich body components to form a glassy layer on the surface.

RECOMMENDED READING

Parmelee, C. W., and C. G. Harmon, *Ceramic Glazes*, 2nd ed., Cahners Books (1973). A comprehensive description of almost every type of glaze composition that has been described in the technical literature. See also References 1 and 2.

REFERENCES

1. Picolpasso, Cipriano, *The Three Books of the Potter's Art (1557)*, R. Lightbrown and A. Caiger-Smith translation, Scolar Press, London (1980). A major part of Picolpasso's discussion is related to the preparation of pigments and glazes for tin-opacified majolica.

2. Weyl, W. A., *Colored Glasses*, Society of Glass Technology, Sheffield, England (1951). Weyl's book is probably a bit too technical for most readers, but it is by far the best general riscussion of colors in glass.

PART IV

STUDYING CERAMIC

OBJECTS

As with all art and artifacts, one can learn to view and study ceramic objects in a way that strengthens and expands both one's pleasure and the understanding it brings. This requires the active participation of the observer, and also a certain amount of discipline. One's background and critical sense are developed by studying a variety of examples so that one begins to know instinctively what is "right" from an overall impression without always being able to articulate the reasons for this opinion.

After sensing an initial general impression, one might want to examine the object more carefully—noting its special characteristics of shape, size, form, texture, design, and color—and enjoy the harmonious way in which the form, color, and line join together. A critical evaluation will include describing the visual appearance, analyzing the form, looking for a dominant motif or basic idea, assessing the object's significance, and determining the method of production. Perhaps this will be the time to observe several similar samples to see the range of shapes and colors and the variations found in a family of ware. A close, detailed examination can tell us much about the processes used in creating the piece and help us to understand its aesthetic effect and visual impact. Knowing something about the history and associations of the ceramic, fitting a particular example into its place in a span of development, considering associations of design elements and methods of manufacture with related wares or other objects, and understanding the determinants of its impact all add to one's appreciation and pleasure in a well-planned, well-executed ceramic masterpiece.

The benefits of object study go beyond added understanding of a particular object. Artisans and artists rarely disclose their methods; for example, the formulas for colored enamels used at the Manufacture Nationale de Sèvres remain secret to this day. In our study of Medici porcelain, we found that formulas given in historical documents are quite simply wrong; in analyzing Kang Hsi enamels, we discovered new evidence of Chinese technical sophistication; by applying our knowledge of ceramic technology to Böttger's porcelain achievement, we opened a new window on the history of European science and technology. For older archaeological material, there are no documents at all. Thus well-preserved objects with a good provenance are our most basic source of data for developing a credible history of the development of our art, our technology, our culture—of all that is most important in the human heritage.

In Chapter 15 we describe methods of study and their application; some are simple enough for readers to pursue individually; others require searching out a specialist. All are founded on correctly visualizing the external and internal structure of the object, on both a macroscopic and a microscopic scale.

In the final chapter, we discuss some of the questions we may ask concerning a ceramic and the plausibility of inferences derived from object examination.

SEEING AND STUDYING CERAMICS

When an object has made an aesthetic impact or is historically important, we wish to learn more about the nature of its appearance, how it was made, and why it stimulates a different response from that of other objects. In our view detailed study should be done sequentially, with simple observations first. Much can be learned from a careful visual examination and by handling the object. A great deal more can be learned by examination with a 10X magnifying glass assisted by a penlight and by probing by fingernail and a needle. For more serious examination in the office, kitchen, or study, a low-power binocular microscope, an ultraviolet lamp (black light), and a few chemicals can add greatly to our store of information. For a more intensive investigation, laboratory observations and tests such as we have applied to the objects described in Part II may be useful. Such tests require special apparatus and skill, are expensive, and should only be employed to answer quite specific questions. If the simpler tests we describe are thoughtfully carried out, most questions can be answered without resorting to laboratory analysis.

VISUAL EXAMINATION

As the first step in visual examination, we like to get a *feel* for the object. It is desirable to pick it up, feel its weight, and judge the thickness of the wall, cross-sectional shape, and degree of symmetry. For the same size, soft-paste porcelain (which contains mostly cristobalite and wollastonite crystals) is lighter than hard-paste porcelain (which contains more dense mullite and quartz crystals). True Wedgwood jasperware made with barium sulfate is heavier than either porcelain or modern replications made with semivitreous earthenware. Occasionally one finds soft-paste porcelain objects with a high lead content that are unusually heavy. The weight is also affected by wall thickness and porosity, so these must be taken into account. A very porous, low-fired earthenware will be lightest of all.

If we hold a plate or bowl on our fingertips and tap it lightly, there will be a bell-like tone for vitreous ware such as porcelain or stoneware. Objects of complex shape must be balanced to allow free vibration. Porosity acts to dampen the resonant tone; thus for a given shape, a longer resonance corresponds to higher firing, less porosity, and better strength, and is usually accompanied by greater translucence. Meissen ware, which has fewer quartz particles with their surrounding cracks, is more resonant than K'ang Hsi porcelain. Both are more resonant than semivitreous earthenware with its higher porosity. Low-fired earthenware and terra-cotta have no ring at all, generally emitting a low thud when tapped.

Another test for porosity that is indicative of the degree of firing and resultant strength is to touch a spot of the body with a drop of water or the tip of one's tongue. The capillary suction that is seen or felt is a sensitive test of the body's porosity—the greater the suction, the greater is the porosity. If a body is not porous, the surface will remain wet.

Finally, holding the object in front of a strong light allows an estimate of its translucence. Light transmission is diminished by impurities in the ware, and also by porosity, as discussed in Chapter 12. If the iron content is low and there is little porosity, as in porcelain, translucency will be high. When both iron impurities and much porosity are present, as in earthenware or terra-cotta, there is no translucency at all. The weight of a piece, its ring, its open porosity, and its translucency help characterize the nature of the ware and the degree of firing.

Sometimes the characteristics of the body surface are concealed by accumulated dirt, but finding a chipped spot that can be lightly cleaned will permit one to see the surface texture of the fracture. Hard porcelain has a dense, uniform, fine-grained fracture, whereas soft-paste porcelain, because of the "horse's teeth" cristobalite present, has a more granular fracture. High-fired wares have a smoother, glassier fracture than low-fired earthenwares, which have a dull surface resulting from a microscopically rough fracture. That is, the texture of a fracture surface depends on the relative proportions of glass and crystals present, the size of the crystals, and the amount of porosity.

From the form of the ware and its surface texture, it can often be described as thrown, molded, incised, free-hand modeled, or made by some combination of manufacturing methods. If it is thrown, upward and outward spiral grooves corresponding to the lines of finger or trimming tool pressure are sometimes seen, and more easily by using a glancing light. Throwing leads to symmetrical shapes that must stand up while the clay is wet; the upper wall thus tends to be thinner than the lower wall before trimming. Ware that is thrown in sections and then joined together in an overlapping joint usually has extra thickness at the join, which can be seen or felt; a butt join results in a thinner band at the join. Molding is used where shapes are undercut, noncircular, and have complex surface designs or considerable horizontal extensions beyond what could be supported by wet clay. Free-hand modeled forms tend to be of uneven thickness and have many undercut surfaces that could not have been formed and removed from a simple mold. On luxury wares external indications of forming are almost always obscured by the final trimming to shape with a scraper or pointed tool. For plates and bowls, the shape of the foot and turning marks are indications of the final shaping method. Indeed the finishing of luxury wares by trimming after shaping more often than not obliterates signs of the forming methods that are readily seen on coarser ware. Trimming grooves, along with fine furrows from displaced temper particles dragged through the clay by the tool, sometimes can be seen on the surface. Molded wares often show signs of seams and raised ridges that result from different orientations of the clay particles at the join; excess thickness at the mold join is often seen on the interior of the ware, the marks of which are obliterated on the external surface. Drawing the fingers over the surface with one hand on the interior and the other hand on the exterior is often the most sensitive method of finding such grooves and irregularities, which are indicative of shaping methods. Use of a light directed from an oblique angle enables visual observations of surface texture.

The glaze and body may be examined for defects that are characteristic of particular compositions and firing procedures. It is only the exceptional piece that does not have at least one join showing shrinkage cracks or separation that can be seen upon close examination. Firing shrinkage can produce deformations such as warping, slumping, and even bloating. Only the very best glazes are free from dimples in the surface where subsurface bubbles have shrunk during cooling. These can be seen best by viewing the surface in reflection from a light source at a low glancing angle. This lighting will also emphasize defects such as pinholes where the bubbles have opened at the surface and not healed over—and crawling or orange peel texture. At the edge of the glaze, there will be an advancing or thickened rim for high-lime and alkali glazes, while lead glazes will tend to "wet out," or run and thin, at the edge. Dip marks and runs where the glaze is thicker can sometimes be seen in a glaze applied by dipping or painting.

When underglaze painting is used, the overglaze surface usually appears smooth upon changing the angle of reflection. This is true even when there are low sloping hills of glaze over heavy underglaze painting, such as seen in the red decoration on Iznik tile. In contrast overglaze enamels reflect differently with slight changes in the angle of illumination. Often there are variations in enamel thickness and raised edges can be seen where a color ends. Sometimes there is a roughened surface from individual brush strokes, indicating a low-temperature or short enamel firing. Because enamels often contain lead, the reflectivity may be brighter than that of the underlying glaze. Some colors require thick or thin applications, which can be noticed at this stage of examination.

The colors of glazes of most traditional wares are more limited and more characteristic than the wide variety of colored stains now available—and this has affected the mode of decoration. Copper as a colorant ranges from a bright green in lead glazes to a typical turquoise in the usual lead-alkaline glaze and a bright blue in lime-free and lead-free alkaline glazes. Cobalt and copper ions in solution behave much like watercolors. The intensity of color of these enamels is not very sensitive to the layer thickness. Darkening the color requires an increased concentration of the coloring ions; that is, a different enamel formulation. On the other hand, colorants based on pigment particles immersed in the glass, such as cobalt aluminate blue or a chrome oxide green, allow shading of the color intensity according to the depth of the color applied. When pigmented enamels began to be used in the eighteenth century, painting achieved a greater degree of sophistication and importance in the decoration of ceramics.

Thus careful visual examination, together with handling an object, allows one to observe a great deal about visual effects, materials, and methods. Simple observations of density, porosity, light transmission, surface reflectivity, fracture surface texture, method of manufacture, defects, and color provide a detailed description of great value.

MAGNIFYING GLASS, PENLIGHT, AND NEEDLE

With three simple tools—a 10X magnifying glass (often called a loupe), a small penlight, and a steel needle—we can extend our level of observation beyond what can be seen with the naked eye (Figure 15.1). The description of visual appearance, tactile feel, and textural quality requires examination of an object at a level of structure just beyond what can be seen with the unaided eye and felt by hand. Magnification lower than 10X should not be considered as it adds little to our capability; the largest diameter glass that can be carried comfortably is best. As museums, collectors' studios, and dealers' shops frequently are poorly lighted, a small penlight is necessary, to provide both direct, local illumination and the glancing-angle illumination required to reveal variations in texture. Finally, a needle mounted in a small wooden or metal handle, commercially available from laboratory or pottery suppliers, is convenient as a test probe, although a rather large sewing needle will do just as well. Used together, these simple instruments, as illustrated in Figure 15.1, will reveal most of the clues that tell us about the visual effects and how and from what an object was made.

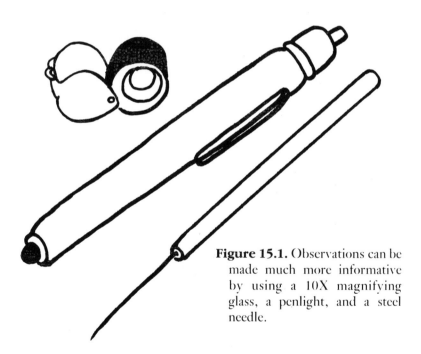

Figure 15.1. Observations can be made much more informative by using a 10X magnifying glass, a penlight, and a steel needle.

The 10X loupe is used to establish the extent and history of restoration. Most of the examples illustrated in Part II have some areas of restoration. Some objects will be found to have been repaired from several similar, but not identical, objects. A magnified view of the painted design and body fabric indicates where linear designs are not followed precisely from one piece to the next and where body color, texture, and types of inclusions are different. Overpainting on a worn enamel using high-gloss paint instead of ceramic enamels can easily be seen. The gloss and specular reflection will be different, as will the hardness when tested with the steel needle. The surfaces of porous wares such as Egyptian faience, quartz-frit-clay ceramics, earthenware, and terra-cotta, when stained, or even coated with a layer of dirt, can be seen with the 10X loupe.

When observed with the penlight held at different angles, the glaze, any slip layer, and the body can be easily distinguished and the thickness of each discerned. One can determine whether a slip layer is an added material, or perhaps only an interaction zone between the glaze and body, as seen in Song Dynasty celadons. The order of application of overglaze enamels and underglaze colorants can be seen and the translucency or opacity of the glaze distinguished more precisely. While European porcelain glazes are almost always transparent, most Chinese and Near Eastern glazes have a softness attributable to the presence of fine bubbles and precipitates. By focusing on the top and bottom surfaces of the glaze, the placement, as well as the size and shape, of bubbles usually can be seen. If a chipped area of the glaze is available, one can characterize the texture of the body, judge the nature and alignment of internal porosity, and note whether there is layering of the body or glaze. Also, the needle can be used to probe beneath the surface accumulations of dirt or weathering to establish friability and the degree of sintering by observing the ease with which one can dislodge a few grains of material and make a small scratch not observable to the unaided eye. The magnifying glass makes visible, in an apparently smooth surface, subtle variations that might indicate underfiring or overfiring, for example, and also distinguishes finer- from coarser-particle bodies, without changing the object's actual appearance.

At 10X magnification, elements of structure that determine the visual texture become clear; for example, characteristic bubble structures of the glazes are revealed. To see the different bubble structures best, the penlight should be aimed toward the glaze at a rather low glancing angle, which will minimize bright, blinding specular reflection and emphasize the contrast between bubbles and particles that refract or scatter the light from the interior of the glaze. Cloudy areas of whiteness, such as in the jun ware, illustrate variations in the composition; transparent precipitate-free areas will be seen where the glaze is thinner and has reacted with the body. Precipitates in quite fluid glazes often flow downward, lining up the particles in a striated pattern, sometimes thought to resemble fur. It is best known in Temmoku ware, but also occurs in our jun sample. Many glazes, such as for the Medici and celadon ware, contain particles of undissolved batch material that the magnifying glass will disclose as opaque, colored lumps or translucent particles. Sometimes compositional heterogeneity in the glaze can be seen as light reflecting in striations or "cords" in the glaze. Bubbles, undissolved batch, precipitate areas, and flow lines are indicative of various visual effects, glaze formulations, and firing methods.

At this magnification with a glancing light, the nature of colorants and stains can often be appreciated. These sometimes occur as coarse particles, such as the black underglaze pigment in the Iznik tile. Diffuse edges of a colored area indicate solution colors such as cobalt and copper. Under magnification these colors appear to bleed, as compared with pigment particle stains such as cobalt aluminate blue or chrome green, which may have the same color hue, but are sharp-edged. The optical density of any decoration and its change with thickness will distinguish enamels using pigment particles from those with solution colors.

The magnifying glass will often allow one to reconstruct the *sequence* of processing procedures. For example, underglaze and overglaze colors are easily distinguished. Prior to the development of cobalt aluminate blue stains, the blue color in a design was painted as an underglaze color fired with the glaze. As a result the details in blue are less precise and defined than would have been true with an overglaze enamel. The order of forming, trimming, and application of slips or glazes can often be ascertained. However, forming marks may be overridden by trimming marks and undercuts are often added to molded appliques. In earthenware particularly, building up by throwing or coil construction, followed by sponging, leaves marks different from the parallel grooves of turning with a metal tool or scraping with a knife. Layers of slip or glaze often overlie scraping marks. Through careful observation one can infer quite a bit about the order in which different operations were carried out to produce the object.

Sometimes the hand of the modeler or painter can be distinguished from that of an apprentice. It is not unusual to find some parts of figures or decorated plates executed with great dexterity and refinement, whereas background scenery, foliage, and edge decoration reflect the use of different tools, with coarser strokes and less attention to detail, form, and expression.

Very often the characteristics of the body are obscured by accrued dirt, particularly on older and more porous pieces. Here is when judicious use of the needle to displace a few grains of surface dirt and disclose the body color and texture will allow examination with the 10X glass. For samples of earthenware with grains of temper, the needle can also be used as to distinguish grains of feldspar and calcite, which the needle will easily scratch, from grains of quartz, which are harder than steel. For glazes the needle will scratch soft lead and borax compositions, but not the lime-alkali-silicate glazes on hard porcelain. (Quantitative hardness scales are based on the size of a microscopic indentation produced with a pointed probe under precisely controlled conditions. A simpler, arbitrary method is the Mohs scale, widely used by geologists, which lists ten minerals in increasing order of hardness—talc, gypsum, calcite, fluorite, apatite, feldspar, quartz, topaz, and corundum. The harder will scratch the softer. Steel has a hardness intermediate between feldspar and quartz, 7.5; a fingernail is intermediate between calcite and fluorite, about 3.5. These two implements, the needle and fingernail, are enough for almost all of our purposes.) Scratches should be observed with the magnifying glass, or with the low-power microscope discussed in the next section.

Of all the methods of study we suggest, use of the 10X magnifying glass with a glancing penlight source is probably the most important. To understand better the visual appearance of ceramic objects, and to conjecture about technology and craftsmanship, a magnified view is essential. Mineral particles, surface texture, bubble structures, drips, pinholes, seams, cracks at mold joins, turning marks, and a variety of other indicators are revealed. If the only result of this book were to get a good 10X loupe and a penlight into the hands of each reader, that would signify a great success.

IN THE STUDY, KITCHEN, OR STORAGE AREA

At the next level of investigation, there is quite a lot more that can be learned about objects with relatively modest apparatus—an ultraviolet illuminator (black light), a low-power binocular microscope, a few simple chemicals, some calipers, a scale, and a camera—for an investment of about $1000. To get started, or for occasional use, these items can be found in a museum conservation laboratory or in a high school science laboratory. However, it is preferable to have them available at home where one will quickly become more comfortable with these devices and more proficient in their use.

Fluorescent lamps are most often used to detect restorations. Plaster epoxy and animal glue, waxes, varnish, and paint pigments look sufficiently different from the original ceramics when viewed in ultraviolet (black light) fluorescence that such restorations can be more easily detected. Fluorescence of different colors can also be indicative of compositional variations. The fluorescent lamp used preferably should have both short-wavelength (254 nm) and long-wavelength (a band about 366 nm) illumination since they often reveal different fluorescent effects. Lamps used for mineral characterization, and which are available from laboratory supply houses, usually contain two separate fluorescent mercury bulbs that can be switched back and forth. The short-wavelength radiation has been found most effective.

The ultraviolet light excites visible fluorescence of different colors from particular chemical constituents of the ware. By using ultraviolet radiation, we first discovered that in early Böttger porcelains (made before 1720) there were clear indications of variable glaze compositions, as shown in Plate XXII. The exact nature of these changes is now being studied by electron microprobe chemical analysis. Böttger porcelain made in Meissen has a creamy fluorescence, whereas the glazes of some samples of later Meissen hard porcelain and modern hard porcelain show a dark purple coloration. In contrast eighteenth century soft-paste porcelain exhibits a bright white fluorescence.

The mercury-vapor short-wave ultraviolet radiation referred to is the same as is used to excite phosphors in ordinary fluorescent light bulbs. Extensive studies of phosphors indicate that the light emitted is critically dependent upon the presence of impurities, which can have an important effect, even in small concentrations, and may act as activators or poisons in the fluorescent process. Because of the sensitivity of phosphors to even small amounts of impurities, and the influence of minor elements such as manganese, antimony, arsenic, and tin as activators, that may be present in varying amounts, it is dangerous to catalog the types of fluorescence always to be expected from a particular composition. These effects in ceramics are one subject of our current research. Thus in identifying Böttger or later hard-paste porcelain, for example, the fluorescent test should be taken as but one indicator. Variations in the intensity or color of fluorescence are always evidence of some compositional difference.

The most useful tool to visualize the structure of ceramics is a binocular microscope with a magnification capability of about 10 to 80X. The most convenient type has a zoom lens that alters the magnification from 1 to 8X, combined with a 10X eyepiece so that the overall magnification is in the range of 10–80X. Less expensive microscopes have a fixed objective lens with a 1X to 3X magnification to which different eyepieces can be added to provide magnifications in the range 10–30X. These microscopes are sufficiently self-contained and simple enough that they can be easily transported to the field or to other museums or collections. They allow characterization of the body structures of what are sometimes described as "gritless" wares in which the individual nonplastic articles cannot be seen with the unaided eye.

Binocular microscopes are simple to use. They extend by an order of magnitude the amount of information that can be obtained with a simple magnifying glass. The considerable expense—several hundred dollars—will be many times repaid in the serious study of ceramic objects. Students working with objects in our own laboratory—whether art historians, archaeologists, or scientists—are regularly urged to spend as much time as possible looking at objects through a binocular microscope. As in other pursuits, the more one looks, the more one sees.

Sometimes it is difficult to fit an entire object under the usual microscope stand, and in the museum conservation laboratory there will be special extension arms for the microscopes. It is usually possible to reverse the base of a small microscope and weight it so that a larger object can be placed beneath it for observation. With the higher magnification available with a binocular microscope, the steadier observation platform, and better illumination, it is possible to observe features of an object much more clearly than with a magnifying glass. The best procedure is first to obtain an overall view of the piece with the low 10X setting. After surveying the object to see the surface structure, bubble structure, body grain structure, marks attributable to turning or trimming, and pigment areas, the magnification can be increased to a level where the individual grains in the glaze are seen, flow marks and scratches on the surface observed, and details of the ware characterized. As with the magnifying glass, the use of a needle to probe individual grains and ensure that one is not studying surface dirt is required.

In the object examinations described in Section II, we saw how the thinness and rougher appearance of the iron coral-red overglaze enamel on a K'ang Hsi porcelain indicated that the preparation of this enamel must have been very different from the other colorants. The presence of a more vitreous underglaze quartz layer in the Egyptian faience chalice was determined with the low-power binocular microscope, leading to the conjecture that glaze effloresced from this layer. The nature of the characteristic hazy-blue underglaze of the Medici bottle was revealed by examination with the binocular microscope to be caused by precipitates and bubbles. Examination of the greenish spots in the jun ware sample led to an understanding of how coagulation of the colloidal red-copper particles into a metallic grain left a clear copper-ion-colored region. Observation of the variations in the appearance of the celadons led to speculation about the variability of firing temperatures and indicated a method of multilayer glaze application; in the best celadons, microscopic examination indicated the presence of cloudy areas of precipitate materials in addition to bubbles, which served as a key to a better understanding of how jadelike visual effects were obtained.

In addition to mere observation, some simple tests can be conducted while the object is viewed at suitable magnifications. Calcium carbonate, quartz, and feldspar all are white and slightly transparent, and are often confused with one another. However, these common elements, as do others, have characteristic shapes that indicate their composition. Calcite grains are often rhombohedral and translucent, whereas quartz grains are concoidal and sharp when ground, but rounded and worn when added as sand. Feldspar particles may also be rounded, but often show right-angle cleavage fractures. A drop of hydrochloric acid applied to calcite will give an effervescence not seen with other minerals. Secondary deposits of needlelike calcium sulfate are often seen in the pores of low-fired ceramics. Indications of weathering can be seen, such as salt particles on a soapy-feeling glaze, as in some ancient alkaline glazes such as Egyptian faience. Iridescence due to weathering can be identified and surface pits resulting from corrosion observed. In addition, tests for hardness, color variation, particle size, amount of porosity, and the presence of particular constituents can take place under the microscope.

In the study or kitchen, it is also found that a few chemical spot tests can help with the characterization of materials. The most commonly used is muriatic (hydrochloric) acid, available from hardware stores and pharmacies. Calcium carbonate effervesces strongly in reaction with this acid and can be positively identified. Other carbonates show weaker effervescence. If a drop of 10 percent hydrofluoric acid is placed on the surface of a body and then a drop of 1 percent potassium iodide applied, a yellow color will indicate the presence of lead. There are other spot tests that can be done in an analytical laboratory without damage visible to the unaided eye, but they require less commonly available chemicals and are best carried out by trained chemists.

Finally, for a precise description and record of an object, the most useful easy method is to take a color photograph with daylight film, either in natural light or using a strobe light attachment to the camera or as illumination for the microscope. Modern positive slides give a better color replication than print in which the printing process can alter the color. (Normally film prints are produced on machines that adapt for "average" color reproduction and may be more influenced by the choice of a background than by the piece itself.) If a centimeter scale is included in the photograph, the record is really quite good; color slides can easily be reproduced as prints and the colors will last for ten years or more without any special storage.

Traditional rendering of shape and size utilizes calipers and graph paper placed behind the object, and also under the drawing paper, to prepare a cross section that will illustrate the proportions, evidence of manufacture, characteristic shape of the foot and rim, and other particularly characteristic features. Such careful drawings show only the profile at one cross section and tend to ignore variations caused by shrinkage, warpage, or variations in manufacture. If such detail is not required, a small sketch can be made from the top, bottom, or side of the ware to characterize the overall form and the location of particularly important features.

Color descriptions of ware are particularly difficult in that what one person sees as robin's egg blue another may see as sea green. In addition the light used for illumination can affect the color seen. The proper science of color characterization based on spectrophotometry and chromaticity matching is rather complex. However, for almost all descriptive purposes, Munsell color charts are recommended as most useful. They specify color in terms of three variables: the hue, or spectral color; the chroma, or intensity of color; and the value or neutral value scale of white and gray that are mixed with the color. Standard color charts and books of color chips are widely available so that a color described in terms of the Munsell notation can be recognized or reproduced throughout the world.

AT THE LABORATORY

If laboratory studies are worth doing at all, they require modern equipment and trained personnel; as a result they are expensive and time consuming. In addition the physicists or chemists or technicians who actually do the laboratory tests cannot be expected to know very much, if anything, about the technology of ceramics, and particularly about any special circumstances that might affect results or conclusions. Thus it is essential that the person ordering the laboratory studies be familiar with the types of measurements that are feasible and desirable—and even then should discuss the project with a professional technical ceramist if possible. While we shall describe a variety of tests as an indication of what is available, our general recommendation is to have as little as possible done at the laboratory.

In general laboratory tests can provide information about the date of manufacture, the internal macrostructure and microstructure, the overall and microcomposition, and various physical properties. But before racing off to the laboratory for any of these determinations, it is sensible to formulate and articulate quite clearly the question you want answered.

Posing a Question

As often as not, laboratory measurements are unproductive, largely because the particular question they are intended to answer is not clearly defined. The types of questions one might pose arise from the examinations described here. These are an absolute prerequisite, as they relate to when an object was made, where it was made, how it was made, by whom it was made, and perhaps why it was made. The simplest application of these questions may be for the identification of imitations, which will be explicitly discussed in a later section.

In the study of individual masterpieces, we have been most concerned with elucidating how the object was made, and why this procedure resulted in a particular visual impact. Knowing how the object was made also allowed us to place it in a stream of developing technology and thus throw additional light on the origin of and the relationships among different ceramic traditions. Questions as to how an artifact was made must be based on keen observation of the external characteristics with magnifying glass and binocular microscope. The nature of the body and the glaze, indications of joins between separately formed parts, tool marks from the finishing process, finger marks and sponge or wiping marks, observation of the order in which operations were done and the types of raw materials used are critical items of information. Following on these observations, laboratory determination of the macrostructure and microstructure of the body and glaze, along with compositional analysis, provide the best added data for reconstructing the technology, characterizing the sources of visual impact, and placing the object in a framework of technical, artistic, and cultural significance. Replication of an inferred method provides strong support for one's conclusions.

Sampling Requirements

When we have described our objectives and our needs, we have found almost all curators extremely helpful. This is true in spite of a widespread belief that any sampling of a piece, no matter how innocuous, is by definition "destructive." The word elicits such negative reactions that it is difficult to suggest that "sampling" and "destructive" are not synonymous. In preparing this book we did not sample any whole objects, but instead, each of the chemical-composition, microstructure, and special tests was performed on shards identical to the object pictured. Dealers, who might be sued for selling a fraud, and many buyers are generally even more receptive to sampling than are curators.

In the best case, laboratory tests can be carried out nonintrusively in a way that does not require a sample to be taken and leaves the object the same as it was before testing. For compositional analysis in particular, this requires some special instrumental modifications that are feasible, but rather expensive.

For many tests a tiny, almost invisible, bit of material scraped off with a diamond point or abrasive, a "microsample," is sufficient. If the chips of material can be seen under a binocular microscope, they can be manipulated and mounted for many methods of analysis. A chip of body or glaze less than a millimeter in dimension is more than adequate for microstructure determination, compositional analysis with an electron microprobe, and constituent identification by x-ray diffraction. However, we do not recommend this approach in general because ceramic wares are often variable in their structure and composition. In evaluating some Song Dynasty glaze techniques, we found that the chemical composition across the cross section of glaze and its microstructure varied in a regular way from the surface to the glaze-body interface. At the interface with the body, there was a general increase in alumina content and formation of a crystalline layer consisting of anorthite crystals. With too small a sample, we would have missed the most interesting point of this research. For some coarser materials, such as primitive shell-tempered earthenware, a tiny sample would be completely unrepresentative. In every case of laboratory analysis, the question of sample adequacy must be addressed.

The best way to obtain a "macrosample" appropriate for compositional analysis, thermoluminescent testing, and microstructure determination is to take a small cylindrical core sample, about 3 mm in diameter and height. This is done with a water-cooled diamond core drill. If the diamond drill is not worn (use a new drill if there is any doubt), and the drill runs true (does not vibrate), there is no danger of breaking the object. Such a sample from an unseen surface of a ceramic sculpture or the side or back of a tile is nondestructive; there has been absolutely no aesthetic alteration of the object. If taken from under the unseen base of a jun plate or celadon jar, it would be nondestructive in the sense that it could be filled with plaster and have no influence on the aesthetics, serviceability, or future study of the piece even though it would be clearly intrusive. Sometimes an old repair can be unmended and the sample taken from the wall before re-mending. If an object is broken, the dust that a conservator normally discards might be saved, as it would be sufficient for many analyses. We do not ever recommend sampling when there is no clearly articulated, significant objective—but we also feel that refusing to consider the advantages and disadvantages of sampling in a rational way is irresponsible.

One aspect of sampling that curators, collectors, and dealers should remember is the potential use of shards, particularly shards with good provenance, as research objects even though they are usually considered unsuitable for sale or display. Indeed, given a choice of examining a whole vessel or a fragment, we often choose the fragment because of the greater amount of information immediately accessible (from the fracture surface, for example).

For any test a sample free of intrusive elements picked up during its life or changes induced by weathering is essential. For instance, the microstructure of an overfired shard is not representative of a normal glaze or body. A repaired object may have cleaning compounds and adhesives sucked up into the porous body. Dirt in surface pores can substantially alter color. Weathering and corrosion, particularly of glazes and glasses that have a high sodium oxide content, result in a different composition than that of the material as originally manufactured. Many samples are highly variable, and before undertaking time-consuming and expensive analyses, one should be sure that an overall visual examination and viewing with a binocular microscope have provided some assurance as to sample uniformity.

Choosing a Method of Testing

There are literally hundreds of methods of testing an object that might be considered. The objectives of most laboratory tests are to differentiate the object from other objects with regard to when and where it was made—that is, the date and provenance—or to find out how a ceramic was made and the relationship of its technology to its cultural or historical environment. These questions should always be amplified on the basis of the visual examination and simple methods of binocular microscope and spot tests previously described. Then it is necessary to be sure that any proposed test is truly applicable to the question posed. Thermoluminescent dating has a range of error of about plus or minus 20 percent; it would be valuable for distinguishing a recent fraud from an authentic T'ang Dynasty object, but not for placing objects in chronological order within the T'ang Dynasty. Determining the bulk chemical composition often does not adequately differentiate between similar sorts of clays; trace analysis through neutron activation is usually much more definite, particularly if there are standards available for the material being tested.

A second consideration in choosing a test method relates to the size of sample required. The best situation is clearly that where the method is nonintrusive, where no sampling is required at all. Or we may wish to rely on the use of a microsample, but sometimes sampling on this scale will not be representative and, although it is technically feasible to use a microsample, it is not sufficient to ensure a representative result. The largest size sample required for any laboratory test with which we are concerned is a macrosample with dimensions of about 3 by 3 mm.

Finally, as illustrated in Table 15.1, the investigator must decide whether the result to be obtained will warrant the level of intrusion necessary for sample selection. This is a rational judgment for which there can be no absolute standard. It seems to us, however, that it would be as irrational to say that a macrosample should be available from every object as to say that no sample should be allowed on any object.

TABLE *15.1*

Steps Required in Choosing a Method of Testing

1. Determine that the test will be applicable to answering the question posed.
2. Determine the sample required:
   a. No sample (completely noninstrusive)
   b. Microsample (less than 0.5 mm).
   c. Macrosample (core drill 3 × 3 mm).
3. Determine that the benefit of answering the question posed is greater than damage, if any, done by sampling the object.

Dating

For archaeological materials, advances in dating with carbon-14 have made the determination of their age our most solid finding—a complete change from only a few decades ago. And most recently the use of linear accelerators for separating carbon-14 from the associated stable isotopes has made it possible to use small samples. As a result ceramics that contain carbon as part of a black core, or as introduced into pores from cooking or for decorative purposes, can be subjected to carbon-14 dating—but test facilities are limited and the absence of calcite must be assured.

For ceramic objects the most common laboratory dating method is to use thermoluminescence, which depends on the fact that the accumulated effects of radiation received by a ceramic over time are retained in the structure and make the sample glow (become luminescent) when it is heated in the range of 100–400°C. Once heated, as in the firing process, this glow energy is dissipated and the thermoluminescent clock starts anew. Thus by carefully measuring the amount of glow during reheating in the laboratory, the age of the object since it was last heated can be determined.

While the overall concept is simple and straightforward, there are many pitfalls in putting it into practice. The luminescence observed depends on the composition of the object, and also on the environment experienced during its lifetime since firing—that is, the radioactivity of the soil in which it may have been buried and perhaps intrusive contaminants. When there is a lot of material available, as for archaeological shards, individual quartz grains are sometimes screened out and cleaned for better accuracy. For whole objects a sample about 3 mm in diameter and 3 mm deep is taken with a diamond core drill and slices made. These slices can also be used for optical microscopy, electron microscopy, compositional analysis, and other tests. If quartz is present, and if the tests are done by skilled operators, the object's age can be determined to within plus or minus 20 percent. (Testers often claim better precision than this, but one should be a bit skeptical.)

For one purpose, disclosing recent frauds, thermoluminescent analysis is very useful indeed. An age of 50–100 years can be clearly distinguished from 300 or 1000 years and the results are quite definitive. As one example, a study was done of T'ang Dynasty tomb figures, many of which were reproduced in China at the beginning of this century using local clays and hand molds. These replications employed the same techniques, the same materials, and the same molds as known during the T'ang Dynasty, so stylistic analysis was not applicable. Identification of the replicas with thermoluminescence was completely effective. On the other hand, attempting to date original T'ang Dynasty figures as being early or late in the dynasty, say, whether from 700 A.D. or 900 A.D. (that is, 1200 or 1000 years ago), would require such care as to be a major research project rather than a routine determination. The possible pitfalls in thermoluminescent analysis necessitate that a full-time tester completely experienced with such determinations be sought for any application other than detecting recent frauds. Dating methods are summarized in Table 15.2.

Visualizing and Describing the Macrostructure (0.05–1 mm)

Structures in the size range below 1 mm are difficult to resolve precisely with the unaided eye and are best visualized and described using the 10X magnifying glass and binocular microscope described previously. The eye can resolve about 0.1 mm.

The classic method of describing a structure in the range down to 50 μm and less is the use of optical microscopes that have a resolution of about 0.5 gmm. Porous ceramic samples of macrodimensions are impregnated under vacuum with an epoxy resin; then one side is ground flat and polished. This suffices for viewing in reflected light and is preferred since

TABLE *15.2*

Dating Methods

Method	Precision	Sample Required
1. Archaeological pottery type, stylistic analysis of design elements	Variable	None—nonintrusive method
2. Linear accelerator	4 percent	1–2 mg of carbon, when available, from a macrosample
3. Thermoluminescence	20 percent	Macrosample (3 mm × 3 mm)

it provides the least chance of introducing changes during grinding. For viewing in transmitted light, the sample is mounted in a well of a petrographic slide and the other side is ground and polished to a total sample thickness of about 30 μm. The same sample can then be used for reflected-light observation of opaque constituents and for transmitted light using standard petrographic techniques, but artifacts such as cracks, pore enlargement, and grain displacement can occur unless extreme care is taken in sample preparation. Since the sample thickness is about 30 μm, this is the minimum size of particle for which the petrographic microscope can be used in transmitted light to determine optical characteristics and identify minerals. The clay particles and those found in fine porcelains are smaller than this, so that the petrographic microscope is most useful for identifying and characterizing nonplastic temper particles in coarse wares.

To understand the internal macrostructure of many samples, the use of x-ray radiography often is advantageous. Plate II, Plate V, and Figure 10.4 illustrate the internal spaces, bubbles, and porous areas of ware formed by throwing, molding, and modeling. Internal cracks frequently indicate where samples were joined, and the orientation of tempering material and porosity is characteristic of the fast wheel-throwing technique. Cracks where coils join together are often visible, and there is a characteristic variation in the internal porosity of materials modeled at low pressure as compared with those formed at higher pressure and extension. The only significant problem with radiography is that a sample exposed to x-radiation cannot subsequently have its age determined by thermoluminescence.

Particularly for illustrative purposes, but also to define more sharply the nature of some porosity, a technique known as xeroradiography, which uses Xerox plates instead of film for recording the image, is useful. Xeroradiography accentuates the porosity and the characteristics of temper additives; it also loses some of the detail available on film and thus has both advantages and disadvantages. Another advantage of radiography and xeroradiography is that the equipment is available in many hospitals, and one can often arrange to use it at times, such as in the evenings, when it is not needed for medical testing. Another imaging method for medical purposes, computer-assisted tomography (CAT scan), provides an x-ray image of a slice of material through the body. The resolution achieved is only about 1 mm, so it is not useful for examining ceramic objects.

Methods of visualizing and describing the macrostructure (0.05–1 mm) are summarized in Table 15.3.

TABLE *15.3*

Methods of Visualizing and Describing the Macrostructure (0.05–1 mm)

1. *Observing a fracture surface.* Site for observation often available at chipped edge, but surface may be contaminated. Breaking a shard or examining a broken object allows characterization of the nonplastic temper, degree of vitrification, and signs of joins, oriented porosity, or other indications of forming procedures. Allows assessment of structure in planning further sampling. Can also be used for microstructure.

2. *Observation of polished cross section.* Requires 1–5-mm sample. Allows study of a flat cross section to determine the nature and amounts of the different phases present. Can also be used for microstructure.

3. *Observation of thin section.* Requires 2–10-mm sample. Allows use of petrographic microscope to identify mineral phases with a particle size greater than about 30 μm. It is more difficult to prepare than a polished sample. Can also be used for microstructure.

4. *Film x-ray radiography.* Several-centimeter sample or whole object required. A high resolution of internal cracks, pore alignment, temper particles, variable density, joins, and wall thickness is obtained. The x-radiation used eliminates the possibility for future thermoluminescence testing.

5. *Xeroradiography.* Several-centimeter sample or whole object is required. A high-contrast image is obtained that enhances cracks, pores, joins, and temper particles having an "edge" image. Less resolution and overall information than with film but faster and cheaper. The x-radiation used eliminates the possibility for future luminescence testing.

6. *Computer-assisted tomography (CAT scan).* This should be a good way to see an internal cross section of a whole object, but the resolution obtained is only about 1 mm, so it is not useful.

Visualizing and Describing the Microstructure (0.05–50 μm)

The use of optical microscopy extends from the macrostructure previously discussed into the region where a resolution of about 0.5 μm can be obtained. The limitation of petrographic microscopes with transmitted light is based on specimen thickness, typically 30 μm. In reflection with sample constituents distinguished by different reflectivities, or by using etched samples, optical microscopes can distinguish a structure with a resolution of 0.5 μm, a limitation imposed by the wavelength of light. Increasingly, however, electron microscopes, which cover a much wider range of resolution and magnification, are taking the place of optical instruments. Typical etchants for optical or electron microscopy of silicate materials might be a 2 percent solution of hydrofluoric acid applied to the sample for 10–30 seconds, or a boiling solution of sodium hydroxide for 2–20 minutes. In either case the etched sample must be thoroughly cleaned of debris in an ultrasonic cleaning solution so as not to leave loose particles on the surface. The same sample and sample preparation can be used for both optical and scanning electron microscope examination.

The most usual examination of samples by electron microscope utilizes "secondary electron emission" in which contrast is generated by the variations in surface elevation resulting from etching or existing in a fractured surface. Another mode of operation, called "back-scattered" electron emission, is used with an unetched polished section. It provides contrast as a result of more electrons being scattered back from higher atomic number constituents. The secondary electron emission mode with an etched sample is particularly good for examining the characteristics of minor crystalline constituents. In each of these methods, it is possible to couple the microscopic observation with simultaneous observation of electron-beam-initiated x-ray emissions, thus allowing the elemental chemical composition of an area as small as 3–5 μm in dimension to be determined. Such x-ray analysis is semiquantitative when proper computer software is available, and is particularly useful in identifying the elements present and their distribution.

In special cases where higher magnifications are required, transmission electron microscopy (TEM) may be appropriate. This method requires thinning a sample to about 0.1 μm with a special ion-thinning process. It is useful when very fine particles or an emulsion are present, as for the Song Dynasty jun ware and Kashan lusterware. In viewing the fine particulates in pigment materials, we have found transmission electron microscopy of value. When the transmission electron microscope is used with a scanning electron beam, it is referred to as a scanning transmission electron microscope (STEM), an instrument most used for the compositional analysis of very-fine-particle-size constituents in the structure.

A comparison of methods for visualizing and describing the microstructure is given in Table 15.4. As ceramists we believe the single, most powerful tool for understanding the structure and processing of a ceramic to be a determination of the microstructure using various techniques, of which the most generally applicable is scanning electron microscopy.

TABLE *15.4*

Methods of Visualizing and Describing the Microstructure
(0.005–50 μm)

1. *Polished-cross-section microscopy.* Requires 1–5-mm sample.

    a. Scanning electron microscopy with back-scattered electron imaging allows polished section to be seen as areas of different chemical composition, with the contrast depending on differences in atomic number. Resolution of about 0.01 μm is easy to attain.

    b. Scanning electron microscopy with secondary electron images requires surface topography to be developed by chemical etching. With proper etching the three-dimensional shape of different crystals present can be seen. Resolution of about 0.01 μm is easy to attain.

    c. Optical microscopy also requires etching to develop different reflectance for different phases. A resolution of about 0.5 μm can be attained.

2. *Fractured-surface microscopy.* Requires 1–5-mm sample. Using electron microscopy a magnified view of the fractured surface can be seen. This is the best method of viewing soft, porous materials, such as earthenwares, that are difficult to polish. However, the fracture surface does not give a picture of the random average structure, since the fracture will occur preferentially in one phase or another. Resolution of about 0.01 μm is easy to attain.

3. *Thin-section transmission electron microscopy.* Requires 1–5-mm sample. This method requires preparing a very thin section only 0.05 μm thick using a special ion-beam apparatus. It is useful where very-fine-scale microstructural detail is required. Resolution of about 0.001 μm is easy to attain.

Compositional Analysis

The simplest chemical determination is a spot test for calcium carbonate using a dilute acid as already described. For special purposes more elaborate tests can be done by analytical chemists using a tiny spot on the sample to carry out a qualitative analysis. For a variety of other purposes related to identifying an object as being within a known group, determining where the object was made and how it was made, and studying the raw materials involved and their sources, quantitative chemical analyses can play a part.

To determine the approximate composition of an entire object, the most useful method that does not require sampling is probably *x-ray fluorescence.* If an x-ray beam is focused on the surface of an object, fluorescent x-rays are generated where wavelength and energy depend on the chemical composition of that object. The method is rapid, can be used on a whole object, and a number of elements present can be ascertained. A disadvantage is that low-atomic-weight elements such as sodium, aluminum, and boron, which are important constituents, cannot be determined. Another disadvantage is that standards must be used that are quite similar to the material being tested since some elements, such as barium, can strongly modify results. By iteration, these compositional effects can be calculated with modern computers, but these are only beginning to be available in museum laboratories. One of the excellent applications is the determination of the presence or absence of particular colorants and opacifiers. Since the method is rapid and can be used for complete objects, the analysis of large numbers of samples to determine whether they are similar or have characteristic differences can be carried out readily. Odd compositions can be identified and the use of modern ingredients in fakes determined.

A method that is similar in principle is the use of an electron beam to induce fluorescence. Since the diameter of the electron beam is small, this technique is described as *electron microprobe* analysis. The method requires that the sample be situated in a vacuum chamber, and so the most common samples are small slices similar to those used for thermoluminescence, except that they must be polished and placed in a special mount. Some electron beam analysis devices now do have a large evacuated chamber and can accommodate entire objects without sampling, but as yet not many are found in museum laboratories and there are some problems in selecting the exact spot for analysis, as well as potential difficulties with variations in composition near the surface. Nevertheless, attaching large vacuum chambers to various instrumental analysis devices is certainly the way of the future. One of the advantages, and disadvantages, of electron microprobe analysis is that a thin sample only a few micrometers in depth and diameter is analyzed. This allows local variations in composition to be identified—for example, the composition of the glass phase bonding together quartz particles in Egyptian faience or Islamic tile. It also may create some difficulties in samples with local variations when an average composition is desired. In determining the area of observation, electron microbeam instruments allow the local microstructure to be observed using back-scattered electrons in the scanning electron microscope mode. Electron microprobe analyses are not as subject to standard requirements as x-ray fluorescence measurements, and this is the analytical technique we have used most extensively for our quantitative microchemical analyses. A related method is to employ a beam of protons to induce x-ray emission (PIXE); there is a greater depth penetration than with an electron beam, but the method is quite sensitive and trace element concentrations can be determined.

Two types of spectroscopic measurements are in wide use. In *optical emission spectrometry*, a small sample, 5–100 mg, is excited in an arc discharge between carbon electrodes or in a laser beam. The emitted light is analyzed for the particular materials present. It is most useful for identifying, in a semiquantitative way, materials that may be present in rather small amounts. A related method, *atomic absorption spectrometry*, takes a somewhat larger, but still small, sample, 10–100 mg, which is put in solution and then passed into a flame through which light of the particular elemental frequency is directed so that absorption rather than emission is measured. Quantitative analysis based on calibration with solutions containing known elements is necessary, but an accuracy within a few percentage points of the actual concentration can be obtained.

For determining sources of materials and identifying mineral deposits, a process called *neutron activation analysis* is effective. A powder sample is placed in a fused-silica or plastic tube, which is then irradiated with a neutron beam in an atomic pile. Individual elements are excited by being transformed into unstable radioactive isotopes. When the sample is withdrawn from the pile, the particular isotopes present and their amounts can be determined by analysis of the emitted radiation. The method is useful since it allows simultaneous quantitative determinations of a number of elements in small samples with good accuracy. The relative ratios of several different elements in one sample can be compared with other samples. Matching of the patterns of several different constituent elements permits strong confidence that two samples have the same geological source. As with other methods, the sampling technique is important since tempers, for example, may have different impurities than the clay constituent. However, the resultant patterns of many elements are less affected by sampling problems than one might expect.

A unique x-ray diffraction pattern is generated by each crystalline material. A determination of the amplitude of the pattern for each of the mineral constituents can be used for mineralogical analysis. Apparatus for x-ray diffraction that utilizes any flat surface of a sample on which the x-ray beam can be focused is available and can be utilized to identify entire objects. More commonly, the method uses a sample prepared in the form of a powder, of which only a small amount is needed to determine the characteristic pattern. For low-fired ceramic clays in which a number of complex silicate minerals of variable composition may give variable patterns, the resulting data require expert interpretation.

There are other special methods of analysis, such as isotope determination and mass spectroscopy, that may be of value in particular researches. Surface analysis by Auger spectroscopy and determining the characteristic valence and surroundings of iron in ceramics by Mossbauer spectroscopy may be of use in some cases. Several methods of compositional analysis are summarized in Table 15.5.

TABLE *15.5*

Widely Available Instrumental Methods of Compositional Analysis

1. *X-ray fluorescence spectroscopy (XRF)*. A flat surface larger than about 5 mm is required. A semiquantitative analysis of elemental composition is relatively easy to obtain. With proper standards and a computer program, the method can be made quantitative. The thickness of the surface layer analyzed depends on the material, typically in the range 20–200 μm. If there is a change in composition with depth, results will not be reliable.

2. *Electron microprobe analysis*. Usually requires a polished cross section, but some vacuum chambers suitable for holding an entire object are being tested. Quantitative determination of elements present in amounts greater than about 0.1–0.5 percent can be done. The method analyzes an area and depth of 2–3 μm so analyses of individual phases present in a microstructure can be carried out. It is the best general method of individual phase microanalysis.

3. *Scanning transmission electron microscope analysis*. Using a section thinned to 0.05 μm, the transmitted electron beam allows semiquantitative analysis of microstructure constituents as small as 0.01 μm in dimension.

4. *Neutron activation analysis*. A powdered sample 50–100 mg in weight is placed in a plastic or silica tube, irradiated in a nuclear reactor, and the "activated" constituents analyzed. By comparison with standards, simultaneous quantitative analysis of several constituents present in trace amounts allows "fingerprinting" of the samples. Making sure the small sample used is representative of the object is sometimes a problem, but this is the best method of identifying sources.

5. *X-ray diffraction*. Any flat surface larger than about a centimeter in dimension can be used, or a 50–100-mm powdered sample is equally satisfactory. Each crystalline phase present gives a pattern that can be compared with standards or data available in tables. Modern machines do all this with a computer.

6. *Optical emission spectroscopy*. A 5–100 mg sample allows analysis of metallic elements present, even in small amounts, to be detected in a qualitative or semiquantitative way. With standards the method can be made quantitative. When small samples are used, care is necessary to assure that they are representative.

7. *Atomic absorption spectroscopy*. With a 10–100-mg sample, analyses can be done of about 50 metallic elements. The method is more quantitative than emission spectroscopy.

Physical Property Measurements

A variety of physical property measurements can be made to characterize particular ceramics. Among these are the *apparent* or *open* porosity connecting with the surface; and the *total* porosity, including closed pores in the interior. Also, such factors as the density, strength, translucence, elastic modules, thermal shock resistance, and impact strength occasionally may be pertinent to a special research objective.

Refiring tests indicate behavior during the original firing and help in defining firing temperature. A change in the thermal expansion behavior is one method used to determine previous firing treatment. A more sensitive method is to heat a sample in an electron microscope or make observations after heat treatment with an electron microscope.

REPLICATIONS AND ETHNOGRAPHIC OBSERVATIONS

The experience of visiting and observing an artisan–potter, a country village enterprise, or a manufacturing plant can be rewarding. It is easy to forget both the challenge and the joy of working with clay, and also the very high levels of skill that daily renewed experience develops.

Replication experiments can be used to evaluate the workability of body constituents, to determine problems that may have limited the production of a particular type or decorative style, and to evaluate methods of forming bodies, shrinkage, finishing, and decoration as they affect particular products. Replication by refiring can be used to reproduce a particular microstructure, and to study the influence of particle size, temperature–time firing envelope, cooling rate, or atmosphere to develop an understanding of what controls the way an object looks and feels. Interpreting the results of replication requires an understanding of the nature of the ceramic variables discussed in Chapter 12 so that one variable does not become confused with others during the tests.

Replication verifies the credibility of a process. For example, the efflorescence glazing method used for Egyptian faience manufacture becomes more understandable when laboratory replications show that the migration of efflorescent salts to the surface will produce a glaze with the same structure and character as those observed in museum samples. Another method of Egyptian faience glazing, which both has been observed in the present-day manufacture of "donkey beads" in Iran and tested by laboratory replication, is to use a glazing powder in which the beads are packed;

transport of the alkalies and copper results in a bright blue siliceous coating. Replications of Indus Valley black-on-gray ware and Greek red-on-black ware, of the temperatures reached in primitive kilns, of burnishing techniques, and of a host of other procedures and ingredients have made significant contributions to important studies.

One of the classic cases of successful ceramic replication was the determination of techniques used to make the black-on-red Athenian pottery produced from the late seventh to the late fourth centuries B.C., which was a high point in the exercise of Greek ceramic skill and painted pottery. The turning point in understanding this process was the reproduction of the ancient black glaze by Dr. Theodore Schumann in 1942 (*Ber. Deutsch. Keram. Gesell.*, *23*, 408, 1952; C. Wiechert, *Arch. Anziger*, 512, 1942). His studies have been extended by A. Winter (*Keram. Zeit.*, *8*, 110, 113, 1956), Marie Farnsworth, (with H. Wisely, *Am. J. Arch.*, *62*, 165, 1958; *Archaeology*, *12*, 242, 1959), and particularly J. V. Noble (*The Techniques of Painted Attic Pottery*, Watson and Guptill, New York, 1965). With increasing elaboration and with excellent laboratory replications, it has been shown that the essential ingredient in forming black-on-red ware was control of the oxidation–reduction process, which changes the reduced black magnetite iron oxide to the red oxidized form, hematite. If the design is painted with a fine-particle-size sinterable slip containing iron oxide, and the ware is fired at about 900°C under reducing conditions, the object in the kiln has a black painted layer over a gray underbody. When the atmosphere is changed to oxidizing during cooling, the sintered black slip is unaffected, or very little affected, because it has become impermeable to the atmosphere, while the more porous body is oxidized to become red. Replication studies of this and other paint processes have shown that the Greek potters controlled both kiln atmosphere and material permeability to determine which parts of their objects would rapidly or slowly change color. This production method was based on a long history of control of glaze color by varying the kiln atmosphere and materials preparation. While in retrospect the nature of the process and its explanation along the lines just described are straightforward, the studies described were undoubtedly an essential part of unearthing the story.

Replication to achieve merely a similar superficial appearance is not enough. To draw inferences about the original artifact, it is also necessary to replicate the microstructure and the composition. Students in our laboratory using modern materials can easily replicate the color and structure of Song Dynasty celadons, but not the bubble patterns that are very sensitive to the particular raw materials used—probably the micaceous clay, but perhaps also the feldspar.

IDENTIFICATION OF FAKES AND COPIES

Reproductions of antiques and attempts to pass them off as genuine have been with us since Roman times, and probably earlier. In the recent past, as prices have soared, imitators have become more proficient and their products more difficult to detect.

The first line of defense is the object's history in terms of provenance and association—these are almost always doubtful in fraudulent replicas. The second line of defense is stylistic analysis, in which the many variables of ware type and design elements are compared. A carefully honed taste is a powerful weapon, but it can be considered as only one type of evidence. History indicates that even the most expert of experts is occasionally fooled.

Replications made with the same techniques, the same materials, and sometimes even the same molds as originals, cannot be detected by stylistic analysis if the replicator is sufficiently skilled. Fortunately the creators of outstanding ceramics of the past began as apprentices when young and spent full time developing their skill. The skills of modern counterfeiters are rarely as well developed. As a result it is often the cruder wares for which faking is most successful.

For a well-made replication, the best test is probably a determination of the approximate date of manufacture by the use of thermoluminescence dating. While the precision of these measurements, only plus or minus 20 percent, is not as good as one would like for historical research, it is more than adequate to distinguish between recent manufacture and ware made more than 100 years ago.

Beyond stylistic analysis, provenance, and dating, the best tests are the visualization of microstructure and compositional analyses. These must, however, be based on comparisons with genuine objects, for which the necessary data are seldom available. We recently published a report on the composition and microstructure of eighteenth century French soft-paste porcelains that were fired in a similar way in similar kilns and have a very similar microstructure to that illustrated for the Boucher figure in Chapter 10. Examination of late-nineteenth-century soft-paste ware made at Sèvres and elsewhere showed a similar overall composition but a very different microstructure.

If we were contemplating spending tens or hundreds of thousands of dollars on an object of uncertain provenance, we would insist on thermoluminescence analysis and a microstructural and compositional comparison with samples known to be genuine.

RECOMMENDED READING

Tite, M. S., *Methods of Physical Examination in Archaeology*, Seminar Press, London (1972). Excellent general discussion of the many different instrumental techniques that can be applied to artifact examination.

Young, W. J. (ed.), *Application of Science in Examination of Works of Art*, Museum of Fine Arts, Boston, Arno Press, New York (1960). Dr. Young was a pioneer in the field and this account of a variety of different applications remains interesting and informative.

(a) Lambert, J. B. (ed.), *Archaeological Chemistry III*, American Chemical Society, Washington, D.C. (1984).

(b) Carter, G. F. (ed.), *Archaeological Chemistry II*, American Chemical Society, Washington, D.C. (1978).

(c) Beck, Curt W. (ed.), *Archaeological Chemistry I*, American Chemical Society, Washington, D.C. (1974).

The foregoing three volumes include several dozen examples of the application of specific methods to particular problems.

Fleming, Stuart J., *Authenticity in Art: The Scientific Detection of Forgery*, The Institute of Physics, London (1975). This authoritative work makes it clear just how serious the problem of authenticity is, and how scientific measurements can help.

CHAPTER 16

INFERENCE FROM ARTIFACTS

A central theme of this book has been that by examination of the object itself we can learn much about the way in which it was created—from raw materials to the final masterpiece—and how this has led to its visual impact. That is, we can infer the history of a particular object by examining the end product—a truly novel capability in the study of ceramics. That information seems to us an important new element now available for a fuller appreciation of ceramic masterworks and their place in the evolution of the art and its craftsmanship.

We have seen that the sources of essential data necessary to infer the story of each object have been close, thoughtful observation of the macrostructure with touch, penlight, and magnifying glass; an even closer observation with binocular microscope; and then determination of the microstructural arrangement of the constituents and their microcomposition using recently developed instrumental techniques in concert with an understanding of ceramic science and technology. These truly revolutionary methods permit detailed internal examination of tiny samples of material. With virtually undetectable sampling, it is possible to reconstruct the undocumented, often secret, procedures used to create a masterpiece.

In addition to the appreciation of ceramic masterpieces, these methods allow inferences from object study that are the meat and bones of developing a narrative description of the history and prehistory of ceramic art and technology. It is only with such a narrative in hand that interpretation in terms of history and culture, pattern and change, can be established. Efforts at this larger application of ceramic object study have not been very productive in the past; understanding why requires an incursion into the nature of inductive reasoning and the validity of derived inferences.

Finding the right answers requires asking the right questions—questions based on some conjecture or hypothesis or theory that can be made more or less credible by the result of our inquiry. More often than not, too little time and effort have been devoted to imagining and defining hypotheses and to anticipating just how effectively laboratory results are going to strengthen or negate them.

Before beginning any laboratory studies, one should evaluate the inferences that can be drawn from outside the laboratory. Provenance of the object, when available, is extremely important, and the level of confidence in the provenance and its importance to one's conclusions should be carefully considered. By and large studies with doubtful samples can lead only to doubtful conclusions. Some scientists feel that stylistic analysis is somehow less reliable than chemical analysis; but nothing could be further from the truth. In addition to questions of provenance and style, the most important observations are the external visual examination with the naked eye, magnifying glass, and binocular microscope, which can give information about the structure and composition of ware, as well as the way in which it was formed.

There are two principal advantages to carefully chosen and defined laboratory studies. First, they add an independent method of testing an idea. Second, they can provide data that would be very surprising, were it not for the proposed conjecture. Testing any idea can rarely find strong confirmation when based on any single piece of evidence, be it documentary, stylistic, or analytical. If our idea is confirmed in two quite different ways, then we can be much more confident. Even more so, if a result that would be completely unexpected, really amazing, and nearly unbelievable standing by itself is found to confirm our idea, our confidence is greatly strengthened. The quantitative precision of laboratory tests sometimes can meet this criterion.

Either as part of a historical study to place an object in a particular scheme of cultural or historical development, or to add to the credibility of its authenticity (or perhaps prove it fake), we may want evidence as to when an object was made. In some cases laboratory tests can be quite definitive; indeed, carbon-14 dating, which allows the age of objects to be determined quite unambiguously, has revolutionized archaeology. For ceramic objects the principal laboratory dating method is thermoluminescent measurement. For glasses and glazes, observation of corrosion products on the surface in a way as is done for obsidian dating might be possible.

As a part of historical or cultural studies, we may want to ask where an object was made. This question might occur in a variety of contexts. Archaeologists and historians studying cultural interactions are often interested in trade patterns. Was an object made where it was found or was it imported, and if so, from where? Was a porcelain bottle found in an Egyptian grave made in Egypt or imported from China? Was a particular soft-paste porcelain figure made in Chantilly or somewhere else? Answering this sort of question is essentially a matching process with both scientific and other evidence. We need a known object or set with which to match an unknown. No single match is likely to be conclusive, so we should always use several different tests, the best of which is probably stylistic comparison. Consideration of style should include not only the drawing or the rim shape or the method of finishing the foot, but also the thickness of glaze, the colors used, and the order of forming. Experience has shown, however, that styles can be cleverly forged, and other tests may be required. (Before the advent of fingerprints, the most common criminal identification system was "bertillonage"—which matched five different body measurements. Even so, it was criticized because these were said to be related to one another, not independent matches.) Other matches that are most often used are chemical analyses. If several different elements give the same pattern in the object as in a known population, it is very likely that the object belongs. Similar reasoning applies to the constituents present and their characteristic patterns seen by x-ray diffraction, thermal analysis, or microstructure studies. Chemical analysis, physical property determinations, microscopic and electron microscope observations of microstructures, and thermoluminescence to determine date of manufacture can each provide independent confirmations that may render a stylistic interpretation more credible.

Inferences about how and from what an object was made have already been extensively discussed. It only remains to say that these results are often ones from which further information as to cultural mind set, technological capabilities, and craft and social organization can be derived, as well as an understanding of the source of aesthetic impact.

We have presented what we think is a convincing case that there has been a revolutionary jump in our capability for determining the story of an object's individual creation and of its place in the flow of history. However, two caveats are required for the overly optimistic. First, the standards needed for finding a result without too much bother are frequently not available. Second, good judgment based on a sound knowledge of a wide range of ceramic materials, processes, structures, and properties is required. Observation and laboratory measurements cannot be expected to take the place of standards and judgment.

RECOMMENDED READING

Kingery, W. D., "Plausible Inferences from Ceramic Artifacts," *Journal of Field Archaeology*, 8, 457–467 (1981). This is a rather longer discussion of some of the topics discussed in this chapter, along with an extensive bibliography.

Polya, G., *How to Solve It*, Princeton University Press Paperback, Princeton, N.J., 1971; also *Patterns of Plausible Inference*, Vol. II of *Mathematics and Plausible Reasoning*, Princeton University Press, Princeton, N.J., 1954. Both of these are focused on mathematics, but are applicable to all sorts of problem solving and inductive reasoning. Outstanding clarity in what is often a murky subject.

SOME SPECIAL
TERMINOLOGY

We have done our best to avoid technical jargon not accessible to readers. Nevertheless, relating technology, composition, and structure to visual impact and other properties requires the use of some special terminology. To avoid repetitious definitions throughout the text, we have collected a short list here that may be helpful.

Alkalies. Reactive elements in the first column of the periodic table, most commonly the oxides lithia (Li_2O), soda (Na_2O), and potassia (K_2O) that are added to ceramic bodies and glazes as fluxes to lower the melting temperature; with silica they form glasses. Alkalies are present in the feldspar minerals, in plant ash, and in mineral salt deposits.

Alkaline earths. Elements in the second column of the periodic table, principally the oxides of calcium (CaO), magnesium (MgO), and barium (BaO). These ingredients are mostly added to ceramic bodies and glazes to lower the melting point, but are not as effective as alkalies. Calcia is derived from limestone ($CaCO_3$) and gypsum ($CaSO_4$), magnesia from magnesite ($MgCO_3$), and baria from the carbonate ($BaCO_3$) and sulfate ($BaSO_4$).

Alkali-silicate glaze. A silicate glaze in which the principal fluxes added to reduce the melting point are alkali and alkaline earth oxides.

Anorthite. A naturally occuring calcium-aluminum-silicate feldspar that also frequently appears as needlelike crystals in ceramic glazes and at the glaze–body interface. The molecular composition of anorthite is $CaO \cdot Al_2O_3 \cdot 2SiO_2$.

Ball clay. A highly plastic clay with good dry strength, but too fine to be used without nonplastic additions. The name comes from the practice of digging "balls" of clay from open pits of a convenient size for carrying, 20 to 30 pounds. The clays are mostly cream colored after firing, and vitrify in the range of 1100–1200°C as a result of silica, potash, soda, calcia, and magnesia impurities.

Bisque, bisquit. A word derived from the appearance of an unglazed body after firing. It is used to describe such a body, which is usually then coated with a glaze and subjected to a second "glost" fire. It is also used to describe the firing process of an unglazed ware, as in bisque firing.

Bone china. A type of porcelain made from a mixture of clay, feldspar, quartz, and bone ash. It has a high translucency because of the high glass content and calcium phosphate formed during firing. It tends to deform during the high-temperature firing so the body is first fired while supported in a powder and then glaze is applied for a glost fire at a lower temperature. Bone ash is made by calcining cattle bones to drive off the volatile and combustible constituents to form white calcium phosphate.

Böttger porcelain. An early European porcelain formulation invented by Böttger at Meissen in 1708. It consists of a mixture of white clay and gypsum.

Burnishing. Rubbing the surface of a clay body, which both compacts and aligns the surface particles to give a smooth appearance. After firing the surface is glossy.

Calcine. Heating a raw material or mixture of materials to eliminate combustible and volatile constituents and agglomerate the particles at a relatively low temperature at which no substantial liquid is formed.

Capillarity. The tendency of a curved liquid surface to move in a direction to become more planar. This force is important for the workability of clay–water pastes and for the firing behavior of ceramic bodies.

Celadon. Chinese wares featuring a soft, lustrous blue-green, green, or olive-green glaze with a texture similar in appearance to jade.

Celsius or centigrade. The temperature scale on which the freezing point of water is 0° and its boiling point is 100°. Earthenware pottery is typically fired at a temperature in the range 700–1000°C; hard porcelain is fired at a temperature of 1300°C–1400°C.

China clay. A clay that consists primarily of the mineral kaolinite, has moderate plasticity, and fires white.

China stone (pentuntse). A partially decomposed igneous rock consisting of a mixture of quartz, kaolinite, mica, and feldspar. Varieties found in China have sufficient kaolin and fine-particle-size mica that the ground rock is plastic enough to be used without added clay. Cornwall stone,

Cornish stone, and pegmatite are the same sort of mineral.

Clay. A fine-particle-size platey material that develops plasticity when formed as a paste with water. The term is usually restricted to hydrated aluminum silicates.

Crackle. A network of hairline cracks in a glaze that is generally considered a defect, but also has been intentionally employed as a decorative feature, particularly in Chinese wares. The effect is the result of a poor "fit," that is, a tendency for the glaze to contract more than the underlying body during cooling; its adherence to the body prevents this contraction and as a result cracks form. A second set of crackle lines can be induced by rapidly cooling the ware by removing it from the furnace while it is still warm. This is called dunting.

Crawling. A glaze defect in which a glaze that has cracked during drying or been applied to an unclean surface draws back from an unglazed spot of exposed body. Alkaline and alkaline-lime glazes have a greater tendency for crawling than lead-silicate or lead-alkali-silicate glazes.

Crazing. Formation of a network of hairline cracks resulting from differences in contraction of the glaze and body during cooling (see crackle). A different form of crazing occurs when the body is porous and takes up water over a long period of time during use or burial; this causes an expansion of the body so that the glaze is pulled apart and cracks. The crazing now seen on many museum objects resulted from this process occurring many years after the ware was first made.

Cristobalite. A high-temperature form of silica that forms from quartz during a long-duration high-temperature firing.

Crystal. A solid with atoms located in an ordered array; that is, a symmetrical, repeated geometric pattern as opposed to a *glass* in which the atoms are randomly arrayed without repeated order or spatial periodicity. Crystals sometimes transform into a different arrangement of the atoms on heating, a process that generally changes the volume of the crystal. One example is quartz, which expands as it changes form at 573°C and then contracts on cooling. This transformation causes the powdering of flint nodules on calcining at high temperature and it is the cause of fine cracks formed around quartz grains in porcelain.

Delft ware. A cream-colored earthenware coated with a white tin-opacified lead glaze and often decorated with a simple palette of cobalt blue, manganese purple, and Naples yellow (lead antimonate). This was the Northern European version of majolica; the same material is called faience in France.

Diffraction. A phenomenon in which light, x-ray, or an electron beam interacts with a crystal to form a pattern that identifies the crystal and its atomic array and dimensions.

Drying shrinkage. The decrease in size as a body changes from a plastic form to a dry form. Shrinkage occurs as lubricating water films are eliminated in the drying process and is mostly complete by the leather-hard state when the particles come into contact with each other. Material with coarser particles has less drying shrinkage than one with fine particles because there are more fine particles in a given length and more water films to be eliminated.

Earthenware. A clay body fired at a temperature between 600 and 1100°C to have a porosity greater than 10 percent and a thudding sound when struck, and which is usually colored red, gray, brown, or buff. Clays for making earthenware are widely available, and have been so used since about 8000 B.C. It is the impurities in earthenware clays that allow a hard product to be made at such a low firing temperature; earthenwares usually include a substantial amount of alkali, lime, and iron oxide.

Efflorescence. A white salt scum that forms, during drying, on the surface of a ceramic body containing soluble salts. This is a defect for most pottery because it creates problems with glaze adherence. In the manufacture of Egyptian faience, the phenomenon was utilized as a source of the surface glaze. After firing there can be efflorescence of calcium sulfate to form a white scum on the surface of some brick.

Egyptian faience. The first contrived white ceramic body, with a blue glaze imitating lapus lazuli and turquoise. It is predominantly quartz with additions of limestone, malachite, and alkali fired at a temperature in the range 800–1000°C.

Enamel. The general term for a pigmented glass painted and fired on the surface of an underlying glaze for the decoration of porcelain or pottery.

Engobe. A general term for a surface coating of different compositions, such as a slip of clay or a layer of quartz, placed between the underlying body and overlying glaze.

Famille rose palette. A group of overglaze enamel colors used in China during the seventeenth and eighteenth centuries, sometimes called "foreign" colors because they were first imported into China from Europe. The most prominent color is based on a gold ruby pigment, but even more important is extensive use of an opaque white pigment mixed with colors to produce a range of tints.

Feldspar. A crystalline compound made from a combination of silica and alumina with one or more alkalies or alkaline earth elements. Feldspars are named for the principal alkali or alkaline earth constituent; for instance, anorthite is a calcium feldspar, orthoclase is a potassium feldspar, albite is a sodium feldspar. Feldspars are insoluble and are used as a source of alkali and alumina in bodies and glazes.

Firing shrinkage. The decrease in size of a ceramic that takes place upon firing. Firing shrinkage begins when a viscous liquid is formed between particles to make the body cohesive; as the temperature is increased, more viscous liquid is formed and the body shrinks with the elimination of pore space between particles. If a sample is overfired, there may be deformation and slumping, or even an expansion of the gas-filled pores to cause bloating.

Fit. A term referring to the relative contraction on cooling of glaze and body. If the glaze contracts slightly less than the body does, it is placed in compression, contributes to the increased strength of the ware, and is said to "fit."

Flint. The form of quartz occurring as hard nodules in limestone deposits. When heated to about 900°C, it breaks down into a fine white powder. The term is now used by potters to mean any finely ground quartz.

Flux. The material used to lower the melting point of another material. Alkalies are the effective flux for silicates, and alkaline earths also lower the melting point of silicate compositions. Lead oxide, bismuth oxide, and borax are other powerful fluxes.

Frit, fritted. The premelting of a silicate composition, and then cooling it as a glass for use in a glaze or body as a powdered raw material. Sometimes frit is used to mean the same as "calcine" or "sinter," that is to fire at a low temperature to eliminate volatile constituents and make the mass cohesive without complete fusion. However, this usage should be avoided in deference to the more precise terms, calcine and sinter.

Glass. A solid consisting of a random array of atoms formed by cooling a viscous liquid without crystallization. When reheated, a glass gradually becomes less rigid and more liquidlike over a range of temperatures rather than at a single temperature.

Glaze. A coating on a ceramic body that is a glass, or a glass matrix, in which a mixture of crystals and bubbles is dispersed. The glaze layer is both decorative and protective.

Glost firing. Firing of a glaze on a previously fired body.

Grain, grain size. A discrete bit of coherent material found in an unfired or fired body or glaze.

Green. Unfired, as in the "green strength" of an unfired ware.

Gypsum. Hydrated calcium sulfate that occurs as a natural mineral.

When it is heated and partially dehydrated, it reacts with water to make molds of plaster of Paris.

Hard-paste porcelain. A porcelain body composed of a white high-temperature clay mixed with feldspar and quartz.

Ion. An atom that has gained or lost one or more electrons to become positively or negatively charged.

Iron red, coral red. Fine-particle-size red iron-oxide pigment mixed with a small amount of glass for use as an overglaze enamel. The iron pigment tends to dissolve in the glass, giving a typical green color such as seen when viewing a window pane edge on. To prevent this, the enamel was thinly applied and special frit compositions used.

Isotherm. A line of constant temperature on a phase diagram.

Isothermal section. A section through a phase diagram at a constant temperature.

Jasperware. A contrived composition invented by Josiah Wedgwood in the eighteenth century based on a mixture of barium sulfate, quartz, clay, and lime. The body was fired to form a compact, unglazed translucent body.

Kaolin. A fine-particle-size platey white-firing clay used in porcelain manufacture and named for a mine site (Kaoling) near Ching-te-Chen in China; also called china clay. Composed of larger particles, it is less plastic than ball clay or montmorillonite.

Lead-alkali silicate glaze. Glazes in which the modifying constituent is a mixture of lead and alkali, widely used for intermediate-temperature applications. In such glazes copper has a turquoise color rather than the green of a pure lead glaze or the blue of a pure alkaline glaze.

Lead-silicate glaze. A glaze in which the principal constituents are silica and lead oxide. Such glazes flow out well over an underlying body and penetrate into the body for good adhesion; they tend to "fit" clay bodies well, and can be fired at moderate temperatures.

Leather-hard. Describing a clay body in which essentially all of the drying shrinkage has occurred but which can be incised, carved, trimmed, or joined with or added to other parts.

Levigate. To wash by mixing clay or other material with water and allowing it to settle so that the coarse particles segregate to the bottom and the fine ones remain on top. Levigation is the means of separating the fine from the coarse fraction by ladling off or decanting the fine particles; it is the same as sedimentation.

Lime. Calcium oxide, sometimes called burnt lime, because it is made from limestone by calcination, driving off the volatile products. Lime is formed when limestone is heated to about 800°C. It is a constituent of glazes. Burnt lime, or quicklime, reacts with moisture in the air to form the hydroxide. Over a long period of time, this is slowly converted back to the carbonate, the final form of lime plaster.

Limestone. The mineral form of calcium carbonate, which is ground for use as a raw material in glasses, glazes, and some bodies; an alkaline earth.

Luster. A metallic-like appearance of a glaze surface caused by fine particles of metals such as silver and copper formed at or near the surface of the glaze.

Macrostructure. The internal and external structure of a material that can be observed with the naked eye without the aid of magnification; radiography is a technique for viewing the internal macrostructure.

Majolica. A tin-lead opacified glazed earthenware in which the body is usually cream or buff colored and tiny tin-oxide crystals give the glaze its white color. This ware served as a white ground for the painting of complex designs in Italy during the fourteenth, fifteenth, and sixteenth centuries, and is still made today.

Melting range. The range of temperature over which melting occurs. While a single crystal melts at a particular temperature, a mixture of crystals gradually liquefies over a range of temperatures from the "solidus" temperature when the first liquid appears to the higher "liquidus" temperature at which the entire composition is molten.

Microstructure. The internal structure of a material or object that requires magnification greater than that attained by the unaided eye for observation; optical and electron microscopes are used as tools to observe microstructure.

Mold. A porous earthenware or plaster form over which or into which clay can be pressed and shaped. The clay is removed after it has dried sufficiently to maintain its shape.

Montmorillonite. A fine-particle-size clay containing appreciable alkali and alkaline earth constituents commonly found in littoral regions and ancient sea beds. The fine particle size usually results in good plasticity and a high drying shrinkage.

Nonplastic. A constituent such as quartz, lime, feldspar, or already-fired clay that is added to a raw clay to affect its plastic properties and decrease its drying shrinkage.

Ocher. Fine-particle-size red or yellow earthy colorant that is composed of mixtures of iron oxides and often contains clay, lime, quartz, and feldspar as impurities.

Opacifier. A constituent that makes a glaze completely or nearly opaque, that is, unable to transmit light. The most commonly used opacifier in ceramic glazes is tin oxide.

Overglaze. Decoration painted with low-fired enamels on top of the glaze surface; contrast with *underglaze*.

Oxidation, oxidizing atmosphere. A condition in which the gas in contact with the body has excess air, or oxygen, present, which is available to combine chemically, first with the surface, and then with the interior of the body. A kiln with excess air results in clay bodies that contain iron being red in color, with the oxidized form of iron oxide, hematite, producing the color.

Parian porcelain. An unglazed white porcelain body made with a high amount of feldspar in imitation of marble; it was first produced in nineteenth century England.

Particle, particle size. A discrete piece of material, which can range in size from very small to moderately small. Its size in most clays is in the range 0.1–10 μ (micrometers); quartz and feldspar grains used in ceramic bodies normally have particle sizes in the range of 50–100 μ.

Phase. A distinguishable portion of a body or glaze that has a uniform composition and structure. Quartz grains would be a phase present in most ceramic bodies, as would the glassy matrix, mullite crystals, and so on.

Plasticity. The property of clays that allows them to be deformed when a pressure is applied, but then to hold a new shape when the pressure is removed.

Porcelain. A white, translucent, high-fired ceramic ware with a sonorous ring and low porosity.

Precipitation. The formation of a crystalline phase from a liquid beginning with a tiny crystallite that subsequently grows; crystallites forming in a viscous liquid often are first formed at the surface.

Quartz. The mineral that is the most common crystalline form of silica (SiO_2).

Quartz-frit-clay body (frit porcelain). A ceramic body that is white and composed of quartz grains glued together with a mixture of clay and glass frit. When fired to near-vitrification, the body has some resemblance to Chinese porcelain. When made with more clay and less frit, the body is weak and friable.

Raw glaze. A glaze in which all of the constituents are natural minerals that have not been premelted before formulating the glaze.

Reduction, reducing atmosphere. The atmosphere in a smoky kiln resulting from fuel-rich combustion that is depleted in oxygen. The flame is long and smoky. In a low-oxygen atmosphere, the iron content of a clay or glaze is "reduced" to a gray or black color.

Refraction. The bending of light from a straight path as it travels from one material to another, leading to a scattering of light as translucency, or even opacification.

Saggar. A box made of refractory clay in which ware is placed during firing to protect it from the flames and ash in the furnace.

Salt glaze, salt glazing. A method of applying a glaze in the kiln at a high temperature by throwing salt into the kiln to vaporize and react with the surface of the vessel to form an alkali-silicate glaze. The most common substance used for salt glazing is ordinary table salt, sodium chloride; most salt glazes tend to have a somewhat uneven orange-peel texture, but this is not necessarily the case.

Silica. The oxide of silicon (SiO_2) found in nature as the mineral quartz in sand beds or as flint nodules and in soft-paste porcelain in the crystalline form of cristobalite.

Sinter, sintering. The sticking together of particles when heated to high temperature to form an agglomerated mass, usually of greater density than the starting material. Complex processes of chemical reaction, densification, and consolidation take place, but without substantial melting. Sintering is used as a term for processes occurring during the firing of a ware and the "sintering" of mixtures to be used in bodies and glazes.

Slip, slip coating. A fine-particle clay mixture with water that can be applied to the surface of a clay body to form a layer or coating, often burnished before firing. Also used as a general term for any suspension, as a slurry.

Slurry. A mixture of fine-particle material with water that can be poured, painted, or dipped onto a surface; glaze is applied as a slurry to form a surface layer on a ceramic body.

Soapstone, steatite. A soft, easily carved material composed of the mineral talc, a magnesium silicate, which becomes hard when fired to a low temperature. Used as a replacement for all or part of the clay in some ceramic bodies.

Solution. The complete mixing of two substances into a homogeneous, uniform-composition product.

Spectroscopy. An analytical method that uses the interaction of a structure with radiation to determine its composition.

Spinel. A natural or synthetic crystal of the general formula AB_2O_4 used as glaze pigments.

Stoneware. Ware based on a clay body that is not white when fired, but has a ring when struck, with low porosity and a dense structure.

Structure. The organization of material into an observable pattern in space.

Temper. A synonym for the nonplastic addition to a clay that affects its properties of plasticity and lowers the drying shrinkage.

Tin glaze. A glaze opacified with fine particles of tin oxide that are insoluble in the glaze at the firing temperature and provide a white opaque coating.

Transfer printing. A process in which a pattern is printed on paper with a ceramic pigment or overglaze enamel and then transformed via the paper onto the ceramic body.

Transition elements. Elements in the periodic table that provide coloring oxides stable at moderately high temperature; the oxides of iron, copper, chromium, cobalt, manganese, nickel, vanadium, and titanium.

Translucency. A condition intermediate between complete transparency and opacity in which some light is diffusely transmitted through a body or glaze. The light is scattered during transmission such that a visual effect of depth is achieved.

Triaxial body. A whiteware body made from the three constituents clay, quartz, and feldspar.

Underglaze decoration. Decoration painted on the ware and then covered over with the glaze before firing.

Vitreous, vitrify, vitrification. To make glassy, to melt and then to cool, to solidify as a glass.

Wedging. The process of mixing and remixing a plastic clay body to eliminate inhomogeneity and bubbles.

Wollastonite. A calcium silicate crystal, $CaSiO_3$, that is a frequent constituent of glazes, giving rise to translucency and matte surfaces; it also occurs as a crystalline constituent of soft-paste porcelain.

Workability. The combination of yield stress and extensibility that makes it possible for a clay body to be shaped and formed.

Working range. The range of water content over which a clay body can be plastically deformed and shaped without slumping.

INDEX

A

Abbasid 112
absorption 214
Abydos 48, 51, 53, 54
Academie des Beaux Arts 179
Addis, J. 91
aesthetic impact 4, 9, 26, 209, 279, 311
agglomerates 36
alabaster (calcium sulfate) 164, 168
Albrechtsburg 166, 168
d'Albis, A. 194
alkali, alkalies 54, 58, 140, 170, 183, 262, 315
alkali additions to clay 37, 183, 228
alkaline earths 262, 315
alkaline earth additions to clay 37
alkaline glazes 11, 229, 237, 315 (see glazes)
Allan, J. W. 121
alum 183
aluminum oxide (alumina) 4, 26, 33, 85, 86, 87, 100, 104, 107, 140, 141, 153, 170, 171, 187, 201, 261, 262, 263, 267, 270, 274
Amenophis III 51, 53
analytical methods 3, 302ff
anorthite 33, 81, 84, 85, 87, 88, 89, 100, 102, 104, 213, 226, 230, 265, 315

antimony oxide 33, 213
application of glaze 55, 58, 62, 76, 85, 97, 132, 138, 153, 169, 245, 261, 264–265, 273, 286
applique decoration 196–197, 200, 241
d'Arcet 197
Argenteuil calcareous clay 13, 183, 187
Armenian bole 129
arsenic oxide 33, 213
Arita ware 41
art ceramics 163, 179–180, 182
ash, ash glazing 8, 85, 100, 114, 140, 153, 245, 276
assembly and joining of clay parts 37, 56, 62, 71, 73, 138, 168, 184, 228, 239, 240, 242ff
Astbury 15
Atil, E. 120, 121
atmosphere 8, 77, 81, 85, 100, 118, 153, 228, 250, 252, 307
atomic absorption spectroscopy 304, 305
atomic structure 18, 20, 195, 211, 216
atomic mobility 224, 226
Attic black–on–red ware 8, 36
Aue 168
Augustus the Strong 14, 165, 166, 167, 168, 173
Auscher, E. S. 194

B

Bachelier, Jean-Jacques   179, 194
bag wall   97
Baines, J., & J. Malek   65
Baldelli Boni manuscript   140
ball clay   15, 152, 195, 236, 237, 238, 315
bamboo ring   240
bamboo tube   76, 265
Bandar Abbas   10
barium carbonate   16, 199, 264
barium oxide   264, 270
barium sulfate   16, 199, 201, 203, 231
Baroque art   182
Bartholomai, Dr.   167
basalte ware   16, 198
Bayezid II   123
Beck, Curt W.   309
Beck, H.   66
Bedford, John   207
Beleek porcelain   230, 231
Bentley, Thomas   16, 198, 204, 205
bentonite   232, 233
Berlin   15, 166, 175
Biavati, E.   147
Binns, C. F.   66
binocular microscope   281, 288, 289–291, 294, 295, 298
bismuth oxide   17, 41, 120, 216, 264, 270, 275
bisque, bisquit ware or firing   3, 76, 138, 179, 180, 192, 241, 255, 265, 273, 316
blanc–de–chine ware   165
bloating   248, 250
Blondeau, Pierre   179
blue color, significance of   54
blue & white wares   41, 49, 135, 136, 151, 164, 165
Blunden, C.   108
Bolton, Matthew   202
bone ash (calcium phosphate)   15, 230
bone china   15, 230, 231, 258, 265, 316
bone–dry   184, 245–246
borax   17, 33, 263, 270, 274
boron   41, 216, 262, 263, 266
boric oxide   262, 274
Boston Museum of Fine Arts   51, 52, 70
Böttger, Johann Friedrich   14, 36, 39, 49,
163–173, 229, 230, 231, 256, 257, 276
Böttger porcelain   4, 5, 21, 163–177, 195, 263, 280, 282, 289, 316
Böttger red stoneware   231
Boucher, François   44, 49, 179ff, 185
Bourbon, Louis Henri de   182
Bourry, E.   259
Bowen, H. K.   226
bricks   11, 241, 258
  bricks, defects in   245
Bristol glazes   264
Brongniart, Alexander   17, 45, 175, 177, 192, 194
Brovarsky, E.   56, 66
bubbles, pores   75, 81, 83, 85, 100, 101, 138, 139, 185, 213, 217, 220, 238, 261, 286
Buddhist art   125
burning lens, burning glass   166, 167, 168, 170, 216, 223
burnishing   7, 39, 85, 88, 89, 107, 222, 246, 250, 275, 316
Burselm   48
Bushnell, S. Q.   161

C

Caiger-Smith, A.   121, 147, 259, 277
Cairo   112
calcia (see lime, limestone)   223, 232
calcine   115, 140, 153, 164, 168, 216, 241, 273, 316
calcined clay   118
calcium antimonate   213
calcium carbonate (calcite limestone)   33, 288, 291, 297
calcium feldspar   33
calcium oxide   (see lime)
calcium phosphate   100, 140, 143, 153 (see bone ash)
calcium silicate   33, 271   (see wollastonite pyroxenes)
calcium sulfate   245, 291   (see gypsum)
caneware   198
Canton   164
capillarity   36, 115, 211, 217–223, 244, 247, 282, 316
carbon   269
carbon–14 dating   297, 312

Cardew, M. 259
Carswell, J. 133
Carter, G. F. 309
carving 246
CAT scan 299, 300
Catherine of Russia 204
cawk 16, 199
Caylus, Count 16
celadon, Song Dynasty 11, 44, 47,
    69–91, 93, 101, 104, 238, 257–258,
    286, 291, 294, 316
  Celadon replications 307
celsian (barium–aluminum–silicate) 202,
    203
cementation glazing 54, 55
centimeter 20
Centigrade 316
ceramic history 7–18, 19, 293, 311
ceramic technology 7–18, 19, 37–43, 45,
    89, 93, 107, 120, 133, 140, 146, 187,
    209, 227–259, 263, 288, 293, 311
ceramic science 18–36, 45, 211–226, 311,
    313–314
ceramic traditions 293, 313
Ch'ai ware 94
Chang, Fukang 90, 108
Chantilly 15, 182
Charleston, R. J. 45
Charlotte, Queen 204, 205
Chelsea 15, 17, 204
chemical revolution 270, 274 (see
    scientific revolution)
chemical symbols 33
Chen, X. 91
Chen, Xian–qui 108
Chetwynd, Deborah 204
Chicaneau, Pierre 182
Ch'ien Lung 152
China clay 236, 238, 316
China Stone 10, 11, 80, 85, 100, 151,
    152, 230, 234, 316
Chinese ceramic practices 10, 39, 40, 41,
    69–109, 133, 149–162, 241, 257, 265,
    273, 274, 286
Chinese glazes 11
Chinese porcelain 5, 224 (see hard paste
    porcelain)
Chinese soft paste 152
Ch'ing Dynasty 49, 149, 165
Ching–te–Chen (Jing de Zhen) 10, 49,

149, 151, 155, 159, 160, 161, 162
  Ching–te–Chen kiln 154, 175, 257
chlorides 244 (see salt)
chocolate pot 165, 195
Chou Jen 90, 91
chromite ferrite spinels 129, 270
chromium oxide 20, 270, 284
chromophores 271
Ch'un (see Jun)
Church, A. H. 207
Cintemani 125
clare de lune glaze 160
clays 33, 34, 35, 37, 141, 168, 216, 316
clay body composition 141, 168, 227–231
clay body microstructures 21, 22, 23, 24,
    25
cloisonne enamels 11
cobalt 20, 42, 115, 123, 125, 138, 139,
    157, 196, 199, 201, 269, 273, 284
cobalt–aluminate blue 214, 284
coil building 239–240
colorants 10, 11, 20, 40, 41, 118, 125,
    155, 211, 213, 214, 215, 269–271,
    287, 303 (see pigments)
color photography 291, 292
complexity of technology 72, 76, 89,
    107, 120, 156–157, 160–161, 287
cones 256
Constantinople (Istanbul) 124, 125
constraints of raw materials 39, 40, 112,
    141, 145, 146, 209, 222
color temperature 256 (see firing color)
cooling rate 26, 76, 77, 97, 98, 107, 224
Cooper, Emmanuel 45
copper 20, 41, 54, 58, 62, 64, 93, 94,
    97, 105, 106, 107, 112, 115, 118, 119,
    123, 125, 157, 169, 214, 269, 284
coral red overglaze enamel 132, 155, 157,
    159, 271, 290
cord 105, 287
Corinth 234
Cornish clay 199, 205
Cornwall stone 199, 205
cracking 237, 243, 244, 263 (see dunting)
crackle 316
craft specialization 160 (see specialization
    or factory system)
craftsmanship 62, 308
crawling 62, 170, 223, 268
crazing 267, 268, 316

creamware   198, 204
Crecy   179
cristobalite   21, 33, 97, 99, 141, 187, 192,
     193, 213, 214, 217, 230, 317
crystal   216, 219, 261, 317
Czechoslovakia   7

D

Damascus   72
Darwin, Erasmus   202
dating methods   297–298
David, Percival   108
Davillier, M. le Baron   135, 146
decalcomania   42
defects   (see glazing defects, firing
     defects, cracking, warping, bloating)
Dehua   165
delayed crazing   268
Delft blue   42, 270, 273
delftware   12, 165, 166, 167, 318 (see
     maiolica)
Derbyshire   16, 199
destructive analysis   294
diamond core drilling   294, 297
diffraction   18, 45, 211, 294, 304, 305,
     318
diffuse reflection or transmission   212,
     214, 215
diffusion   118, 119, 199, 307
dirt   286, 287–288, 295, 301
division of labor   17
Dolne Vestonice   7
dolomite   126
draft   76, 77, 97, 132, 153, 174, 256, 257
dragon kiln   76, 77, 78, 79, 258
draw trials   153, 202, 256
drawings   184, 200
     drawings as documentation   292
Dresden   163, 166, 167
drying   54, 62, 152, 184, 185, 220, 221,
     232–236, 238, 244–245, 247
drying shrinkage   37, 39, 56, 75, 114,
     115, 138, 163, 185, 200, 228, 232,
     233, 236, 237, 238, 240, 241, 245,
     263, 265, 283, 318
Dubois brothers   182
Ducret, S.   176
Du Halde   17

dunting   267
Dutch East Indies Company   164

E

earthenware   7–9, 40, 217, 224, 225,
     227–229, 231, 282, 286, 294, 318
     firing of   247–251
     microstructure   235, 248, 249
earth's crust, composition of   26
Ebelman, J. J.   161
Edirne   125
efflorescence   54, 55, 58, 62, 65, 114,
     229, 244, 245, 263, 275, 306, 318
eggshell wares   245
Egypt   47, 51–67, 112, 123, 135
Egyptian blue   270
Egyptian faienc   9, 39, 49, 51–67, 93,
     223, 238, 244, 246, 275, 286, 290,
     303, 306, 318
Egyptian faience chalice   51–67, 72, 290
Ehli Hiref   123
electron microprobe   44, 115, 141, 157,
     294
electron microscopy   18, 21, 62, 63,
     300–302 (see scanning electron
     microscopy, transmission electron
     microscopy)
electronic ceramics   4
Eler brothers   15, 195
emulsion   26, 100, 103, 104, 107
emulsion formation   28, 30, 101, 104
enamel   318 (see overglaze enamel)
encaustic painting   198
energy dispersive–xray analysis
     (EDS)   301
engine turning lathe   16, 37, 39, 200, 204
England   229, 230
engobes   138, 231, 272, 318
etchants   301
Etruria   204
European ceramic practices   89, 98, 107,
     152, 160, 163–193, 253, 257, 270, 286
eutectic   223

F

factory system   42–3, 149, 155, 163, 204,
     206

faience   12, 47 (see majolica, delftware)
fakes   297, 308, 309, 312, 313
famille rose pallette   16–17, 37, 41, 151, 270, 318
famille verte palette   12, 41, 150, 271
Farnsworth, Marie   307
fast wheel   239 (see throwing)
fat clay   232
Fatimid   112
feldspar   14, 22, 23, 26, 33, 34, 35, 80, 82, 138, 140, 143, 152, 173, 174, 229 230, 231, 238, 251, 263, 267, 288, 291, 318
Ferdinando   141
Ferrara   135
ferrous sulfate   155
finishing   39, 75, 115, 138, 153, 168, 184, 185, 186, 241, 245–246 (see trimming)
fireboxes   175, 183, 253, 257
firing   97, 174–175, 186, 247–258, 265–266, 306 (see kilns)
firing behavior   223ff
firing behavior of
  earthenware   247–249
  glasses   216
  iron oxide   250
  hard paste   27–28, 80, 115, 220
  quartz bodies   115, 117
  lusters   119
  Medici porcelain   141
  soft paste   187, 191, 192
firing color   41, 71, 118, 153, 173, 247, 256
firing defects   258, 283
firing shrinkage   163, 186, 202, 252, 265, 319
firing supports   186, 265
firing temperatures   10, 11, 13, 14, 15, 21, 26, 36, 40, 88, 100, 101, 104, 115, 132, 138, 153, 155, 164, 166, 168, 170, 173, 186, 187, 192, 201, 202, 229, 230, 247, 252, 271, 275, 276, 277
Fisher, the potter   167
fit   319 (see glaze fit)
Fleming, Stuart J.   309
flint   140, 159, 195, 199 (see quartz), 217, 229, 238, 319
Florence   48, 49
flues   255, 256 (see draft)

fluidity   224, 261 (see viscosity)
fluorine   269
fluorspar   41, 270
flux, fluxes   27, 32, 140, 167, 216, 217, 263, 264, 270, 274
foot wedging   238
fracture strength   21, 192, 216
fracture texture   21, 190, 192, 216, 282, 283
  importance of   295
Franchet, L.   108, 121
Frankenthal   15
French Academy of Science   166
French Royal Academy   165
Frederick I   166
frit   10, 13, 112, 116, 126, 129, 146, 230, 231, 255, 264, 276, 319
frit porcelain   115, 135, 246 (see quartz–clay–frit porcelain)
fritted glaze   55, 56, 262, 263
fuel   253, 257
Fujian (Fou-Kian)   165
Fulton, Matthew   200
Fulvy, Orry de   182–183
function   165
furnaces   167 (see kilns)
Fürstenburg   15, 173, 175

G

galena   (lead sulfide)   275, 276
German stoneware   10 (see soft glazed stoneware)
German mining resources   165, 229
Gibbs, J. Willard   27, 223
gilding   41, 274–5
glass   18, 20, 33, 61, 80, 81, 126–130, 155, 156, 170, 172, 173, 183, 191, 192, 193, 202, 203, 212, 214, 216, 217, 218, 219, 224, 229, 247, 248, 250, 251, 258, 264, 266, 319
glass blowing and melting   9, 264
glass formation   27, 34, 35, 216, 218, 219, 223, 224 (see sintering)
glass formers   32, 262
glass frit   112, 229 (see frit)
glass houses   166
glassy liquid in glaze   21, 22, 23, 24, 25, 26, 115, 214
  in body   251

glass technology 65, 264
glazes 3, 14, 81–90, 93, 94, 212–215, 223, 225, 230–231, 264–266, 319
glaze, alkali silicate 140, 229–231
glaze application 264–5, 275 (see application of glaze)
glaze defects 170, 267–268, 283, 284
glaze fit 40, 267–268
glaze, lead alkali silicate 157, 159
glaze surface 266–267
glaze thickness 54, 58, 72, 75, 76, 132, 140
glost firing 262, 319
goethite 214
gold 42, 153, 166, 264, 269, 270
Gombroon or gomroon ware 10, 115, 182
Gompertz, G. St. G. M. 90
grain, grain size 319
Granger, M. A. 194
Gravant, François 183
Greek black on red ware 40, 250, 251, 307 (see Attic)
green (unfired) 319
green color, significance of 54
green strength or dry strength 184, 246
grinding (see milling, polishing)
grog 37
gum Arabic 186
Gussoni, Andrea 136
gypsum 14, 16, 183, 199, 229, 230, 231, 237, 241, 319

H

Hackwood, William 196–197, 200
Hajji Firuz 234, 235
Halaf 8
Halle, A. F. 194
Han Dynasty 230
hardness (scratch or Mohs scale) 288
hard paste porcelain 21, 22, 23, 26, 34, 35, 149–162, 163–177, 205, 224, 238, 251, 252, 282, 320
Harmon, C. G. 277
Harris, J. R. 65, 67
Harrison & Alders 198
Hathor 56
health hazards 192, 264

heat transfer 256–257
Heatherington, A. L. 91, 108
Hebei (Hopei) 94
Hellot, Jean 183, 194, 197
hematite 33, 157, 159, 214, 228, 250, 307
Henan (Honan) 94
High–tech modern ceramics 3, 4
high temperature processes 211, 223–225
hill climbing kiln (see dragon kiln)
historical precedents 4–5
Hobson, R. L. 108
Höchst 15, 175
Honore d'Urfe 72
Horoldt, Johann Gregor 175
horseshoe kiln 97, 98
Hungary 123
Hunger, Christoph Konrad 175
hydrochloric acid (muriatic acid) 291

I

ice 223
illite 232, 234, 235, 246
I–Hsing ware (Jiaxing) 14, 163, 165, 168
Imari ware 41
imitation, semi- and precious stones 49, 51, 53, 64–65, 69, 93, 123, 125, 133, 167, 179, 186, 199
  metals 49, 51, 53, 111, 118–120, 168
  textiles 125, 126, 133
imitations of Chinese ware 163, 165, 168, 182
imitations of Near Eastern wares 182–183
incised decoration 58, 62, 75, 184, 245–246
index of refraction 212, 213, 217
India 112
Indian porcelain 136
Indus Valley black–on–grey ware 307
Industrial revolution 14, 16, 165, 195, 197, 202, 204, 205, 206
intermediates 262
ion 320
Iran 115, 121 (see Qom beads)
iridescence 45
Irminger, Jacob 168, 169
iron 20

iron oxide   7–8, 33, 85, 88, 98, 100, 107, 115, 123, 129, 168, 214, 228, 229, 230, 274
  firing behavior   250–251
  impurity   45, 62, 64, 117, 126, 152, 155, 187, 229, 230, 244, 269, 270
iron oxide red color   125, 129, 132, 320 (see coral red)
iron sulfides   214
Ishii, T.   91
Islamic lusterware   (see lusterware)
Islamic ceramic practices   49, 111–133 esp. 133
isotherm, isothermal section   35, 191, 320
Istanbul   123–125
Italy   12, 118, 135
Iznik tile   10, 12, 39, 41, 48, 49, 115, 123–133, 272, 303

J

jade   49, 69, 81, 89
jasper   167
jasper porcelain   168
jasperware   16, 49, 50, 195, 231, 271, 282, 320
jiggering   153, 243
Jin Dynasty   73, 94
Jingdezhen   47 (see Ching–te–Chen)
joining   (see assembly)
Jungfernbastei laboratory   167, 173
junware glaze   26, 28, 29, 30, 31, 224, 291, 301
  blue color   28
  white cloud effect   30
junware   11, 43, 44, 47
junware bowl   93–109

K

Kaczmarczyk, A. & R. E. M. Hedges   67
K'ang Hsi porcelain & glaze   17, 36, 41, 49, 132, 149, 151, 152, 153, 159, 162, 165, 173, 175, 192, 202, 270, 274, 280, 290 (see hard paste porcelain)
kaolin   10, 15, 151, 152, 168, 173, 176, 197, 230, 232, 246, 320
kaolinite   33, 38

Karanova, Yugoslavia   248
Kashan   10, 48, 111, 114, 121
Kassel kiln   175
Keir, James   202
Kerma   56
Kiangsi province   151
Kiefer, C., & A. Allibert   54, 66
kilns   10, 76–79, 107, 112, 132, 140, 151, 153, 154, 155, 165, 166, 168, 170, 174, 229, 252–258 (see horseshoe kiln, dragon kiln, draft, muffle kiln)
Kingery, W. D.   90, 91, 108, 109, 146, 194, 226, 314
Konigstein   167

L

laboratory analysis   281, 292–306, esp. 293, 308, 309, 312
La Danseuse   179–181
Lambert, J. B.   309
landscape painting, Chinese   149
Lane, A.   121, 133, 146
lapis lazuli   51, 53, 64, 167
Lau, M.   91
Lawrence, W. G.   226
lead   118, 199
  analysis of   291
lead–alkali–silicate glaze   33, 49, 123, 128, 129, 133, 231, 275, 320
lead antimonate   213
lead arsenate   213
lead glazing   11, 112, 139, 140–143, 231, 266, 276
lead oxide   33, 115, 116, 126, 140, 143, 155, 223, 231, 262, 263, 264, 266
lead—silicate glaze   33, 263, 275, 320
lean clay   232
leather hard   39, 75, 184, 220, 221, 236, 244, 245, 246, 320
Liebnitz   14, 166
Leiden   165
Leipzig   168
Leventine   136, 140
Levantine porcelain   135 (see quartz–clay–frit porcelain)
Levigate   320 (see settling)
Li Jiazhi   91, 108
Lightbown, R.   147, 259

Lime (CaO) 11, 26, 54, 58, 62, 85, 86, 100, 101, 114, 126, 140, 145, 153, 167, 168, 170–171, 183, 187, 223, 228, 229, 230, 237, 267, 270, 271, 273, 320

limey clay bodies 10, 11, 183, 228, 229, 232, 238

limestone 33, 58, 85, 183, 250, 321

Limoges 175

Linru xian 94

liquid—liquid phase separation 101

liquidus temperature 145, 223

Lister, Martin 13, 176, 182, 183, 194

lithage 33, 263

Liverani, G. 147

Liverpool 17, 42, 198, 204

Longquan 48, 69, 70

lotus 58, 59, 75

Louis XV 183, 197

loupe (magnifying glass) 281, 285–288, 298

low power microscopy 43–44 (see binocular microscope)

Lucas, A. & J. R. Harris 65, 67

Lunar Society of Birmingham 202

Lung Ch'uan (see Longquan)

luster, lusterware 11–12, 41, 111–121, 126, 135, 212, 274–275, 301, 321

luster painting 118–120

M

Macao 165

MacIver and Mace 53, 66

Macquer, P. J. 197, 202

macrostructure 18, 43–45, 211, 293
    impt of 20, 298–300, 313, 321 (see individual objects, manufacturing methods, visual effects)

magnesia 33, 114, 140, 187, 270 (see dolomite)

magnetite 33, 214, 228, 250, 307

maiolica (or majolica) 12, 39, 135, 140, 146, 205, 228, 272, 273, 321
    glazes 16

malachite 9, 53, 64, 270

manganese 20

manganese dioxide 8, 42, 125, 138, 139, 157, 269, 271

Manufacture Nationale de Sèvres 184, 280

manufacturing methods 283, 293, 299
    manufacturing sequence 287, 293 (see shaping, application, throwing, etc.)

marble 179, 182

marketing 200, 204, 205, 206

marzacotta 13, 140, 141

masterpieces 47, 53 (see ceramic masterpieces)

matte glazes 198, 267

measurement 18, 20, 292

media for overglaze enamels & gilding 275 (see organic additives)

Medici, Cosimo I de 135

Medici, Francesco I de 13, 49, 135, 141, 146, 230, 231

Medici porcelain 5, 13, 49, 135–147, 223, 229, 231, 280, 290

Medici porcelain bottle 135–147, 290

Medley, M. 108, 161

Meir, Egypt 54

Meissen 15, 17, 48, 49, 163, 166, 195, 230

Meissen production 14, 163–177, 246

melting range 27, 145, 191, 216, 223, 321 (see firing temperature)

melting temperature 27, 166, 216, 223
    of SiO_2 27 (see phase diagrams, firing temperature)

Mendeleef 27

Mennecy 15

Menzhausen, I 176

mercury 166

Mesopotamia 8, 45, 53

Metegard, Eliza 206

Metropolitan Museum of Art, New York 138, 164, 196

mica 80, 152, 229, 230

microchemical analysis 18, 44, 81–82, 126, 140, 141, 187, 201, 302–306 (see electron microprobe analysis)

micrometer 20

microprobe analyses (see electron microprobe)

microstructure 18, 44, 45, 52, 58, 82, 83, 211, 293, 300–302, 306, 321
    analysis of 20–21, 289, 290, 291
    of celadon 81–88

Egyptian faience 60, 61, 62
  of Iznik tile 128
  of jun ware 100–103
  of lusterware 115–119
milk glass 13
millimeter 20
mill additions 264
milling 85, 101, 107, 112, 116, 118, 126, 140, 155, 157, 183, 200, 237, 238, 264, 273
Minai ware 12, 274
Ming Dynasty ceramic practices 12, 49, 94, 98, 107, 132, 135, 149, 164, 165
modeling (pinch forming) 37, 54, 65, 71, 73, 185, 238–239, 283
models 184, 200
modifiers 262
Mohs hardness 288
mold, molding & mold making 8, 39, 54, 56, 62, 65, 114, 126, 133, 137, 138, 152, 153, 155, 163, 164, 169, 180, 184, 185, 186, 187, 192, 241–242, 283, 321
molecular weight 262
montmorillonite clay 33, 112, 114, 116, 232, 238, 321
muffle kiln 132, 155, 275
mullite 21, 22, 23, 26, 27, 33, 34, 35, 80, 82, 155, 156, 170, 172, 173, 213, 214, 217, 229, 230, 251, 265, 267
Munsell color determination 292
Musée de Louvre, Paris 188
Musée National de Céramique, Sèvres 124, 136, 137, 138, 139, 180, 184
Museo Internazionale delle Ceramiche di Faenza 138, 141

N

nanometer 20
Naples yellow (lead antimonate) 213, 270
natron 9, 40, 62, 64, 264
Near Eastern ceramic practices 7, 11, 39, 40, 51, 53, 65, 140, 146, 228, 229, 239, 241, 246, 253, 264, 274, 286
needle tool 281, 285–288, 290
Nehmitz, Michael 168
neoclassicism 198

neutron activation analysis (N.A.A.) 296, 304, 305
Newcommon kiln 175
New World ceramic practices 241
Nicaea 125
nickel oxide 269, 273
Noble, J. V. 66, 307
nonplastic inclusions 37, 114, 238, 251, 299, 321
nonplastic minerals 228
Nordhausen 168
northern celadon (yaozhou) 69
Norton, F. H. 45, 226
Nubia 53
Nymphenburg 15, 175

O

object examination 43–45
ocher 7–8, 41, 118, 214, 245, 321 (see iron oxide)
oil painting 266
oil—vinegar salad dressing 26, 100–101 (see emulsion)
opacifiers 120, 212–214, 269–271, 322 (see tin oxide)
opalescence 93, 97, 100, 101–103, 105, 106, 107
opaque glazes 4, 101, 212, 230
optical density 287
optical emission spectroscopy 305
optical microscopes 300, 301 (see binocular microscope)
  petrographic microscope 299
optical properties 18, 211–226 (see visual effect, visual impact)
orange peel texture 268, 284 (see salt glazed stoneware)
organic additives, binders, impurities 114, 118, 129, 155, 184, 186, 232, 237, 238, 246, 247, 265, 273, 274, 275, 289
Osiris 53
Ottoman Empire 123
overfiring 250, 251, 286 (see slumping & bloating, glaze defects)
overglaze enamels 12, 41, 149, 150, 151, 155, 157–161, 262, 266, 274–5, 284, 322

overglaze painting   41, 155, 158, 163, 284
oxidation   8, 71, 228–9, 250, 322 (see atmosphere)

P

Pabst von Ohain, Gottfried   163, 165, 166
paddle and anvil forming   39, 240
painterly decoration   12, 37, 40, 49, 111, 112
Pan-po (Banpo)   107, 253, 254, 255, 257
Paquier, Claudius Innocentius du   175
Parent, M.   175
Paris   49
Parian porcelain   322
Parmelee, C. W.   277
particle orientation or alignment, 243, 246, 250
particle size   36, 85, 86, 101, 118, 129, 157, 159, 183, 212, 217, 220, 228, 232, 233, 238, 264, 269, 270, 271, 322 (see milling)
pearl ash   33 (see potassium carbonate)
pegmatite   42, 270
Peking   149
penlight   281, 285–288
Percival David Foundation of Chinese Art   150
Père d'Entrecolles   (Father François Xavier d'Entrecolles)   15, 17, 150, 151, 152, 153, 155, 157, 160, 161, 176, 177, 197
periodic table   27, 32, 33
permeability   227, 247
Petrie, W. M. F.   66
Petsopoulos, Y.   133
Petuntse   11, 15, 151, 152, 176 (see china stone)
phase   18, 32, 322
phase diagram   27, 34, 36, 104, 141, 145, 170–171, 187, 191, 192, 223, 224
phase equilibria   223
Philon, H.   121
phosphorous oxides   216
Piccolpasso, Cipriano   135, 140, 147, 228, 230, 231, 241, 253, 256, 259, 265, 277
piece molds   242
Pier Maria   136

pigments   7–8, 155, 269–271 (see colorants)
pine ash   11
pinholes   268, 284
pit firing   253, 254
plaque of unfired clay for setting ware   76
plaster molds   137, 138, 152, 169, 184, 200, 241, 244
plaster-of-paris (see plaster molds)
plasticity and formability   26, 152, 183, 187, 220, 221, 222, 227, 232–233, 238, 322, 323
platey particles   232
Plauen   168
polishing   186, 199, 246, 275 (see imitation stone, gilding)
Polya, G.   314
Pompadour, Mme de   179, 183
porcelain   72, 230, 231, 322 (see soft-paste, hard paste, quartz-clay-frit)
porosity   73, 144, 152, 185, 201, 214, 238, 240, 247, 266, 282, 286, 306
Portuguese   164–165
potash   40, 228, 246, 263 (see potassium carbonate)
potassia   33, 86, 100, 101, 104, 153, 157, 187, 232
potassium carbonate (potash, pearl ash)   33, 114, 115, 116, 126, 140
potassium nitrate   159, 183, 274
Poterat, Edme and Louis   182
potter's wheel   8, 37, 94, 95
pottery, definition of   72
Preaud, T.   194
precipitation   269, 287, 322 (see opacifiers, pigments, crystals)
preparation of body composition   183–184, 237–238
Priestley, Joseph   202
proton—induced—x-ray—emission (PIXE)   303, 304, 305
provenance, importance of   312, 313
purple of Cassius   42, 270, 271
pyrometer   202, 253, 256
pyroxenes   141

Q

Qāsim, Abūl   115, 116, 118, 121

Qing Dynasty (see Ch'ing Dynasty)
Qom beads (blue Iranian donkey
    beads) 40, 52, 54, 276–277, 306
quarter mold 240
quartz 9, 10, 21, 22, 23, 24, 25, 27, 33,
    34, 35, 54, 58, 61, 62, 80, 81, 84, 97,
    99, 112, 114, 115, 116, 126, 128, 129,
    130, 138, 140, 141, 143, 152, 153,
    155, 156, 157, 173, 183, 186, 192,
    193, 213, 214, 216, 217, 229, 230,
    231, 237, 251, 274, 288, 291, 297,
    322
quartz frit body 39 (see Egyptian faience)
quartz-frit-clay body 10, 111–134, 231,
    237, 238, 246, 286, 322 (see Islamic
    lustreware or Iznik tile)
quartz-clay-frit porcelain (same as
    quartz-frit-clay body)
quartz paste 229, 230, 231, 265, 273
Queensware 204

R

R, RO, R₂O, R₂O₃ 262
Raby, J. 134
radiography 240 (see xero–radiography
    and x–ray radiography)
random network array 216, 218, 219
rate of deformation 233
rate of production 242
rate of reaction 226
raw glaze 262–264, 322
Rayy 114, 121
Reaumur, Rene 15, 151, 176, 177, 197
Reaumur porcelain 15
red clays 64, 229
red flashing 120
red heat 247 (see firing color)
red lead 33, 263
red stoneware 163, 165, 166, 167, 168,
    271 (see I–Hsing ware)
reduction 8, 100, 118, 153, 157, 228,
    229, 250, 269, 322 (see atmosphere)
reflection, reflectivity 45, 69, 102, 119,
    120, 186, 187, 190, 212, 214, 215,
    266, 271, 284
refraction 323
Reilly, Robin 206
Renaissance 136
    ceramic practice 259

replication 45, 54, 55, 155, 168, 170,
    173, 293, 306–307
research, evidence of 159, 163, 165, 166,
    168, 173, 175–6, 199, 202, 205 (see
    scientific or chemical revolution)
resist decoration 272
restoration 286, 289, 308
rib or ribbing 184, 240
rice grain porcelain 10, 246
Ringer, Johann Jakob 175
risk in execution 62
Rococo art 182
Rouen 182
rouge 42 (see iron oxide)
Royal Society 202
Ruhle, Christolph 167
Russell, R., Jr. 207

S

Sadler and Green 42, 198
Sagger 76, 77, 78, 79, 97, 115, 153, 154,
    155, 168, 173, 175, 255, 258, 265,
    323
Saladin, Sultan 72
salt, saltwater 140, 141, 183, 223, 228,
    233, 244, 275, 276
salt glazing, salt glazed stoneware 14, 40,
    175, 195, 198, 276, 323
Salvatat, L. A. 161
sampling 294–295
    representative sample 294
    microsample or macrosample 294
    sample size 296
    sample preparation 298, 299, 301, 303
sanbornite (barium silicate) 202, 203
sand 54, 126, 140, 141, 153 (see quartz)
sang–de–boeuf red glaze 269
Saqqara 54
Sato, M. 108
Savage, George 206
Savill, R. 194
Sayer, G. R. 162
Saxony 165, 167
scanning electron microscopy
    (S.E.M.) 44, 156, 159, 160, 172,
    174, 193, 301, 302, 306
scattering 214
Scherzer, E. 161
Schnorr earth 168

Schulle, W.   170, 176
Schumann, Theodore   307
scientific revolution   163, 165, 195, 197, 199, 202, 205, 270, 274, 280
screening   238, 264 (see filtration)
scumming   245
Searle, A. B.   259
Seger, Hermann   262, 263
Seger formula   262, 263
Selim I   123
Seljuk   10, 114
Senwosret I   65
sericite   232, 234
setting   252, 258, 265
settling   152, 183, 237, 265 (see levigation)
Sèvres   17, 39, 41, 179, 183, 192, 194, 195, 246
   Sèvres blue   42, 270
   Sèvres blue-black   42, 270
sgraffito   246
Shang Dynasty   10, 72, 229
Shanghai   165
shaping   8, 72, 93, 94, 96, 97, 152–153, 209, 220–221, 227, 232–234, 238–247, 283
shell temper   237
shivering   267
short clay   232, 237, 243
shrinkage   (see drying or firing shrinkage, thermal expansion, crazing)
silica   33, 104, 140, 153, 170–171, 183, 187, 201, 216, 262, 323 (see quartz)
silicates   26, 27, 202, 216 (see wollastonite, feldspar)
silicon dioxide $(SiO_2, silica)$ 26, 27
silver   41, 112, 118, 119, 269
Sinan, Agha   125
sinter   13, 36, 146, 183, 220, 221, 228, 230, 231, 264, 323
sintering   8, 61, 140, 141, 220, 221, 224, 228, 247, 250, 266, 286, 307 (see capillarity)
skove kiln   253
slab making   184
slab building   37, 239–240
slips and slip coatings   7, 9, 36, 39, 100, 126, 133, 184, 199, 200, 228, 230, 231, 245, 272–274, 323
slip casting   39, 244

slow wheel   239
slumping   220, 221, 223, 225, 232, 248
   avoidance of   250–252
slurry   58, 61, 140, 238, 241, 245, 265, 323 (see suspension)
smalt   273
smear glazes   40, 277
soapstone   15, 152, 323 (see talc)
soda   33, 62, 63, 64, 114, 126, 140, 141, 153, 187, 192, 222, 232, 237
soda ash (sodium carbonate)   33, 182, 263
soda–lime–silicate glaze   33 (see glass)
sodium carbonate   33
sodium fluoride   213
soft paste porcelain   39, 44, 49, 141, 237, 246, 251, 252, 258, 265, 282
   glazing   16
   French   5, 13–14, 21, 24, 25, 26, 165, 202, 205, 214, 217, 230, 231, 289, 308
   Chinese   152
   sculpture   179
Soho   205
solar furnace   165, 166, 223
solidus temperature   223
soluble salts or alkalies   263, 264 (see efflorescence and fritting)
solution and solubility   262, 323
   solution colors   269
Song Dynasty wares   11, 47, 69, 72, 73, 93, 94, 107
Spain   112, 118, 136
spalling   237 (see glaze defects)
spark plug insulators   4
specialization   155 (see factory system)
spectroscopy   18, 211, 304, 305, 323
specular reflection or transmission   212, 214, 215
spinel   214, 323
spode   15
spot tests   291, 302
spraying   265
sprigged decoration   200, 201, 241
Sprimont, Nicholas   15
St. Cloud   13, 15, 16, 49, 136, 165, 166, 182, 183, 195
St. Petersburg   15
Staffordshire   15, 17, 195, 198, 204, 205, 276
stains   271, 275

standards 313

stenciled decoration 129

Stoke–on–Trent 198

Stone, J. F. S., & L. C. Thomas 65

stoneware 39, 229, 231, 265, 323

  English 40, 223–224

  clay 236

stone working technique 53 (see polishing)

Strasburg 15

Stöltzel, Samuel 175

stress concentrator 21

structure 3, 211, 285, 324

structure–properties–processing relationships 18, 26, 43, 45

Stull, R. T. 91

sulfur 269

Süleyman the Magnificent 123

Sung Synasty (see Song Dynasty)

Sung, Ying–Hsing 162

surface energy 222

surface tension 222

surface texture 211, 212, 223

suspension 116, 118, 152, 228, 263, 264, 272 (see slurry)

Sweden 167

Syria 135

T

Taiwan 164

talc 33, 152

T'ang Dynasty (and wares) 9, 112, 297–8

Tang Ying 161 (see Ts'ang Ying–hsuan)

T'ao–Lu 162

T'ao Shuo 109, 161

T'ao Ya 162

technology 4, 227

temper 228, 237, 324 (see nonplastic inclusions)

temperature effects 223–226, 252

Templeton, Lady Elizabeth 195–197, 200

termal shock resistance 21, 173, 198

terra sigilata 229, 251

thermal expansion 216

  contraction 228, 237, 267, 272, 306

thermodynamics 27

thermoluminescent dating 296, 297–298, 299, 308, 312

throwing 39, 65, 73, 93, 94, 96, 114, 152, 184, 192, 200, 222, 239, 241–243, 283

Thutmosis III 51, 53

Tichane, R. 161

tiles 114, 241, 265

time–temperature envelope 225, 226

tin chloride 42

tin glaze 231, 324

tin oxide 11, 12, 33, 115, 116, 117, 138, 140, 213, 231, 270, 271

titanium dioxide 213, 244

Tite, M. S. et. al. 66, 309

tournette 239

Tragear, M. 90, 108

transfer printing 42, 197, 204, 324

transition elements 20, 32, 214

translucency 45, 64, 81, 89, 99, 116, 117, 139, 140, 151, 212

  of body 26, 163, 164, 167, 182, 186–187, 190, 192, 200, 202, 214, 215, 282, 286, 324

transmission 119, 192, 212, 215, 282, 284

transmission electron microscopy (T.E.M.) 45, 103, 119, 301, 302

triaxial porcelain 145, 223, 230, 324

tridymite 33

trimming 13, 96, 152, 153, 192, 200, 243, 245

Trou, Henri 182

tunnel kiln 258

Turkey 135

Ts'ang Ying–hsuan 151, 159 (see Tang Ying)

Tschinhaus, Count Ehrenfried Walther von 49, 163, 165, 166, 167, 170, 216, 223

turntable 239

turquoise 51, 53, 64

Tuscany 135

U

ultrasonic cleaning 301

ultraviolet light (black light) 173, 288–289

Uhlmann, D. R. 226

undercut 241–242

underglaze coating 126, 231, 284 (see slip)

underglaze colorants 123, 125, 126, 129, 138, 272–274

underglaze decoration 133, 138, 212, 272–274, 284, 324

underglaze red 273

updraft kilns 175
    medieval & Renaissance 255

uranium oxide 4, 270

V

Vandiver, P. 66, 67, 91, 108, 109, 146

van Malcem, Gerhard 167

vapor glazing 40, 245, 275, 276

variability of product 72, 73, 94, 96, 184
    of composition 116–118, 118–120, 157, 161
        of temperature 175
            of optical quality 224
    of clays 232
    of color 268, 270–271
    of microstructure 308

Venetian porcelain 13

Venice 15, 135, 140

Venusbastai 163

Victoria and Albert Museum 95, 113, 127, 138

Vienna 14, 175

Vincennes 14, 15, 48, 49, 141, 179, 182, 184, 195, 197 (see Sèvres)

vinegar 41, 118, 263

viscosity 101, 192, 216, 217, 224 (see firing behavior)

visual effect
    Egyptian faience 58
    celadon 77, 80, 244
    jun 94, 96, 100, 101, 224
    lusterware 111–112, 120
    Iznik tile 125–126, 127, 129, 132, 133
    Medici bottle 14, 136, 138
    K'ang Hsi plate 149
    Bottger tea caddy 163–164
    Boucher soft paste 179, 186, 192
    general 211–217, 285

visual examination 281–284, 295, 296, 311, 312

visual impact (see aesthetic impact)

vitreous stoneware 229, 324

Vogt, G. 161

W

Walcha, Otto 176, 177

warping 138, 141, 223, 244 (see slumping)

wasters 77, 89, 141

water color painting 155, 158

water content of clays 184, 185, 217, 220, 221

water films 232

Watson, O. 121

Watt, James 42–3, 202

wavelength of light 20, 192, 213, 300

wax 222 (see organic)

weathering (pitting corrosion iridescence, etc.) 291, 295, 312

wedging processes 152, 184, 238, 324 (see preparation of clay body)

Wedgwood, Josiah 15, 16, 39, 49, 50, 151, 195–207, esp. 198, 256

Wedgwood Jasperware 195–207, esp. 199, 246 (see jasperware)

Wedgwood, Thomas 198

West, R. R. 226

wetting behavior 222

Weyl, Woldemar 269, 277

white clays 126, 141, 164, 170, 198, 229, 230

white ground 100, 120, 125, 141, 150, 158, 159, 212, 230, 274

white lead 33, 157, 159, 263, 274

Wieldon, Thomas 198

Wildenstein, Paul 166, 167, 170, 173, 177

wine lees 13, 140, 141, 231

Winter, A. 307

Wirgin, J. 90, 162

Wittenburg 166

wollastonite 24, 25, 26, 33, 81, 87, 88, 89, 101, 104, 105, 107, 191, 192, 193, 213, 214, 224, 230, 267, 324

Worcester 15, 152

workability of clays, working range 73, 228, 324

Wulff, Hans E. 66, 115, 121, 133

Wu San–Kuei rebellion 149

X

xeroradiography   44, 56, 57, 59, 73, 74, 299, 300
x–ray diffraction   (XRD)   (see diffraction)
x–ray fluorescence (XRF)   302–303, 305
x–ray radiography   44, 185, 188, 189, 299, 300
Xuzhou   48

Y

Yale University   223

yield point   232, 233, 245
Yi–Hsing ware   14 (see I–Hsing or red stoneware)
Young, W. J.   309
Yuan Dynasty   11, 69, 77, 81, 90, 94, 107
Yue wares (or Yueh)   72, 81, 90, 263

Z

Zhou (Chou) Dynasty protoporcelain   10
Zhuo Zhen Xi   108
zinc oxide   264, 270
Zwickau   168